Get Updates and More on Nolo.com

Go to this book's companion page at:

www.nolo.com/back-of-book/TRD.html

When there's an important change to the law affecting this book, we'll post updates. You'll also find articles and other related materials.

More Resources from Nolo.com

Legal Forms, Books, & Software
Hundreds of do-it-yourself products—all written in plain English, approved, and updated by our in-house legal editors.

Legal Articles
Get informed with thousands of free articles on everyday legal topics. Our articles are accurate, up to date, and reader friendly.

Find a Lawyer
Want to talk to a lawyer? Use Nolo to find a lawyer who can help you with your case.

NOLO
LAW for ALL

⚖ NOLO

The Trusted Name
(but don't take our word for it)

"In Nolo you can trust."
THE NEW YORK TIMES

"Nolo is always there in a jam as the nation's premier publisher of do-it-yourself legal books."
NEWSWEEK

"Nolo publications…guide people simply through the how, when, where and why of the law."
THE WASHINGTON POST

"[Nolo's]…material is developed by experienced attorneys who have a knack for making complicated material accessible."
LIBRARY JOURNAL

"When it comes to self-help legal stuff, nobody does a better job than Nolo…"
USA TODAY

"The most prominent U.S. publisher of self-help legal aids."
TIME MAGAZINE

"Nolo is a pioneer in both consumer and business self-help books and software."
LOS ANGELES TIMES

12th Edition

Trademark

Legal Care for Your Business & Product Name

Stephen Fishman, J.D.

TWELFTH EDITION	AUGUST 2019
Editor	JANET PORTMAN
Book Design	TERRI HEARSH
Proofreading	SUSAN CARLSON GREENE
Index	SONGBIRD INDEXING SERVICES
Printing	BANG PRINTING

Names: Fishman, Stephen, author.
Title: Trademark : legal care for your business & product name / Stephen
    Fishman, J.D.
Description: Twelfth edition. | Berkeley, California : Nolo, 2019. | Includes
    index.
Identifiers: LCCN 2019006321 (print) | LCCN 2019007539 (ebook) | ISBN
    9781413326666 (ebook) | ISBN 9781413326659 (pbk.)
Subjects: LCSH: Trademarks--Law and legislation--United States--Popular
    works. | Business names--Law and legislation--United States--Popular works.
Classification: LCC KF3180.Z9 (ebook) | LCC KF3180.Z9 E43 2019 (print) | DDC
    346./304/88--dc23
LC record available at https://lccn.loc.gov/2019006321

Please note

We believe accurate, plain-English legal information should help you solve
many of your own legal problems. But this text is not a substitute for
personalized advice from a knowledgeable lawyer. If you want the help of a
trained professional—and we'll always point out situations in which we think
that's a good idea—consult an attorney licensed to practice in your state.

Acknowledgments

I would like to acknowledge the invaluable contributions of attorneys Stephen Elias and Richard Stim. Stephen was the original author of this book, and Richard became coauthor after Steve's death in 2011. Many of their words live on here.

Stephen Fishman

About the Author

Stephen Fishman has dedicated his career as an attorney and author to writing useful, authoritative, and recognized legal guides for a nonlawyer audience on intellectual property, business, and taxation matters. He is the author of several Nolo books, including *The Copyright Handbook*, *The Public Domain*, and *Deduct It! Lower Your Small Business Taxes*. You can visit Stephen's website at www.fishmanlawandtaxfiles.com.

Table of Contents

20 Frequently Asked Trademark Questions

Below are brief answers to 20 of the most common questions about trademarks.

1. What does it mean to "trademark" a business or product name or logo?
When people say they plan to "trademark" a name or logo, they generally mean they intend to register the name or logo with the U.S. Patent and Trademark Office (USPTO). Though federal registration provides important benefits, trademark ownership is actually determined by who uses the mark first in a commercial setting. A trademark is created, and trademark ownership is established, when someone uses a name, logo, or other symbol to identify goods or services in the marketplace.

2. What is the difference between a trademark and a service mark?
Legally, there is no difference between the two. A trademark distinguishes a product from competing products. A service mark distinguishes a service from competing services. Throughout this book, the term "trademark" refers to both trademarks and service marks unless otherwise indicated.

3. How long does it take to get a trademark registered?
The typical time it takes to federally register a trademark is between 12 and 18 months.

4. Suppose I register a trademark for a particular product. What happens when I want to use the same trademark for a different product?
Each product or service must be registered within one or more classes (a class is a category of goods or services). If you begin using your trademark on a product or service in a different class than the one for which you originally registered your mark—for example, you use your logo on a paint product when you originally registered it for painting services—you should file another application to register the new use of the mark (in the appropriate class). However, check first to see whether the mark is being used by another business for a similar product. If it is, you might need the assistance of a trademark attorney before proceeding.

5. Can I apply to register a logo, name, and slogan all in one application? What happens if I want to use them separately?

If you want to use and protect each separately, you should register each separately. However, you can—if you wish—register them as one trademark and claim rights for the cumulative use.

6. What happens if I register my mark and later find out that someone else was already using the mark but never got around to registering it?

If the product associated with the other mark was distributed nationally, as is the case with most catalog and Internet sales, then your trademark registration may be subject to cancellation. In any event, the registration will not protect you from an infringement suit if the first user can establish that your use of the mark has created a likelihood of customer confusion. If the other mark was being used locally only, you will probably be entitled to use the name in any region of the country where the first user had not established a presence.

7. I've been told to do a trademark search before applying to register my mark. Why should I, if the USPTO does one when it gets my application?

In general, there are three good reasons for doing your own search:

- Don't waste your money. The filing fee for an electronic application for federal trademark registration ranges from $225 to $400. The fee for a paper application is $600. There is no point in filing an application—and paying these fees—for a name that the USPTO will reject because it's already owned by someone else.
- The USPTO's search will be limited. The USPTO search primarily covers the federal trademark register, which does not include trademarks that are in use but not registered. Because use, rather than registration, determines ownership, the USPTO search will not be as complete as your own search of both registered and unregistered marks.

- The USPTO's decision to register won't shield you from an infringer's lawsuit. The USPTO might find a potentially confusing mark in the course of its search but still decide to register your mark on the basis of its internal guidelines. However, the USPTO's decision to register your mark doesn't get you off the hook if the owner of the existing mark decides to take you to court (see the paragraph just above).

8. What is a "common law" trademark, and what rights does it give me?
A common law trademark is any device (name, logo, slogan, and so on) that its owner uses to identify a business's goods or services in the marketplace, which the owner hasn't registered with a state government or with the USPTO. The owner of a common law trademark that is used in more than one state can use the federal courts to enforce its rights in the parts of the country where the mark is being used.

9. Why should I bother to register a trademark I'm already using on my business or products if I already have rights under the common law?
It's a lot easier to win a federal lawsuit against infringing later users by establishing certain presumptions. Presumptions are facts that you don't have to prove in court and that the other side must rebut. Federal registration gives you two presumptions: that you are the mark's owner and that the later user deliberately copied the mark. These presumptions also make it easier to prove infringement and collect damages and attorneys' fees.

10. Can I do the trademark application myself or should I hire an attorney?
Most people can handle their own trademark applications without attorneys. The USPTO provides easy-to-use instructions for filing your own trademark registration online using its Trademark Electronic Application System (TEAS) at its website (www.uspto.gov).

If, however, you have questions that the USPTO or online registration help files don't answer, you should consult with an attorney. Also, if the mark you are planning to register is unusual (a color, sound, or scent, for example), or if for some reason the USPTO doesn't want to accept your application, you will need to consult an attorney.

11. What if I find an exact match or near-exact match in my search? Can I still use my proposed trademark anyway? What's the worst that can happen if the other trademark owner finds out about my use?

Practically speaking, if you are able to keep the dispute out of court by immediately stopping your use of the mark, you may escape with only having to pay all or part of the trademark owner's attorneys' fees incurred up to that point. This is usually true if you are a small business, because the owner would have no reason to try to reach your shallow pockets. However, the larger your business, or the more your business competes with the owner's, the more likely it is that any settlement will also involve some cash to make up for harm caused by your infringement, real or imagined.

If you are sued for damages, the court may order you to pay any or all of the following:

- actual money damages suffered by the owner as a result of your infringement, or the amount of profits you earned while using the mark
- punitive damages in the amount of three times the amount of actual money damages or profits awarded the owner, and
- attorneys' fees incurred by the owner in bringing the infringement suit.

In addition, of course, the court can order you to stop using the mark, which might result in additional expense, as well as the need to rebuild goodwill around a new mark.

12. Can I register my domain name/Internet website address as a trademark?

Yes, you may apply to federally register your domain name as a trademark, provided that you are using it to market goods or services on the Internet. If, on the other hand, you aren't using the domain name to sell goods or services—for example, you're using it only for personal or family reasons—the USPTO will deny your request.

13. What's the difference between state and federal trademarks?

A state trademark is one that its owner registered on the state's trademark list and uses within the state. A federal trademark is one that is used in more than one state or in any commerce regulated by Congress.

14. If my trademark search finds a mark identical or similar to mine and I find out that the owner is no longer in business (or that the mark is no longer being used by that business), am I free to use it? Can I register it with the USPTO?

Not necessarily. Even if the original owner is no longer in business, the mark itself may have been assigned to another business that is using it. The same is true if the original owner is still in business but no longer using the mark. Finally, if the mark is a creative graphic, such as a logo or trade dress, it might still be protected by copyright law (which protects creative works or expression).

15. If I combine my business or product name with a logo, does the combination distinguish the name from other names that are already registered or in use?

If the name accompanying your logo is the same as or very similar to a name that is federally registered or in use, the owner of the federal trademark can prevent you from using your name/logo combination, even though the appearance of your name/logo combination is completely different. Similarly, the USPTO will refuse to register your name/logo if it is likely to be confused with the registered mark.

16. How thorough should my search be?

At the very least, you should search the federal trademark register for names or other marks that possibly conflict with yours. In addition, you should search relevant trade publications, as well as the Internet.

17. What is the *Official Gazette*, published by the USPTO, and who reads it?

The *Official Gazette* is read by anyone whose business involves keeping up with the latest USPTO announcements and rules—mostly patent and trademark attorneys, patent agents, and so on. In addition, all trademarks proposed for federal registration are published in the *Gazette*, which gives the public advance notice and the opportunity to object to registration. For this reason, you might find it quite useful. You can read the *Gazette* for free online at the USPTO website (www.uspto.gov/learning-and-resources/official-gazette).

18. I've learned that I'll have to renew my trademark registration in a few years. Will the USPTO notify me when the time comes, or do I have to keep track of this date myself?

In 2015, the USPTO began sending courtesy email reminders of registration renewals to owners who:

- had live registrations in progress
- provided the USPTO with a valid email address, and
- authorized email communication from the USPTO.

The USPTO does not send reminders by regular postal mail, and it does not attempt follow-up on emails that were returned as undeliverable. The USPTO's failure to provide such courtesy email reminders does not excuse an owner who fails to file documents on time. If you miss the deadline, your trademark registration will be cancelled. This does not affect your ownership of the mark, assuming you are still using it, but you will have to reregister the mark to maintain the benefits of registration. To assist you in tracking trademark dates, the USPTO's Trademark Status and Document Retrieval (TSDR) system includes a "Maintenance" tab that lists documents that must be filed to maintain registration and when they are due. To locate this tab, search for your registration in the TESS database and click the TSDR button.

19. How do I get the official USPTO form to apply for a federal trademark registration?

The USPTO discourages the use of paper applications and has changed its filing fees to reflect this preference (see below). (In fact, the USPTO no longer even provides a paper form for trademark applications.) For this reason, we have not included a blank application form in this book and discourage paper applications. The online application process, with its interactive help, is less likely to result in errors for first-time filers. Filing electronically also gets you directly into the USPTO system and allows you to file an application from anywhere.

Currently, when applying for registration, you can use the TEAS program to file the application online at the USPTO website in one of three ways: TEAS Plus (currently a filing fee of $225 per class), TEAS Reduced Fee (currently a filing fee of $275 per class), and TEAS Regular (currently a filing fee of $400 per class). You can also prepare a paper application (currently $600 per class). Chapter 7 explains the registration process in more detail.

20. How do I get an international trademark?

There is no such thing as an international trademark. However, it is possible to file one trademark application for a group of countries using a procedure known as the Madrid Protocol. The Madrid Protocol includes 119 countries. In addition, you can file one application and obtain protection (known as a Community Trademark) in 28 European countries. Otherwise, you must seek protection on a country-by-country basis.

Your Legal Companion for Trademarks

Twenty-five years ago, a local business could reasonably expect its marketing activities to be limited to a neighborhood, town, city, county, or even one state. As long as its name (usually its only trademark) didn't conflict with any in use by other local businesses, there was little likelihood of customer confusion and therefore of any legal conflict. Today—because of the Internet—the concept of local is rapidly disappearing for many types of businesses. Doing business online increases the scope of your business from local to national and, because of that, there are new rights and responsibilities. Now, you must pay attention to how your name or other trademarks fit within the vast sea of trademarks that is U.S. commerce. In short, knowledge of trademarks (or branding, as it is fashionably known these days) has become a prerequisite for operating a business.

On the other hand, let's be realistic. Your trademark is only one of many concerns you have in your day-to-day business operations. The good news is that you don't need to become a trademark expert—you only need the basic knowledge in order to protect your business name. Our goal in writing this book is to do just that—to give you everything your business needs to secure and protect your name efficiently and at a reasonable cost.

With that in mind, this book plots a course for small business owners. The first half of the book deals with choosing and registering a trademark, and the second half deals with preserving your rights and staying out of legal trouble.

To achieve our goals, this book explains:
- how trademark rules affect business
- how to choose the best trademark for your business
- how to find out whether other businesses are using similar trademarks
- how to federally register your trademark
- the relationship between domain names and trademarks

- how to maintain your trademark rights
- how to evaluate claims of trademark infringement, and
- the basics of international trademark protection.

Because your chances of being sued over a trademark dispute are slim—fewer than 5,000 trademark-related lawsuits are filed in federal courts each year (and many of these are counterfeiting disputes)—our explanation on how to sue or defend a federal or state court lawsuit for trademark infringement is limited. Nor do we explain the intricacies of handling a case brought before the U.S. Patent and Trademark Office (USPTO)—usually filed when someone opposes your trademark registration. However, we do explain how to respond to the many minor issues that might arise in the course of navigating your trademark application.

Complex proceedings, such as lawsuits and USPTO disputes, will likely require the assistance of an attorney skilled in trademark law. You might need an attorney's help in other situations, and we will alert you to these throughout this book. In short, if things should become more complex, we advise you when and how to seek professional help.

Those pesky problems aside, you should be able to handle most trademark issues with the aid of this legal companion (and without the aid of an attorney). After you've chosen and secured your name and your business is operating smoothly, place this book among your other business references, ready to be pulled into action if you need additional practical advice.

Although we've been harping on legal issues and concerns, keep in mind that our biggest goals are that your business prospers and that consumers associate your trademark with excellent quality and service.

Get Updates, and More, Online

If there are important changes to the information in this book, we'll post them at:

www.nolo.com/back-of-book/TRD.html

You'll also find other useful information there, including author blogs and videos.

A Trademark Primer

This chapter provides an introduction to the basics of trademark law. It will give you the background necessary to understand your rights and obligations in choosing and using a trademark to identify your business and products in the marketplace.

Trademarks and Trademark Law

What's in a name? To Shakespeare, "A rose by any other name would smell as sweet." But what is true in love can be the opposite in business. IBM would not smell half so sweet by another name, nor would Google, Apple, McDonald's, or Levi's. In the business world, the name of a successful product or service contributes greatly to its real worth. Every day, names such as Allendale Auto Parts or Building Blocks Day Care identify these businesses for their customers, help customers find them, and (assuming they provide a good product or service) keep the customers coming back again and again.

And it's not just a clever business or product name that pulls in the customers. Equally important in the vast U.S. consumer marketplace are the logos, packaging, innovative product shapes, cartoon characters, website address names (domain names), and unique product characteristics that businesses are using to hawk their wares. Even the look and feel of a business's website is important in identifying the business and its products in the marketplace.

All of these devices—business and product names, logos, sounds, shapes, smells, colors, packaging—carry one simple message to potential customers: Buy me because I come from XYZ Company. To the extent that these devices are unusual enough to distinguish their underlying products and services from those offered by competitors, they all qualify as trademarks.

If a small business owner were to remember only one point in this book, it should be this: The instant a business or product name or any other identifying device is used in the marketplace to sell goods or services—be it in advertising, on a label, on an Internet site, or in any other way intended to reach out to potential customers—it falls within the reach of trademark law. Trademark law will determine who wins a dispute over the use of the name. Few business owners can afford to disregard or run afoul of this body of law.

What Are Trademarks?

Trademarks fall into two general categories: marks that identify goods or products (known as trademarks) and marks that identify services (known as service marks). Though you may occasionally see this distinction in action, these terms are, in fact, legally interchangeable, and the even more general term "mark" is commonly used to refer to each. In this book, we tilt towards the terms "trademark" and "mark" and seldom use "service mark."

Technically speaking, a trademark is any word, design, slogan, sound, or symbol (including nonfunctional unique packaging) that serves to identify a specific product brand—for instance, Canon (a name for a brand of printers and cameras), Just Do It (a slogan for Nike's shoes and sportswear products), Apple's apple with a bite missing (a symbol for a brand of computers and other electronic products), and the name Coca-Cola in red cursive lettering (a logo for its brand of soft drink).

A service mark is any word, phrase, design, or symbol that operates to identify a specific brand of service—for instance, McDonald's (a name for a brand of fast food service), ACLU (a name for a brand of legal organization), Netflix (a name for a brand of video streaming service), the U.S. Postal Service's eagle in profile (a symbol for a brand of package delivery service), Google's distinctive red, yellow, blue and green lettering (a symbol for various Internet services), and the Olympic Games' multicolored interlocking circles (a symbol for a brand of international sporting event).

In addition to trademarks and service marks, federal trademark law protects two other types of marks—certification marks and collective marks.

Certification marks are used only to certify that products and services that are manufactured or provided by others have certain qualities associated with the marks. For example, the Good Housekeeping Seal of

Approval (a product approved by a homemaking magazine), Roquefort (a cheese from a specific region in France), and Harris Tweeds (a special weave from a specific area in Scotland) are all certification marks. Among the characteristics that this type of mark may represent are regional origin, method of manufacture, product quality, and service accuracy.

A collective mark is a symbol, label, word, phrase, or other distinguishing mark that signifies membership in an organization (a collective membership mark) or that identifies goods or services that originate from the member organization (a collective trademark). For example, the letters ILGWU on a shirt are a collective mark identifying the shirt as a product of members of the International Ladies Garment Workers Union. It distinguishes that shirt from those made by nonunion shops.

Another example of a collective membership mark is the familiar FTD found in many flower shops. This mark means that the flower shop is part of a group that participates in a national flower delivery system. To belong to that group—and thus obtain authorization to use the FTD mark—the shop must pay steep membership fees and conform its practices to the rules set out by the group.

Because a small business's need for collective or certification marks is relatively rare, we don't address them further in this book. If you need help in creating and protecting this type of mark, consult a trademark attorney. (See Chapter 14, "Help Beyond This Book.")

Although most small businesses rely on their business names as their primary trademarks, there are many other ways for a business to inform consumers about itself, its services, and its products.

Logos

Next to a name, the most popular commercial identifier is the logo, a pure graphic or a combination of a graphic and some aspect of the business name. Examples abound. The block-lettered Ford set against a blue oval, the distinctive Amazon name above the arrow connecting the A and Z, the purple and orange FedEx logo (with its "hidden" arrow between the E and X), the gold McDonald's arches, the universally recognized swoosh used to denote Nike products, and the blue cross used to denote Blue Cross's health care services all demonstrate how powerfully a logo can garner instant product or business recognition.

Slogans

Another popular form of trademark is the marketing slogan. "Obey your thirst" (Sprite); "It's everywhere you want to be" (Visa); "Let's go places" (Toyota); and "Just Do It" (Nike) are all devices designed to build customer recognition of the underlying businesses and their products, and therefore each qualifies as a trademark that deserves the same protection under trademark law as a business name.

Packaging, Decor, Product Shape, and Web Pages

In recent decades, a type of trademark known as trade dress has become more important to businesses trying to build customer recognition. Trade dress includes product packaging, external and internal store decor, product shapes, and perhaps the look and feel of a business's Web page. As long as the appearance of the product or its packaging operates as a trademark, it will be treated and protected as a trademark, assuming it meets other trademark requirements, such as distinctiveness. (See "Trade Dress and Product Designs" later in this chapter for more information.)

Colors

Colors help to distinguish products and services. For example, a pale blue box indicates Tiffany's products, a bright green tractor signifies it's from the John Deere Company, and a brown truck indicates UPS delivery services. When color is used with a name or graphic design of a trademark (such as the red lettering and blue star of Converse footwear or the yellow and black coloring of the Cliffs Notes book series), it is registered as an element of the trademark.

It was not until recently that the United States began to protect combinations of colors or single colors by themselves—that is, without any additional text or graphics. In the 1980s, Owens-Corning registered the color pink for its fiberglass insulation and, in 1995, the Supreme Court ruled that a manufacturer of dry-cleaning press pads could claim registration for a green-gold color. (*Qualitex v. Jacobson Products*, 514 U.S. 159 (1995).) Also, a federal appeals court has ruled that a color combination (signifying different tensions in an exercise band) could be protected. (*Fabrication Enters. v. Hygenic Corp.*, 64 F.3d 53 (2d Cir. 1995).)

To obtain protection, the owner of a potential mark for color must establish that, given its use in the marketplace, consumers have come to associate the color with the owner's products or services, as indeed was the case with the Owens-Corning pink fiberglass and the green-gold color for the dry-cleaning pads.

Cases in recent years demonstrate the continuing challenges when registering and protecting colors as trademarks:

- Despite 30 years of continuous use, a company could not acquire trademark protection of the color blue for its endoscopic probes. The Third Circuit held that that the color was **functional** when used in connection with an endoscopic probe and further that the company had failed to demonstrate **secondary meaning**. (*ERBE Elektromedizin GMBH v. Canady Technology LLC*, 629 F.3d 1278 (Fed. Cir. 2010).) (Bold terms are defined in the glossary in Appendix B.)
- Cigarette maker Lorillard could not convince the Trademark Trial and Appeals Board (TTAB) that its color combination of orange lettering and green background (as used in connection with its Newport brand advertising) was a protectable combination. The problem for Lorillard was that the color combination was not used on the packaging or cigarettes, only on advertising. And, even in those cases, it was not always consistent. Hence, there was an insufficient demonstration of **secondary meaning**, despite having sold half a trillion Newport cigarettes. (*In re Lorillard Licensing Co.*, 99 U.S.P.Q.2d 1312 (TTAB 2011).)

- In a 2013 case, the Second Circuit overturned a district court holding that a single color can never serve as a trademark in the fashion industry. The court held that the red soles of the plaintiff's high-end shoes qualified as a trademark, and the defendant was prevented from marketing any shoes bearing outsoles in the same shade of red. (*Christian Louboutin S.A. v. Yves Saint Laurent Am. Holding, Inc.,* 709 F.3d 140 (2d Cir. 2013).)

Internet Domain Names

Internet domain names are the names assigned to Internet sites for the purpose of uniquely identifying the sites and providing an intuitive way for potential visitors to locate them. (We discuss domain names separately in Chapter 2, "Trademarks, Domain Names, and the Internet.")

"No" to Orange Flavor

Flavors, like odors and colors, can be federally registered as trademarks. The challenge is to demonstrate that flavor is identified with the source of the product and is not functional. For example, the Trademark Trial and Appeals Board refused to permit federal registration of an orange flavor as a trademark for antidepressants. The Board stated that the orange flavor was functional and therefore incapable of serving as a trademark—because orange is a preferred flavor for orally administered pharmaceuticals. (*In re Organon N.V.,* 79 U.S.P.Q.2d 1639 (TTAB 2006).)

What Is Trademark Law, and Why Do You Need to Know About It?

In the real world, once customers come to associate a mark with a particular business or product, would-be competitors frequently copy some or all aspects of the mark—its sound, its appearance, its meaning—in an effort to lure customers away from the original business. Even a well-intentioned business owner may violate trademark laws by unwittingly picking a new business name, logo, or other type of trademark that conflicts in some way with a mark already in use somewhere in this large country of ours.

For these and other reasons, the U.S. marketplace is rife with trademark conflicts. It is the job of trademark law to sort out these conflicts in an equitable and consistent manner. It is this book's job to introduce you to how trademark law works, so that you will know how to avoid legal trouble when choosing a name for your business, products, and services. We'll also explain what to do if, despite your best efforts, you end up in a trademark conflict anyway.

Sources of Trademark Law

Three basic sources of law govern the use of trademarks:
- the federal Lanham Act
- state statutes governing trademarks, and
- the common law of trademark and unfair competition (based on court decisions, not statutes).

The coverage of these laws overlaps frequently—in fact, an infringer might violate all of these at once. Below, we explain how to apply these sources of law for purposes of trademark registration and trademark-related disputes.

The Federal Lanham Act

The federal statute known as the Lanham Act (17 U.S.C. §§ 1051 et seq.) provides for a system of registering trademarks. If your mark meets the requirements (see Chapter 7, "Federal Trademark Registration"), the USPTO will approve your application and will place your trademark on the Principal Register.

In addition to providing for the registration of marks used "in commerce," the Lanham Act includes a provision—17 U.S.C. § 1125(a), also known as Section 43(a)—that prohibits false advertising, trade libel, and trademark infringement for unregistered marks.

In 1996, Congress amended the Lanham Act to prohibit dilution of famous marks, an activity previously only prohibited by state laws. Dilution is the use of a famous mark in a way that would diminish the mark's strength or tarnish its reputation for quality. This law allows the owner of a well-known mark to stop the use of a similar mark without having to establish the likelihood of customer confusion. (For more on dilution, see Chapter 10.)

In 1999, Congress amended the Lanham Act to prevent cybersquatting, which it defines as registering, trafficking in, or using a domain name with the intent to profit—in bad faith—from the goodwill of a trademark belonging to someone else. Lawmakers were stepping in to end the practice of buying up domain names that were the exact name, or similar to the name, of an existing business with the intent of selling the names back to the business. (For more on cybersquatting, see Chapter 10.)

In 2006, Congress enacted the Trademark Dilution Revision Act, which established dilution standards, clarified certain activities relating to dilution, and defined key dilution terms. We provide more detail on this law in Chapter 10.

State Trademark and Unfair Competition Laws

States have four types of laws that deal with trademarks:

- A number of states have antidilution laws. Like the federal antidilution statute, these laws allow the owner of a well-known mark to stop the use of a similar mark without having to establish the likelihood of customer confusion.
- All states have statutes providing for a trademark registration system.
- All states have statutes that govern trademark disputes.
- All states have statutes or bodies of court-developed common law that prohibit unfair competition.

State trademark statutes and the state rules against unfair competition usually dictate that the first to use a distinctive mark will have trademark precedence over a second user when the potential for customer confusion exists. State trademark rights apply on a statewide basis only.

State trademark registers are most useful when your mark is used within your state only. However, even if you plan to acquire a federal registration, it won't hurt to also register in your state. The fees are usually quite modest, and you never know when someone local who wants to use your mark will search only your state's trademark register. You can obtain state trademark registration application forms and other information about your state's trademark agency through the links provided at All About Trademarks (www.ggmark.com).

Common Law of Trademarks

Both state and federal courts have developed bodies of common law that cover trademarks. This law originated in judge-made decisions, but over the years, much of it has been placed in statutes (codified). In general, this court-made law applies to all trademarks, registered or not, and reflects the principles we set out in this chapter—that to be protected, a mark must be inherently distinctive or must have developed secondary meaning. And for a legal conflict to exist, there must be a likelihood of customer confusion.

When one trademark owner sues another, standards and principles derived from the common law are usually among the litany of claims. However, common law claims, by themselves, rarely provide the basis for modern trademark decisions— judges usually reach their decisions based on state or federal laws.

Basic Principles of Trademark Law

Trademark law is the body of principles that the courts use to decide disputes regarding names or other devices being used to identify goods and services in the marketplace.

Trademark law comes from many sources: federal and state trademark statutes, federal and state statutes defining and prohibiting "unfair competition" between businesses, and federal and state cases interpreting these laws. (Unfair competition refers to the legal rulings and statutes that protect against unethical business practices.) The federal law that governs trademark rights and registration is known as the Lanham Act. Although there are subtle differences in all these sources of law dealing with how businesses use commercial identifiers, federal trademark statutes and case law govern most trademark disputes. (Later in this chapter, we provide more information on these sources of trademark law.)

Here, briefly, are some basic concepts of federal trademark law that you will need to understand before we go any farther (we provide more details as we go along):

- The first business to use a trademark in the marketplace owns it when challenged by later users.

- To qualify as a trademark, a name, logo, or other device used by a business in its marketing activities must either: (1) be unique enough to earn customer recognition on its own (referred to in trademark law as "inherent distinctiveness"), or (2) have earned customer recognition through its continued use over time (known in the trade as "acquired distinctiveness" or "secondary meaning").

- A trademark owner can sue in federal court to stop another business from using the same or a similar trademark if the owner's mark is **famous**, or if the use by the other business would cause potential customers to confuse one business or product with the other.

- The more distinctive a trademark is, the easier it is for its owner to get the court to stop its use by others.

- The usual court remedy in trademark disputes is to order the losing party to stop further use of the trademark in question. This can be painful because business goodwill often is intimately connected with the business's mark, and because all of the items that carry the mark will have to be pulled from use.

- If the court finds that one business deliberately used a famous or distinctive mark belonging to another business, the offending business can be ordered to pay substantial money damages to the trademark owner.

- The court will usually find that a mark was deliberately copied if the mark was listed on the federal trademark Principal Register at the time it was copied.

Ideally, just knowing basic trademark principles should be enough to answer all your questions and get you started on the road to choosing a clever name for your business or product. But not so fast. The phrases "customer confusion" and "distinctive mark" need some explanation. Unfortunately, Congress has avoided hard definitions and instead opted to let judges decide, on a case-by-case basis, whether a particular mark is famous or risks confusion by customers with an existing mark. Although we provide some guidelines in this book for you to use when you are faced with interpreting these terms, the rock-bottom rules for dealing safely with the ambiguities in trademark law are these:

- Don't choose a business or product name that is the same as one that is used nationally by a large company. Even if you're in the right on some abstract level, the big company will most likely try to legally terrorize you into dropping the mark.
- Don't choose a trademark that is the same—in appearance, sound, or meaning—as a federally registered mark, unless the registered mark is used for a product or service that is very different from the ones offered by your business.
- Don't try to piggyback your marketing efforts on a well-known trademark belonging to another business. For example, don't call your new mobile game app "Angry Burps."
- Don't choose a domain name for your business that is the same as the trademark of an existing business. If you do, you might be accused of infringement (if you have similar products or services), dilution (if the existing business has a famous trademark), or cybersquatting (if you acquired the domain name in bad faith).

These rules are easy to understand. A fifth rule is not: Stay away from existing marks that resemble yours if there's a likelihood that customers would be confused by use of the two marks. Using the guidelines we lay out later in the book (see Chapter 3, "How to Choose a Good Name for Your Business, Product, or Service"), you should be able to select an appropriate name or to recognize when you need a professional opinion.

SEE AN EXPERT

When a trademark lawyer might help. If any of these rules get in your way (you've got a hot name for your business and you want to run with it), a trademark lawyer can help you decide whether your situation is an exception to these rules and what you risk by going ahead with your proposed mark (see Chapter 14, "Help Beyond This Book," for information on how to find a trademark lawyer).

Strong Marks Versus Weak Marks: What Trademark Law Protects

Trademark protection is based on a "strength" classification system. Distinctive trademarks are strong and protectable. Trademarks that are not distinctive are considered weak and cannot be registered or protected unless the trademark owner creates consumer awareness.

Strong marks include coined words (such as Google), **arbitrary** terms (such as Apple for computer products), or terms that have a **suggestive** quality without describing the goods or services (for example Roach Motel). These marks are all born strong and are so memorable or clever that they are classified as "inherently distinctive."

Weak marks, such as Healthy Favorites, Beef & Brew, or Chap Stick, describe some quality, ingredient, or characteristic of the goods and services. Many businesses prefer to use weak trademarks because a descriptive mark provides information about the product to the consumer. For example, consumers know immediately that Food Fair is the name for a supermarket and Raisin Bran is the name for a cereal made with raisins and bran. A weak mark can acquire distinctiveness if, through extensive sales and advertising, the public becomes aware of the mark and associates it with a particular source.

In Chapter 3, the section "What Makes a Distinctive Trademark a Legally Strong Trademark?" revisits in more detail the subject of what makes an effective trademark. The question of what makes one mark strong and another mark weak often is the key to understanding and resolving trademark disputes.

Ownership of a Trademark: The First-to-Use Rule

In the United States, the first business to use a trademark owns it.

Two Types of First Use

There are two ways to qualify as a first user of a trademark:

- **Actual use:** being the first to use the trademark on a product that is distributed in the marketplace or, in the case of a service mark, the first to use the mark in connection with advertising or marketing of a service available to the public, or
- **Intent to use:** being the first to file an intent-to-use application with the U.S. Patent and Trademark Office provided that (1) the applicant files the application before the trademark is actually used by another party, and (2) the applicant later puts the mark into actual use and completes the registration process (see Chapter 7 for more on intent-to-use applications).

EXAMPLE 1: In 2018, Jonah begins publishing *Geezer Tennis*, a magazine for aging tennis players. In 2021, a competing magazine sends Jonah a letter stating that Jonah is infringing on its federally registered trademark Geezer Games. Jonah does a little investigating and learns that Geezer Games was first used as a mark in 2019, a full year after Jonah started using the mark. Jonah would be considered the owner of the Geezer mark and could even require Geezer Games to change its name, because the products of the two businesses compete and would therefore likely lead to customer confusion.

EXAMPLE 2: Now assume that, in 2018, Geezer Games had applied for federal trademark registration of the mark on an intent-to-use basis. If Jonah started actual use of the Geezer mark in March 2018, and Geezer Games filed its application for registration in April 2018, Jonah would still be considered the owner. However, if Geezer Games filed the application before Jonah's actual use, Geezer Games would be the ultimate owner once it put the mark into actual use.

What constitutes actual use and intended use is discussed in more detail in Chapter 7, "Federal Trademark Registration."

Two Different Businesses Can Own the Same Mark

It is possible for a mark to be "owned" by two or more separate businesses as long as no customer confusion is likely to result. If the underlying products or services of two businesses are quite different and don't compete, then customer confusion is unlikely. Similarly, if the underlying products or services are distributed and marketed in different channels or parts of the country, there is little likelihood of customer confusion. For example, one U.S. district court ruled that the mark *Aisle Say* used for theater reviews could be owned by two different entities—one that published its reviews exclusively on the Internet and another that published its reviews in print in the New York metropolitan area. (*Albert v. Spencer,* 1998 U.S. Dist. LEXIS 12700 (S.D. N.Y., 1998).) But, as we pointed out earlier, the more famous or distinctive a mark is, the more likely it is that customer confusion will result (and the less likely it is there will be more than one owner).

When Dual Users Come Into Conflict

What happens if a mark is owned by more than one business, each of which operates in a different geographical market, and one of the businesses decides to expand into the other business's territory? Or suppose that dual ownership has been possible because one business used the mark on sportswear and another on lawn mowers, and both businesses decide to move into gardening clothes? In these situations, some rules kick in that help a court decide the respective rights of the owners. The rules revolve around such questions as:

- Did the second business to actually use the mark know of the first business's previous use?
- Is the first user's mark federally registered and, if so, did the second use begin before or after the registration?
- Is the second user's mark federally registered?
- How broad were the first user's marketing efforts when the second use began?

(Chapter 10, "Sorting Out Trademark Disputes," deals with all these issues and tells you how the courts are likely to resolve them in specific scenarios.)

The Role of Customer Confusion in Trademark Law

As mentioned in the Introduction, virtually all trademark disputes that make it to court are resolved on the basis of the answer to one simple question: Is simultaneous use of the marks likely to cause customer confusion? If customers are not confused, then the courts see no reason to intervene. (Courts sometimes make an exception to the customer confusion rule when dealing with famous marks, which, by law, are entitled to be free from other uses that would dilute their strength or tarnish their reputation for quality. See below for more on dilution.)

It's important to understand that two different marks can be confusingly similar for a number of reasons. Take, for example, the well-known mark Microsoft. Could a business avoid the likelihood of customer confusion by using a name that sounds the same as Microsoft but looks different, such as Mikkrowsought or Mike Crow Soft? Or that looks the same but sounds different, such as Macrosoft? Or perhaps a fanciful arrangement of the words and letters, such as

MI
CRO
SOFT

The answer to all these questions is no. Why? A mark that is similar to another only in sound, appearance, or meaning is still similar and therefore likely to confuse potential customers. However, the weaker the original mark, the less concerned the courts will be about possible customer confusion and the more acceptable changes in appearance, sound, or meaning will be as a way to distinguish one ordinary mark from another.

Even if two marks are exactly the same, customer confusion will not be likely (and infringement won't occur) if the goods or services identified by the marks aren't related in some way. For instance, Delta Faucet and Delta Airlines can both use the Delta mark because customers aren't likely to confuse one with the other due to the difference in their products and services. But clothing and items that are both sold in sporting goods stores may be considered related products—because they are marketed in the same channel—and, therefore, a judge could conclude that customers are likely to be confused as a result.

(Chapter 6, "How to Evaluate the Results of Your Trademark Search," provides an explanation of what standards are used to measure customer confusion.)

Special Treatment for Famous Marks: The Dilution Doctrine

In 1995, Congress passed the Federal Trademark Dilution Act (FTDA), a statute that gives the owners of certain famous marks protection against copycats even when there is no likelihood of customer confusion. This protection becomes stronger when the original owner can show dilution of the famous mark's distinctive quality. The FTDA defines dilution as "the lessening of the capacity of a famous mark to identify and distinguish goods or services." Courts have extended this definition to include two factors:

- blurring of the famous mark (which means detracting from the mark's uniqueness), and
- tarnishment (which means negatively affecting the famous mark's reputation for quality).

In 2006, Congress enacted the Trademark Dilution Revision Act of 2006 which eliminated the need to demonstrate actual or likely confusion, competition, or actual economic injury when the owner of a famous mark brings a dilution claim. The law also provided definitions for "famous," "blurring," and "tarnishment," and it carved out exceptions for activities such as parody and commentary. We provide more detail on the 2006 Act in Chapter 10.

In addition to the FTDA, which has national application, about half of the states have their own dilution statutes that differ to a greater or lesser degree in how they define dilution. The main point you need to know is that famous marks may be protected against use by others even if consumers are not likely to be confused by the dual use.

How Trademark Law Protects Trademarks

The trademark system depends on trademark owners to protect their marks (government lawyers are not out there, looking for instances of infringement). If you don't do anything about your business name or other mark getting ripped off by a competitor, no one else will. So, even though the law provides "protections," you will have to step forward and use the tools the law makes available.

As a general rule, these tools are very limited. In some situations it is possible to resolve a dispute by filing an administrative petition or complaint with the USPTO (see Chapter 7, "Federal Trademark Registration"). However, the vast majority of trademark disputes that can't be settled by negotiations are resolved by filing a federal court lawsuit claiming trademark infringement or, in the case of a dispute between a mark and a domain name, by a federal lawsuit or an administrative arbitration.

Typically, an infringement lawsuit asks the court to immediately order a suspected infringer to stop using the mark in question and to award monetary damages for harm caused by the infringer. Once the judge rules on the request for immediate relief, the parties typically settle the case. If the court grants the immediate relief requested by the plaintiff, the case usually is settled on terms favorable to the plaintiff. If the judge denies the relief, the defendant usually fares better. Few trademark cases make it all the way to trial and, consequently, few cases result in damage awards—although large amounts of money may change hands as part of the settlement.

 TIP

Litigation can get expensive in a hurry, easily running into tens of thousands of dollars in legal fees. The cost of litigation teaches one very important lesson when it comes to trademark disputes: Be flexible and don't get carried away by the right or wrong of the situation. Always treat the issue as a business decision—try to resolve it in the manner that will most benefit (or least harm) your business. Remember that negotiation is an option, and there are many ways to structure a settlement. Using a cease and desist letter if the law is on your side is a first step. (For more on cease and desist letters, see Chapter 11, "When Someone Infringes Your Mark.")

The Role of Federal Registration in Protecting Trademarks

Trademarks can be registered with the USPTO under a federal statute known as the Lanham Act. Trademarks are commonly registered with the USPTO using one of two methods:

- The trademark owner files an application based upon use of the mark in commerce regulated by the federal government.
- The trademark owner files an application (known as an intent-to-use or ITU application) based on an intent to use the mark in commerce regulated by the federal government and subsequently uses it.

Chapter 7, "Federal Trademark Registration," explains how to complete the application process for federal registration.

Registration can increase a trademark owner's ability to win an infringement lawsuit and provide additional benefits as discussed below. Although registration increases protection, it's important to understand that in many cases, it is possible for the owner of an unregistered trademark to stop someone from using a confusingly similar trademark. That's because, with the exception of ITU applications (discussed in Chapter 7, "Federal Trademark Registration"), trademark rights are held by the party who first uses the mark in commerce, not who first files an application for registration with the USPTO. In federal court, a holder of a registered trademark is presumed to own the mark, but this can be rebutted with proof of earlier use of the mark. Thus, registration provides a trademark user with the presumption of ownership, but not actual ownership, of the mark.

The Principal Register

The USPTO keeps two lists of all trademarks that it has decided to register—the Principal Register and the Supplemental Register. In addition to the trademarks themselves, these registers include the following information:

- the owners of the marks
- the dates the marks were registered

- the types of goods or services identified by the marks, and
- other potentially useful information, such as how the marks were described by their owners in the application process.

Of the two lists, the Principal Register is by far the more important. Placement on this list provides a trademark with the protection that makes it worthwhile to register the mark in the first place.

Qualifying for Placement on the Principal Register

To be placed on the Principal Register:

- The mark must be in actual use in commerce involving two or more states or across territorial or international borders. Even if the owner has filed an application for registration based on intended use, the mark will not be registered until the owner puts it into actual use.
- The mark must be sufficiently distinctive (inherently or acquired through use over time) to reasonably operate as a product or service identifier in the marketplace.
- The mark may not be confusingly similar to an existing mark in a context where the confusion of customers would be likely.
- The mark may not fit within one of the categories that Congress has deemed to be off limits for trademarks (such as using "U.S." or the name of a living person without his or her consent).
- The mark may not consist primarily of a surname or a geographical name (unless the mark has become well known over time or the geographical term is clearly arbitrary but not deceptive).
- The mark may not consist of the title of a book, play, recording, or movie that is a single-issue artistic work (as opposed to a series or serial) unless the title has become well known over time.

Benefits of Registration on the Principal Register

Registration on the Principal Register provides these protective benefits:

- exclusive nationwide ownership of the mark (except where the mark is already being used by prior users who might not have registered the mark)

- official notice to all would-be later users that the mark is unavailable
- the right to put an ® after the mark, which also puts users on notice that the mark has been registered
- the right to immunize the mark from certain challenges if the registrant keeps the mark in continuous use for five years after the registration date, and
- a legal presumption that the registrant is the owner of the mark (which means the registrant won't have to prove ownership if a dispute over the mark ends up in court, unless a contender has evidence of earlier use).

Taken together, these benefits make it easier to win an infringement lawsuit and make it more likely that large damages can be collected for the infringement (which means there will be money to pay the attorneys and make it worthwhile to bring the lawsuit in the first place). (See Chapters 10 through 12 for more on infringement lawsuits.)

The Supplemental Register

The Supplemental Register is an option for marks that aren't distinctive enough to qualify for placement on the Principal Register. This lack of distinctiveness means that the courts are unlikely to give the mark much protection in the event of a lawsuit.

As a general rule, placing a mark on the Supplemental Register does not help much if a dispute over the mark ends up in court. However, anyone doing a standard trademark search to find out whether the same or a similar mark is available for use will discover the registration and most likely will decide to choose another mark, just to be safe. Also, placement on the Supplemental Register entitles the mark's owner to use the ® symbol which, to the public, signifies a registered trademark. And finally, if the mark continues in use and remains on the Supplemental Register for five years, it is easier to apply to have the mark placed on the Principal Register (on grounds that it has acquired distinctiveness through continued use over time). The bottom line is that the Supplemental Register provides some practical benefits and therefore provides a sensible alternative if the USPTO denies placement on the Principal Register because of the mark's lack of distinctiveness.

State Trademark Registers

All states maintain separate trademark registers. The main function of these is to provide notice to would-be later users that a mark is already in use in a state. Unlike federal trademark registration, placing a mark on most state registers confers few benefits other than an indication of when trademark rights in the mark were first claimed by the registrant. Because of the relative unimportance of state trademark registrations, we don't devote the space to explaining how to handle them. However, if you want more information on your state's trademark registration procedure and trademark laws, contact your state trademark registration office. You can also obtain more state trademark information at the All About Trademarks website (www.ggmark.com).

Not All Business Names Are Trademarks

The most common method adopted by a new business to identify itself in the marketplace is its name. For the purposes of trademark law, there are two main types of business names:

- the formal name of a business, called its trade name, and
- the name the business uses to market its products or services, alternatively referred to as a "trademark," "service mark," or just plain "mark."

For most small businesses, this is a distinction without a difference. Almost all legal problems involving business names arise when a business name is used as a trademark—that is, used to build a customer base for the business—and not when the name is used as a trade name simply for billing, banking, and tax purposes.

The distinction between a trade name and a trademark can be a little confusing at first, because many businesses use at least a part of their trade name as the name they use to market their goods or services. For instance, every time a small business named something like Pete's Graphic Designs, Elmwood Copymat, or Good Taste Organic Foods puts its name on a store sign, window display, or brochure, it is using its trade name as a trademark. On the other hand, large businesses often use different names for each type of subsidiary activity. For instance, Ford Motor Company puts its name on its cars but also uses a subsidiary mark for each type of car (for instance, Escort, Ranger, and Mustang) and a different mark entirely for its auto parts division (Motorcraft).

Corporate and Fictitious Names

A corporate name is simply the name of a corporation as registered at the time of incorporation. It must generally be approved by a state official, such as the secretary of state or corporations commissioner (the names vary from state to state), and followed by a corporate identifier, such as Inc. or Corp., as in Time, Inc., or Sony Corp. A corporate name is a trade name in that it identifies the corporation and not necessarily any product or service the corporation offers.

Another form of trade name is the fictitious business name, which is any assumed business name or alias. When a person or partnership does business under a name not its own (and this also applies to a corporation doing business under a name other than its corporate name), that person (or partnership) must usually file a fictitious business name statement with the county or state. For example, Laura Smiley uses a fictitious business name when she conducts her sole proprietorship business as Le Petite Cafe or Laura's Bookkeeping, but not if she operates under the name of Laura Smiley Enterprises. Similarly, if the partnership of Fishman, Stim, and Elias operates as the Reader's Corner Bookshop, it is using a fictitious business name.

Trade Name Formalities

Almost all businesses are required to register their business names with a local or state agency charged with keeping track of business names. The particular agency you'll need to use usually depends on whether your business is a corporate entity or a sole proprietorship. Here we provide an overview of the steps you'll likely have to take to get your particular business name registered with the appropriate agency.

Trade Name Registration Requirements

All names that identify business entities—corporate names; fictitious business names; assumed names; partnership names; the names of nonprofit, charitable, religious, and educational institutions; and the names of sole proprietorships—are trade names. With a few exceptions, every business is required by state law to take certain legal steps to list its trade name with a public agency. These vary somewhat depending on the form of the business—for instance, corporations must follow a different procedure than partnerships use. Corporations usually register with their state's secretary of state or corporation commissioner's office. Unincorporated businesses must usually register with an agency that keeps track of fictitious or assumed names.

In addition to providing a registry where members of the public can check on a business ownership, these name registration procedures are designed to screen out the use of identical or very similar names within the state or county where the business is based. However, as we will see, they don't do a perfect job in accomplishing this. Rather than describe the specific requirements of all 50 states, we will explain generally the requirements for most of the states and give you enough information to easily find the rest on your own.

Corporate Name Registration

Corporations are creatures of state law. By a legal fiction, they are considered persons—artificial persons. When they are created, we say they are incorporated (literally translated, "given a body").

This process involves filing articles of incorporation, paying a fee (and possibly an advance on corporate taxes), picking a board of directors, and, most important for our purposes, registering the corporate name with the secretary of state, state department of corporations, or corporations commissioner. Although state laws on name registration vary a bit from state to state, registering a corporate name typically involves three steps for everyone.

Check Your Secretary of State's Website

Most corporate name registration agencies maintain websites. A few states allow you to register your corporate name online and this practice is expected to increase, so make sure and check to see what online services your state agency offers. You can find a listing of the website for each state's agency at www.business.gov/register. (Select "Explore State and Local Resources.")

Step 1. Select a permissible name.
All but three states (Maine, Nevada, and Wyoming) require you to include a word or an abbreviation indicating corporate status, like "corporation," "incorporated," "company," or "limited." Several states also require that the name be in English or Roman characters. In addition, most states forbid including words that imply a purpose different from the one stated in the articles of incorporation or that mislead or deceive the public. For example, if you are forming a corporation that will help people fill out their medical insurance forms, you probably shouldn't call it Oil Drillers, Inc. In addition, states may require that corporate names do not include words that are obscene, falsely suggest associations with government entities, promote unlawful activity, or are prohibited for business use by any state law.

Step 2. Clear your name.
Next, you will need to make sure that your corporate name is distinguishable from every corporate name already registered in your state.

The reason is simple: Your state won't register a corporate name that too closely mimics a name already on file. To ease your task, the secretary of state or other corporate filing agency will do a search for you prior to authorizing the use of your name. In about half the states, you may phone to check on the availability of a name in advance. In the others, you must submit a written request. Often you may request a search of more than one name at a time. A corporation that is fairly confident that its name is unique can simply submit its articles of incorporation without a search, though this risks rejection if the name is already taken. (If your name is rejected, some states might require you to repay the filing fee when you submit under a new name.)

Generally, the state agency will compare your name with registered and reserved names of other corporations incorporated in your state and with those incorporated elsewhere that have registered to do business in your state. How thorough the search will be varies from state to state; and each state has its own rules on how different your name must be from an existing name. In every state, however, if your name is found to be confusingly or deceptively similar to another name, you will have to change it so that it is distinguishable from the existing name. This is true even if the two corporations are in very different fields—unless the owner of the registered name gives written permission for the similar name to be registered.

Step 3. Reserve your corporate name.

A corporation can usually reserve a name prior to actual incorporation if the name otherwise qualifies for registration. Reserving a name freezes out other would-be registrants of that name (or one deceptively similar) during the period of reservation, usually 60 to 120 days. Most, but not all, states permit you to extend the reservation for one or more additional periods for additional fees. Also, some states allow corporations to reserve their names without doing business in the state and even to renew those name registrations annually, which provides the equivalent of long-term name reservations for out-of-state corporations. Check with the secretary of state to discover more about these options if you wish to use them.

CAUTION
Registering your corporate name with a state agency might give you far fewer legal rights than you think it does. As discussed below, it does not necessarily give you the legal right to use that name to identify your products or services, only to identify the corporation.

Fictitious Business Name or Assumed Name Registration

In all states, any person who uses a trade name other than his or her surname, and any organization that goes by a name other than the last names of the owners, must register the name with the state or county as a fictitious or assumed name.

This process, which is analogous to a corporate filing with the state, usually means paying a fee and filing a certificate with the county clerk stating who is doing business under that trade name. Many states also require a business owner to publish a statement, often called a DBA (doing business as), several times in a local newspaper. A DBA statement allows creditors to find the people behind the business.

Not every type of business must file a fictitious business name—it varies by state. In almost all states, fictitious business name laws apply principally to individuals (sole proprietorships) and general partnerships. Because corporations are required to give information to the state regarding the business owners, creditors have a place to look for that information. Consequently, fictitious business name laws do not apply to corporations, except in the fairly rare situation in which a corporation does business under a name different from its corporate name. In most states, fictitious business name laws also do not apply to limited partnerships because other laws govern their registration. In some states, the law also covers nonprofit organizations and corporations, including churches, labor unions, hospitals, and so on.

Unlike registering a corporate name, registration of an assumed or fictitious business name does not necessarily prevent others from registering the same name. Because many states do not maintain a central register of fictitious business names, few states "clear" a fictitious business name by checking it against any other lists before registering it. As a result, several businesses might use the same trade name in the same state.

This means that if your state has no central fictitious name register, the only way to be sure that no one else in your state is using the same trade name is to check the fictitious business name records of every county, not just your own. But, as we discuss below, whether someone else is using the same trade name as yours is of less practical importance than if they are using the same trademark. For this reason, we aren't suggesting you check every county list if all you are concerned about is use of a trade name.

The Legal Relationship Between Trade Names and Trademarks

As mentioned, people often think that once they have complied with all the registration requirements for their trade names, they have the right to use them for all purposes. Because this point is so important, let us again emphasize that this isn't so. As we have seen, there are two very different contexts in which a business's name may be used:

- the formal name of the business for purposes of bank accounts, creditors, and potential lawsuits (trade name), and
- the name that the business uses to market its goods or services (trademark or service mark).

The business registration requirements address the first context only. They don't address the second. That is, Backyard Fantasies, Inc., may be properly registered as a corporate or fictitious business name (trade name) but—because of the previous use of that name by someone else as a trademark—it may be legally unusable as the name the business puts on its signs, displays, advertising, and products (trademarks, service marks).

A trade name acts like a trademark when it is used to identify a product or service. This can sometimes be a tricky determination, especially when comparing trade names and service marks, because they often appear in similar places—on letterheads, advertising copy, signs, and displays. But some general principles apply:

- If the full name is used and appears with an address and phone number, it's probably a trade name. For instance, consider "The Goodnight Meat Company." It appears with an address, and the eye scans it, registering it as information only. This impression is intensified if an obvious trademark that also belongs to the company ("Sunrise Sausage") is used alongside it. Sunrise Sausage serves as the identifier of goods, while the Goodnight Meat Company only identifies the company.
- If a shortened version of the name is used (for instance, "Goodnight Meats"), especially with a design or logo beside or incorporating it, the trade name becomes a trademark. Large companies, such as Consolidated Agriculture, often use a shortened version of their trade names (for instance, ConAgra) alongside marks for specific goods that they produce, including Swift Meats, Hunt-Wesson Oils, Peter Pan Peanut Butter, and Banquet Frozen Dinners. Used this way, the name ConAgra acts like a mark because it has a design surrounding it, and it is sufficiently different from the full corporate name, which is Consolidated Agriculture.

Simply put, if the name you have registered as a corporate or fictitious business name was already in use or federally registered as a trademark or service mark by someone else, you will have to limit your use of the corporate name to your checkbook and bank account. The minute you try to use the name in connection with marketing your goods or services, you risk infringing the existing trademark or service mark. (See Chapter 10 for more on infringement.) If your corporate name figures into your future marketing plans, you must search for use of the name as a trademark in addition to complying with the corporate name registration requirements. If you plan to market your goods or services on the Internet, then you'll also want to check to see whether your proposed name has already been taken as someone else's domain name, which would mean, at the least, that you'd have to use a slightly modified name (because every domain name is unique). See Chapter 2, "Trademarks, Domain Names, and the Internet," for more about domain names.

Trade Dress and Product Designs

Trade dress refers to the total image of a product or service including such features as size, shape, color or color combinations, texture, graphics, or even particular sales techniques. Product design, a subcategory of trade dress, refers to the shape and appearance of a product, for example, the appearance of a line of clothing or furniture.

To the extent that the decor of a business, the packaging of a product, or the shape of a product are distinctive and intended to operate as marks, these indicia will be treated as marks and can even be registered with the USPTO. Visitors to a Hard Rock Cafe, for example, can identify various features that distinguish this chain of restaurants from competitors. In a liquor store, you can distinguish the bottles of Absolut vodka from those of its competitors. And, most everyone can tell the difference between Lyft's logo (pink and white) and Uber's mark (black and white). Because each of these devices signals to customers that the product or service originates from a particular source, they are all examples of trade dress that qualify for trademark protection.

Basic legal principles that apply to trade dress are presented below and might be helpful, particularly in relation to the use of product and service names with trade dress elements.

Distinctiveness

Whether a particular trade dress qualifies for protection as a trademark depends on several basic factors. First, is the trade dress distinctive?

Inherent Distinctiveness

Some types of trade dress may be considered distinctive simply on the basis of the trade dress itself (this is called "inherent distinctiveness"). For example, the U.S. Supreme Court found that a Mexican restaurant chain's decor could be considered inherently distinctive because, in addition to murals and brightly colored pottery, the chain also used a specific indoor and outdoor decor based upon neon-colored border stripes (primarily pink), distinctive outdoor umbrellas, and a novel buffet style of service. (*Two Pesos, Inc. v. Taco Cabana, Inc.,* 505 U.S. 763 (1992).) However, product designs such as the appearance of a line of children's clothing are not considered to be inherently distinctive and can only be protected if they acquire distinctiveness through sales or advertising. (*Wal-Mart Stores, Inc. v. Samara Brothers, Inc.,* 120 S.Ct. 1339 (2000).) And speaking of trade dress (with the emphasis on the "dress" or lack of it), in 2009, the Trademark Trial and Appeals Board refused to register the cuffs and collar design mark used by Chippendale's exotic male dancers, finding that it was not inherently distinctive trade dress. (*In re Chippendales USA, Inc.,* 90 U.S.P.Q.2d 1535 (TTAB 2009).)

Acquired Distinctiveness (Secondary Meaning Rule)

Secondary meaning is a demonstration that the consuming public associates a mark with a single source, usually proved by advertising, promotion, and sales. If the trade dress is not inherently distinctive, distinctiveness can, with exceptions, still be acquired through extensive sales and advertising. A red star might not be inherently distinctive, for example, but when it is used extensively in advertising for gasoline sales and automotive services ("Look For the Big Red Star") then it may have acquired secondary meaning.

Some types of trade dress—such as a single color or a product design—may never be considered inherently distinctive because customers would have no way of associating the trade dress with the underlying products or services, or their source, without becoming familiar with them over time. For example, the use of a single color could not be inherently distinctive because consumers would not immediately associate a color with one product or company. In that case, the color sought to be protected must have acquired distinctiveness under the secondary meaning rule.

Wal-Mart v. Samara: The Supreme Court Makes It Difficult to Protect Product Designs

In *Wal-Mart Stores, Inc. v. Samara Brothers, Inc.*, 120 S.Ct. 1339, 146 L.Ed. 2d 182 (2000), the Supreme Court ruled that product designs, like colors, are not inherently distinctive. Samara created a line of children's clothing that featured one-piece seersucker outfits decorated with appliques of hearts, flowers, and fruits. Wal-Mart asked another clothing company to copy Samara's designs and then sold the knock-offs at a lower price. Samara brought a federal lawsuit against Wal-Mart. The trial court ordered Wal-Mart to pay Samara $1.6 million in damages, and the ruling was upheld on appeal. The Supreme Court overruled the appellate decision, finding that the Samara designs were not protected under trademark law because product designs were not inherently distinctive and Samara had not demonstrated secondary meaning. The result is that no matter how creative a designer is when making a product's appearance or shape, the product will be protected under trademark law only if the owner can demonstrate that the public associates that product design with a single source.

Trade Dress Can Be Registered With the USPTO

As a general matter, distinctive trade dress can be registered with the USPTO and will receive extra protection as a result. However, as with trademarks generally, distinctive trade dress also qualifies for protection against copying even if it's not registered.

Likelihood of Confusion Is Required

As with other types of trademarks, infringement of trade dress occurs only when there is a likelihood of customer confusion between the underlying goods or services, or their origins. Even when two different trade dress packages are similar in appearance, if customers have an easy way to tell one product from the other, courts have been reluctant to find that infringement has occurred. For example, a federal court found that there was no trade dress infringement in the case of two skin care products with similar lettering, colors, and graphic design. The court determined that the prominent use of each company's name on its own product would prevent consumers from being confused by the similar trade dress.

Functional Trade Dress Is Not Protected

The trade dress feature for which you seek protection cannot have a functional purpose other than to distinguish the product or service in the marketplace. This may seem confusing, because all trade dress features have at least some utilitarian function. For instance, packaging protects products against wear and tear, and a uniquely shaped bottle holds the bottle's contents. But if the design elements are not essential for the underlying product's purpose (for instance the curved shape of an Absolut or a Coca-Cola bottle isn't a necessary part of the product), then the trade dress is considered nonfunctional in a legal sense. On the other hand, the blue dot on Sylvania flashcubes (used on old cameras) was considered too functional to qualify for separate trademark status, because it served the utilitarian purpose of indicating when a bulb was used (when the blue dot turns black). Some examples of products that may have nonfunctional design features are furniture, automobiles, sweaters, and notebooks. If the design features of any of these items become well established as means of identifying their sources, and are nonfunctional, they may qualify as protectable trade dress.

If Your Product Design Is Both Functional and Novel

If your design is functional and novel, you should research whether it can be protected as a utility patent. For example, let's say you have created a unique method of packaging compact disc recordings. If it is functional and not protected under trademark law, it may still be protectable under patent laws. For more information, review *Nolo's Patents for Beginners*, by David Pressman and Richard Stim (Nolo).

Can Trade Dress Dilute a Famous Trademark?

As explained earlier in this chapter (see "Special Treatment for Famous Marks: The Dilution Doctrine"), dilution occurs when a famous mark is tarnished or blurred by a similar mark. After the passage of the Trademark Revision Act of 2006, it's also possible to assert a claim of dilution based on unregistered trade dress. To do so, the trade dress owner must prove: (1) The claimed trade dress, taken as a whole, is not functional and is famous; and (2) if the claimed trade dress includes any mark registered on the Principal Register, the unregistered portion of the trade dress, taken as a whole, is famous separate and apart from any fame of such registered marks.

The Difference Between Trademark and Copyright

The general public often uses the terms "trademark" and "copyright" interchangeably. However, trademark and copyright serve different purposes. Trademark protects expression that is used to identify and distinguish a product or service in the marketplace. Copyright protects all creative expression except for slogans, names, titles, and short phrases, the very things that are protected by trademark. Let's take a closer look at what copyright does protect, because when it comes to logos, trade dress, and graphics used on Web pages, trademark and copyright may both apply.

Copyright provides writers, artists, photographers, musicians, software programmers, and other creators of expressive works the exclusive right to control how their works are used. But it is important to understand that only the expression itself is protected—not the ideas being expressed. For example, assume that Lloyd Sagal, a self-identified but unknown philosopher, writes a book exploring the religious implications of life on other planets. Under copyright law, other philosophers are free to use any or all of Lloyd's ideas in their own books (and don't even have to give him credit, although most would because of professional scruples). However, each of these other authors will have to do their own writing. They can't just copy verbatim how Lloyd has expressed the ideas. (For a good explanation of the difference between expression and ideas, see *The Copyright Handbook*, by Stephen Fishman (Nolo).)

A copyright attaches to a work of expression the instant the work takes a tangible form—for instance, on paper, hard drive, or canvas. It is common to give notice of the copyright by placing, next to the author's name, a © and the year the work was published. The creator can also opt to register the work with the U.S. Copyright Office to gain some additional protections. Whether registered or not, the copyright lasts for the life of the creator plus 70 years, with some exceptions.

Copyright covers many types of creative expression, including: advertising copy, catalogs, directories, compilations of information, fiction, interviews, lectures, speeches, leaflets, letters, magazines, newspapers, newsletters, periodicals, journals and other serial publications, nonfiction, plays, poetry, reference books and technical writings, screenplays, song lyrics, textbooks, music, art, graphic designs, motion pictures, sculptures, videos, websites, software of all types, architectural designs and blueprints, choreographic works, pantomimes, photographs, and slides.

Copyright law and trademark law commonly intersect in logos, packaging, websites, and advertising copy. Trademark law protects the name of the product or service, any distinctive slogans used in the advertising or on a website, and distinctive features associated with the name or logo, such as its color or lettering style. Copyright law protects any additional literal expression that the ad or website contains, such as the text, artwork, music, or software. (For more information on the protection of trademarks in websites, see Chapter 2, "Trademarks, Domain Names, and the Internet.")

The Difference Between Trademark and Patent

By filing for and obtaining a patent from the USPTO, an inventor is granted a monopoly on the use and commercial exploitation of the invention described in the patent for a limited time. There are several types of patents. The most common is what's called a utility patent, which lasts for 20 years from the date the application was filed or at least 17 years from the date the patent was issued. A utility patent protects the functional features of a machine, process, manufactured item, composition of matter, or new use for any such items. To qualify for a utility patent, an invention must be novel and surprising (nonobvious) to somebody who is familiar with the field of technology in which the invention falls. Although entrepreneurs use trademarks in conjunction with the sale of patented products or services, the types of protection offered by patent and trademark law is distinct with little, if any, overlap.

It is also possible to obtain a design patent on an innovative design of a manufactured item if the design serves an ornamental rather than a functional purpose. A design patent lasts for 15 years from the date it was issued. Because trademark law protects a product shape that is nonfunctional, it is sometimes possible for a product design or shape to be protected under both patent and trademark law.

Book and Movie Names Can't Be Trademarked

Can the name "Braveheart" be used by anyone, given its wide recognition as the title of a blockbuster Mel Gibson movie? Yes, because as a general rule, the titles of books and movies, as used only on the book or movie, are not considered trademarks. This is because each title is unique to that particular item and not an indicator of the product's source or a means to distinguish it from competitors. When a movie or book title is used as part of a series—for example, *The Matrix*—or when the title develops secondary meaning because of ancillary product sales—for example, *The Lion King*— then courts will protect the title under trademark law.

Trademark, Domain Names, and the Internet

D omain names have various functions. They can serve as an address (whitehouse.gov), as a trademark (amazon.com), or as an expression of free speech (governmentsucks.com). Unlike a trademark, a domain name is awarded to the first person to pay for it. That's why, for many businesses on the Web, acquiring the right domain name is more important than whether the name qualifies as a trademark. In this chapter, we'll explain how to acquire a domain name, and we'll discuss the relationship among your business, domain names, trademarks, and the Internet.

RELATED TOPIC

Domain name disputes. Disputes occasionally arise between domain name owners and trademark owners on the Internet. For information on these cyberdisputes and how the owners resolve them, review Chapter 10, "Sorting Out Trademark Disputes."

RELATED TOPIC

Registering a domain name as a trademark. For information on registering a domain name as a trademark, see Chapter 7, "Federal Trademark Registration."

How to Clear and Register Domain Names

A domain name is the unique Internet "address" that directs your computer to a website on the Internet. For example, typing in www.nolo.com takes you to the website for the publisher of this book. Most companies want domain names that are the same as or similar to their business or product names, for example, fedex.com, pbs.org, or staples.com.

Because domain names, unlike trademarks, are granted on a first-pay, first-serve basis, many businesses have been surprised to find that the domain names they want have already been purchased, either by those with a legitimate intention to use them, or by speculators who hope to make money selling them. How crowded is the world of domain names? One survey found that of 25,500 standard English words found in a dictionary, 90% had already been purchased as domain names. As this edition went to press, there were over 334 million registered domain names, over half of which were .com and .net domains.

The Click-Through That Changed the Web

In 2003, Google began offering AdSense, a service that allows any website to generate revenue by placing targeted ads adjacent to website content.

For example, if you have an article about grammar at your website, the Google AdSense program would analyze the text in the article, realize it was about grammar, and deliver ads that are appropriate and relevant to the subject matter (for example, you might see an ad for a book on writing content for the Web). Alternatively, ads may be delivered based on the user's search history. An ad generates revenue to the original website owner when a visitor to the website clicks on it (referred to as click-through revenue). In our example, the owner of the website with the grammar article would get paid if a reader clicked on the book ad.

This innovation dramatically changed the way people perceived and used domain names. Previously, a website owner had to create a site and seek out and attract advertisers, usually cheesy banner advertisers that were not targeted to the website's visitors.

Now, anyone with a domain name (or a blog or any webpage) can generate targeted advertising revenue instantly through Google AdSense (or through one of Google's competitors).

You'll also see, when we discuss domain name disputes in Chapter 10, how click-through advertising has created a new type of cybersquatter, one who earns advertising money immediately upon creating a webpage. Later in this chapter, we discuss keywords and how they are sometimes used to deceive consumers who use search engines (see "The Controversy Over Keywords").

Check Domain Name Availability

How do you find out if the domain name you want is already taken? The easiest way is to check availability at one of the dozens of online companies that have been approved to register domain names. You can access a listing of these registrars at either the InterNIC site (www.internic.net) or at the ICANN site (www.icann.org). ICANN is the organization that oversees the process of approving domain name registrars. Every registrar provides a search system to determine if a domain name is available.

> EXAMPLE: We accessed www.internic.net, clicked "Search Accredited Registrar Directory," clicked "Registrars Alphabetical by Company Name," and selected Register.com from the list. We typed in our choice for domain name, "goodgrammar.com," and were informed that the domain name had been taken and was not available for registration.

Check Domain Name Ownership

In addition to determining whether a domain name is available, you might want to locate information about the owner of the domain name. For example, if a domain name is taken, you may want to contact the owner to discuss acquiring, sharing, or disputing ownership of the name. You can check the WHOIS records (a database of domain name information) at Network Solutions (www.networksolutions.com/whois) or at www.whois.net. When you type in the domain, the site will provide registrant name or contact information.

> EXAMPLE: We accessed the Network Solutions site and typed in "nytimes.com." Network Solutions reported that the site was owned by New York Times Company and provided contact information including a phone number for the registrant.

Be aware that some registrants, especially those acting in bad faith, might supply false information about domain name ownership and, in these cases, there's not much you can do to track down the domain name holder. Don't let this stop you if you believe you are dealing with someone who is holding a domain name for ransom. As we explain in Chapter 10, "Sorting Out Trademark Disputes," there are ways to wrestle a domain name from a bad-faith registrant even if you don't know the identity of the registrant or where the registrant is located.

Keep in mind that if you have a federally registered trademark, someone else might still have the right to own the domain name. Many different companies can own the same trademark for different services and products, but only one company can obtain the domain name. For example, yours may be one of many different companies that have federally registered the trademark Executive for goods or services. Each of these companies might want www.executive.com, but the first one to purchase it—in this case, Executive Software—is the one that owns the domain name.

Register the Domain Name

If the domain name you have chosen is available, you should consider acquiring it. But before you do, you need to be sure that nobody else is using it as a trademark for similar goods and services. If another business is selling similar goods or services with a similar name, that business can terminate your use of your domain name through arbitration or litigation as discussed below (see "Fight for the Name").

> EXAMPLE: Bob registers the domain name ahab.com to sell artwork depicting whales. Jim has a catalog company, Ahab, that has been selling ocean-themed artwork and merchandise since 2000. Jim has registered the Ahab trademark with the USPTO and can stop Bob's use of the domain name ahab.com.
>
> If Bob had registered the domain name with the intention of selling fishing gear, his use of ahab.com would not infringe Jim's trademark.

To check whether your choice of a domain name is being used as a trademark, review Chapter 5, "How to Do Your Own Trademark Search." Keep in mind, you need to be concerned about using someone else's trademark only if the trademark is famous (such as Wal-Mart or McDonald's) or if your company is selling or likely to sell similar goods or services.

Once you are confident that the domain name won't conflict with another's trademark for similar goods or services, you should register the domain name. Access any of the domain name registrars approved at either InterNIC (www.internic.net) or ICANN (www.icann.org) and complete the online form indicating basic contact information (name, telephone number, and address). The fee is usually $25 (or less) per year, and you can pay online by credit card. The whole procedure takes a matter of minutes, and you will be notified by email of your domain name ownership, which is effective immediately.

Now That You Own a Domain Name ...

When you pay the annual fee for a domain name, all you acquire is an address on the Internet. To use it with your business, you must establish a Web hosting arrangement with an ISP (Internet service provider), usually for a fee of approximately $20 or less per month. You must also construct and upload a website and coordinate the reassignment of the domain name from the domain name registrar (the company that sold you the domain name) to the ISP.

Domain name registration grants you exclusive ownership, and no one else can stop you from using it, unless:

- **You fail to pay annual domain name fees.** Domain name ownership, *unlike trademark ownership*, must be renewed annually (or, in some cases, every two years). If you fail to pay the renewal fees, your domain name ownership will be terminated and could be sold to another buyer.

- **You are a cybersquatter.** If you registered a domain name in bad faith—for example, for the purpose of selling it back to a company with a similar name, your domain name can be taken away from you under federal law or under international arbitration rules for domain name owners. (The standards and procedures for these domain name disputes are discussed in Chapter 10, "Sorting Out Trademark Disputes.")

- **You are an infringer.** If your domain name is likely to confuse customers because it is similar to another trademark, you might have to stop such use. For example, if you registered adoobie.com for the purposes of selling software, it's likely that the Adobe company, makers of graphics software, could sue successfully to stop your use.
- **You are a diluter.** If your domain name dilutes the power of a famous trademark, the owner of the famous mark can sue you under federal laws to stop your continued use. Dilution occurs when you are using your domain name for commercial purposes thereby blurring or tarnishing the reputation of a famous trademark. For example, if you registered guccigoo.com for the purpose of selling baby clothes, the owners of the Gucci trademark could probably stop you from using the domain name. (The standards and procedures for these dilution disputes are discussed in Chapter 10, "Sorting Out Trademark Disputes.")

What to Do When the Domain Name You Want Is Already Registered

People register domain names for one of two reasons: The registrant might be using or already have a good-faith intention to use the domain name, or the registrant might have invested in the registration in hopes of selling it.

Usually, it's easy to determine whether the domain name has been registered for use or sale. Type the domain name into your Web browser. If a functioning website appears that bears some relationship to the domain name, the registrant is probably using the domain name in good faith. If a site comes up that says "This domain name is for sale" or something similar, then the name is for sale by the registrant. If a webpage appears that states, "Site Is Currently Under Construction" or something similar, then the registrant's intentions are unclear, because many cybersquatters use this designation—but so do legitimate domain name owners who have not yet constructed a website. In these "under construction" cases, you should contact the person listed as the registrant.

Choose a New Domain Name

If the domain name you want is already registered, the easiest solution is to choose another domain name that's available. Many domain name companies will suggest alternatives if your domain name is taken. For example, a registrar informed us that "goodgrammar.com" was taken and suggested several available alternatives.

Buy or Share the Domain Name

If you have sufficient funds, you can try to buy the domain name rights from someone who acquired the domain name in good faith. For example, altavista.com was being used in good faith by a company with trademark rights to the term "alta vista." Compaq, the computer company, wanted to use the domain name for its Alta Vista search engine and was willing to pay $3.3 million for the domain name.

Many people buy domain names through brokering services such as Sedo.com, Afternic.com, and buydomains.com. Of course, as you can expect, the price of domains is much higher than purchasing through a domain name registrar. (For example, at BuyDomains, the domain names "haunting.net" and "antiquemirrors.net" were each being offered for about $2,000.) In other cases, the domain holder might sell directly (some websites even have "for sale" signs on the webpages).

Many domain names can have difficulty achieving protection under trademark law because they are highly descriptive of the services—for example drugs.com, loans.com, or cinema.com—and this generic quality can prevent a term from acquiring trademark protection.

However, many Internet companies are prepared to sacrifice some trademark rights for an easy-to-remember domain name such as forsalebyowner.com.

In rare cases, companies can agree to share the domain name. For example, if two companies in different states operate under the name First Washington Bank, they can share the domain name firstwashingtonbank.com. An opening page at the website would allow a viewer to click on either bank to access its services.

Fight for the Name

A registrant who has taken a domain name based upon your trademark primarily for the purposes of selling it to you is a cybersquatter and is violating the Lanham Act's anticybersquatting provisions. You can pursue the cybersquatter in federal court or you can arbitrate against the cybersquatter (a less expensive alternative) using procedures created by ICANN (www.icann.org). (For an explanation of anticybersquatting rules, see Chapter 10.) You are also free to buy the domain name from a cybersquatter if you choose. There is nothing illegal about buying a domain name from someone who is effectively strong-arming you. Many cybersquatters are aware that the cost of fighting a domain dispute averages between $1,500 and $3,000 and price the domain name accordingly.

Domain Names and Trademarks

Two things are certain about the legal relationship between trademarks and domain names:

- Registration of a domain name does not automatically grant trademark rights.
- You can be sued by a trademark owner if your domain name is likely to dilute a famous trademark or to confuse customers.

Domain Name Registration Does Not Guarantee Trademark Rights

Domain name registration, by itself, does not empower you to stop another business from using the name for its business or product. For example, if you acquire the domain name greatgrammar.com, that does not mean you can stop others from using Great Grammar for services or products online or off. It means only that you have the right to use that specific Internet address. Your domain name will function as a trademark only if you use it in connection with the sale of goods or services, and customers associate the name with your business. When that happens, you can stop others from using a similar name so long as those others weren't using the term in the marketplace before you.

You're Not Limited to .com

As you are probably aware, every domain name consists of two parts. The .com portion is termed a top-level domain name (TLD), while the section with the business name (or other identifier) is termed a second-level domain name (SLD).

You can choose from hundreds of TLDs. Many, like .com and .net are classified as generic (gTLDs). Others, like .coop (for cooperatives) and .aero (for the air transport industry), are referred to as sponsored TLDs. And many are country-code TLDs (for example .ca for Canada). You can view the complete listing on the Internet Assigned Numbers Authority webpage (www.iana.org/domains/root/db). There is a TLD for every purpose, from religion (.bible) to pornography (.xxx).

The .com extension is by far the most popular, primarily because it is the default extension that people use when trying to locate a company's website. However, you can choose among a vast array of other top-level domains, some of which will support your company's branding needs. For example, some companies intentionally register their television shows with the country code of Tuvalu (an island in the South Pacific), in order to secure domains with a TLD of .tv.

Consider Amazon.com, a domain name that functions as a trademark because customers associate the name with a certain company and its services. Amazon.com achieved trademark status because the company was the first to use this distinctive name for online retail sales, and the name has been promoted to customers through advertising and sales. If another company were to sell books online or offline under the name Amazon, the owners of Amazon.com could sue under trademark law to stop the use.

In short, to be protectable as a trademark, your domain name must meet the standards described in Chapter 1: The name must be inherently distinctive or must achieve distinction through customer awareness, and you must be the first to use the name in connection with your type of services or products.

Trademark Owners Can Sue Over Your Domain Name Use

You could run into a problem if your domain name legally conflicts with an existing trademark. For example, if you launched a website with the domain name Xon.com to sell automobile accessories, you might be asked to stop using the name by the owners of the Exxon trademark; Exxon has the right to stop look-alike and sound-alike business names that are likely to confuse customers seeking a wide range of auto products.

Whether your domain name would legally conflict with an existing trademark depends on (1) which was first put into actual use, (2) whether use of the domain name would confuse customers regarding the existing mark, or (3) whether the existing mark is famous. The legal standards used in these conflicts are no different than in other trademark disputes. (In Chapter 10, "Sorting Out Trademark Disputes," we provide more detail on how these disputes are resolved.)

Other Trademark Issues in Cyberspace

If you are establishing a website for your business, there are other trademark concerns besides domain names. Be careful about misusing other company's trademarks within your links, programming code, or content. Deceptive and misleading uses can open the door to angry letters, lawyers, and lawsuits. Below we provide a summary of common website issues.

As a general rule, word links—where text such as the word Nike is used to link to another site—are not likely to create trademark problems. However, graphic links—where a graphic trademark logo such as the Nike swoosh is used—might raise trademark issues. Although not required, you might want to include a prominent disclaimer to minimize liability for any trademark questions or issues that could occur when a visitor goes to a linked website.

The Controversy Over Keywords

Most people find their Web destinations via search engines, which have two types of listings: relevant (results determined by the search engine), and sponsored (listings provided by advertisers).

Sponsored listings typically appear with relevant listings, usually appearing at the top of the page and in the right margin. You can become a sponsored listing by purchasing (or bidding on) keywords through a search engine company. For example, at Google.com, you can click on the "Advertising" link at the bottom of the page and register to buy keywords (Google calls them "Adwords") for a small setup fee (approximately $5). Keywords are the terms that people type into the search engine. For example, if you purchase the words "crochet" and "baby," your ad would pop up whenever a user searched for crocheted baby hats. In other words, even though it might not be as relevant, buying a keyword ensures your listings will appear prominently in search results. So, what happens when a company buys a keyword that is a competitor's trademark? For example, several companies have purchased the keyword "Nolo" (the trademark for the publisher of this book). When a person types "Nolo" into a search engine, the competing business's sponsored link appears at the top of the page. Does that use infringe on Nolo's trademark rights?

The answer, in short, is probably not. Courts have routinely allowed companies to purchase a competitor's trademarks as keywords, as long as the competitor's trademark did not appear in the actual advertisement.

In 2011, for example, the Ninth Circuit allowed Network Automation to purchase a competitor's trademark—ActiveBatch—as a keyword. When users searched for "ActiveBatch," Network's own advertisement appeared at the top of the page as a sponsored ad. The court held that this was not trademark infringement because it was unlikely to cause customer confusion. The court reasoned that Internet users have become sophisticated enough to understand the difference between search results and sponsored advertisements. The court also held that the similarity of the marks and marketing channels used were not appropriate factors to consider in keyword advertising cases, because the user is not seeing and comparing the two marks. (*Network Automation, Inc. v. Advanced Systems Concepts, Inc.*, 638 F.3d 1137 (9th Cir. 2011).)

Sample Linking Disclaimer

By providing links to other sites, [*name of your website*] does not guarantee, approve, or endorse the information or products available at those sites, nor does a link indicate any association with or endorsement by the linked site to [*name of your website*].

You *are* permitted to use another company's trademark in your website if you are commenting upon or criticizing the other company. For example, if you have an Internet newsletter and write an article criticizing Microsoft, you can use the Microsoft logo. Keep in mind that your right of free speech doesn't prevent a trademark owner from hassling you with a lawsuit. The high cost of defending a lawsuit is often enough to silence critics despite their free speech rights. On the other hand, if your website is offering goods and services as part of its criticism, or your website is likely to confuse users as to its sponsorship, that may be grounds for a trademark infringement or dilution lawsuit.

How to Choose a Good Name for Your Business, Product, or Service

Now that you have absorbed some trademark basics in Chapter 1 and learned about the relationship between trademarks and domain names in Chapter 2, it's time to set about choosing a trademark for your business or its services and products. Because most developed trademark principles apply to names rather than other types of business and product identifiers, we focus on names in this chapter.

The goal of this chapter is to help you choose a name that will:

- do a good job of identifying your products and services in the marketplace, and
- have enough legal strength to give you the exclusive right to use it.

Not all readers will care about these goals. For instance, the name Rob's Pastry Center might be just the ticket for the bakery Rob Johnson plans to open, but the name certainly won't leap out and grab the average consumer's attention. Nor would the law give such a name much protection, because of its ordinary and descriptive nature.

What follows, then, is the type of information you'll need if you share the goals mentioned above or at least want more information before you decide whether to pursue them.

Much of the information in this chapter is explained more fully in Chapter 9, "Evaluating Trademark Strength." Chapter 9 is for people who need to evaluate the legal strength of their marks when a trademark search turns up a conflicting mark, or when real-world trademark disputes arise. This chapter, on the other hand, is intended as a brief introduction to the difference between strong and weak trademarks, so that you can make an informed decision when choosing a mark for your business or product.

Anatomy of a Product or Service Name Trademark

It's always important to distinguish between the name you choose for your products or services and the name of the underlying class of goods or services. You can protect the former but not the latter. Here are some basic principles.

A Trademark Cannot Be the Generic Term for the Underlying Products or Services Offered by the Business

As we have mentioned, for a name or other symbol to qualify as a mark, it must be unique enough to distinguish the underlying product or service from others in the marketplace. Sometimes, however, a mark chosen for a product or service is very close or identical to the generic name for the underlying type of product or service. For example, assume that a business names its new soft drink product Diet Cola. As it turns out, "diet cola" describes a group of carbonated soft drinks with cola flavoring and some form of sugar substitute. That fact makes the would-be Diet Cola mark generic and not a trademark at all, because it could refer to any of several brands of the underlying diet cola product. Shasta, however, qualifies as a trademark for diet cola because it specifies one particular brand of the several diet colas available on the market. Other examples of generic terms are lite beer, super glue, softsoap, matchbox cars, and supermarket.

In summary, the USPTO will not register, and courts will not provide protection for, a mark that is essentially the generic name for an underlying product or service.

A Trademark Can Include Generic Terms

Sometimes, a trademark includes a generic identifier of the goods or services. For example, Wildside Pet Shop has two elements: the term Wildside, which distinguishes this from other competing businesses, and the generic term "pet shop," which describes the class of services. However, while the full name of the business can be protected as a trademark, the term describing the class of services (pet shop) will never be separately protectable. The applicant for registration must disclaim the separate use of the generic term. That way, anyone is free to use the words "pet shop" as long as they are in combination with terms other than the term "Wildside."

Distinctive Names Make Legally Strong Trademarks

As we have mentioned, the more unique a business, product, or service name is, the easier it is to protect the name from use by others. Because distinctive names make legally strong trademarks, it behooves you to choose a unique name. A product or service name can be unique for a number of reasons, including:

- The name might be coined (made up), as in Exxon petroleum products.
- The combination of words and letters in the name could be so creative that no one else has come up with it, as in Tumblr for online services.
- The name might carry a clever double meaning, as in Pea in a Pod maternity stores.
- The name could have a clever appearance, as in Subway's use of white letters for "Sub" and yellow letters for "Way" combined with arrows.
- Certain words in the name might be completely arbitrary in the context and therefore highly original, as in Diesel, a chain of bookstores.

Whatever the reason, a unique name is by nature considered to be a distinctive name and therefore protected as a trademark. We explain how to make your mark distinctive later in this chapter.

When deciding whether a trademark is legally strong or legally weak, you have to look to the whole mark. For example, many marks that the law will protect are completely made up of ordinary words. Consider the example of Pea in a Pod as a name for a maternity store. There is nothing terribly unusual about any of the words, but the phrase is clever—because of its double-meaning suggestiveness of a uterus (the pod) and an embryo (the pea)—and would definitely qualify as a distinctive mark.

How Trademark Law Treats Marks With Ordinary Terms

So far, you should know that on a protection scale of one to ten, generic terms rate a zero while distinctive marks are near the ten end. Now let's lump all the rest of the terms that businesses frequently like to use as names of services or products into a category we will call "ordinary names."

Though this subject is taken up in detail in Chapter 9, the basic rules that apply to marks containing ordinary terms are these:

- If the overall mark is distinctive, it will be protected no matter how many ordinary terms are used.
- The owner of a trademark using ordinary terms cannot claim ownership to the terms themselves, but only to the overall mark.
- If the ordinary terms in a mark do not create a distinctive or clever whole, the mark will not be given protection unless (a) the terms are distinctive in the context of the product or service (for instance the ordinary word "apple" becomes distinctive in the context of computers), or (b) over time, consumers come to associate the mark with the underlying product or service, as in Best Buy (retail electronic products).

Let's examine these rules in a little more detail.

Most Ordinary Words Are Not Protected

Ordinary terms include all sorts of words that aren't usually distinctive by themselves but that aren't generic either:

- place names (Downtown Barber)
- personal names (Harris Sales, Rubin's Assembly Service)
- words that describe a product or service (Slim-Fast Diet Food), and
- laudatory words or words of praise (Tip-Top Pet Shop).

Misspellings or alternative spellings (like "lite" for "light") cannot make an ordinary term distinctive. Nor do common foreign language equivalents, like "le" for "the" and "casa" for "house."

Because marks that use ordinary terms in ordinary ways are, by definition, not distinctive—that is, the terms aren't unusual or surprising in the context—they receive little legal protection at the outset of their use. This means that under the principles of trademark law, it's more difficult to keep others from using them or something similar.

For example, the mark Dependable Dry Cleaners merely describes the business, without distinguishing it from its rivals. In fact, some of the rivals might also need to advertise their services as reliable or efficient. If trademark law prevented such ordinary uses of common terms, our language would be seriously depleted. As a result, Dependable Dry Cleaners gets little protection as a mark from the courts. Does this mean you can't protect the trademark of a dry cleaner? Of course not. A fanciful name like Cinderella Dry Cleaners (if it's not already used by someone else) is a distinctive and therefore fully protectable trademark.

Ordinary Marks Are Entitled to Protection Once They Acquire Secondary Meaning

Although weak marks are difficult to protect initially, they can become distinctive—and therefore legally protectable—when consumers associate the mark with a single source. This is called the "secondary meaning" rule. Many of the most famous and effective marks, like McDonald's or American Airlines, originally consisted of ordinary terms that over time became widely recognized as product and service identifiers and thus were transformed into strong marks (McDonald's is probably one of the strongest marks in the world).

Even Dependable Dry Cleaners might make it into the ranks of secondary meaning marks if a "Dependable" franchise became a household name through extensive marketing activities.

Using a mark that can't be protected until it has acquired secondary meaning can be a serious drawback to the small business owner. Either the business owner must accept the fact that the mark will be weak—and therefore subject to use by others—until the mark's reputation has been built up over time, or the owner must be prepared to spend a lot of money to promote the mark when it is first used, so that the public recognizes it sooner. Unless money is no object, it might be better to start out with an unusual word, phrase, or design that is protectable from the outset as a mark.

We discuss secondary meaning in detail in Chapter 9, "Evaluating Trademark Strength."

Real Ray's Best Famous Original Pizza

Here's a Big Apple anecdote that illustrates the problem with trying to protect a name that's not distinctive. In New York City, which many view as pizza heaven (along with Chicago), there has been a proliferation of Ray's Pizzas, some of which are known for great pizza. There now are more than two dozen in the city, most of them under separate ownership. They call themselves Ray's Original Pizza, Real Ray's, Famous and Original Ray's, and variations on that theme. From a pizza lover's point of view, when two people set a date to meet at Ray's, no one knows which pizzeria anyone means. (Ray's on 7th Ave.? Ray's on Christopher St.? Which Ray's on 2nd Ave.? Or is it Ray's on Houston?) Consumers never know what quality to expect because they don't know which Ray's pizzerias are related. The pizza parlors get each other's mail and complaints, and none of the owners can sort it out. Resort to the courts has failed because, with so many Ray's, no owner can prove that consumers associate the name Ray's with any one pizzeria. So none is distinctive enough to be protected as a trademark.

What Makes a Distinctive Trademark a Legally Strong Trademark?

Let's explore why distinctive marks make legally stronger marks. A distinctive mark has a greater ability to ward off copiers than does a common name, for three reasons:

- The more distinctive a mark is, like Google, the greater an impression it makes on the customer's memory, and the more likely it is that a similar mark, say Googal, will remind the customer of the original mark. That can lead to confusion. The customer may think Google and Googal are the same brand, or that they are related. They may use one instead of the other, or they may be misled into thinking the reputation of one applies to the other. In either case, the customer is confused, and the rightful owner of the Google mark will have probably lost profits.

• The more distinctive a mark is, the more likely it is that potential customers will assume that all products and services carrying the mark originate from one source. This is the opposite of what consumers are likely to think when confronted with ordinary marks that are similar to each other. For instance, it's reasonable to assume that Double Rainbow Ice Cream is manufactured by one company, whereas you wouldn't make that same assumption for several ice cream outlets that use some combination of words including Tastee in their marks. The greater the likelihood that customers will associate a product or service carrying a particular mark with a particular source, the greater the need to protect against the confusion that would likely result if the same or a similar mark was adopted and used by another business.

• The more time, money, and creativity that goes into making a mark distinctive, the more sense it makes to provide the mark with adequate protection. And if the distinctiveness comes from widespread customer recognition over time (the secondary meaning rule), it also makes sense to protect the business goodwill that has been built up under the mark. Although the main reason for the trademark laws is to prevent customer confusion, the dilution principle (discussed in detail in Chapter 10) recognizes that the value of a well-known mark should be protected in its own right, whether or not customers are confused.

> ### State and Federal Unfair Competition Laws Can Provide Limited Protection to Weak Trademarks
>
> There's one more important point to understand about ordinary words or phrases used as trademarks. Though they are not effective as trademarks without secondary meaning, ordinary names can receive certain kinds of limited protection under state statutes or cases barring activities that amount to unfair competition.
>
> Protection from unfair competition is most useful when the second user of your trade name or mark is trying to create the impression that its business is affiliated with your business. In other words, unfair competition laws can help you if someone isn't making it clear through a variety of ways that they are not connected to your business.
>
> We discuss unfair competition more fully in Chapter 10, "Sorting Out Trademark Disputes."

Guidelines for Making a Mark Distinctive

Short of words that have been coined for the precise purpose of operating as trademarks, such as Exxon, the quality of distinctiveness in a mark is most likely to arise from downright cleverness. For a name mark to be clever and therefore distinctive, it doesn't need to use words that are unusual or even weird. For example, distinctive trademarks often consist of ordinary words used creatively in an unusual context (example: Camel for cigarettes, Apple for computers), several ordinary words combined in an interesting way (Thistle Dew Inn) or with an innovative design (the red and white bullseye, for Target), and words that evoke fanciful associations (Double Rainbow Ice Cream).

Also commonly used for distinctive marks are ordinary words that indirectly suggest what the underlying product or service is all about without describing it outright. Examples of these suggestive marks are: Buzz Feed (for online news services), Banana Republic (for a store that originally specialized in safari-styled outdoor clothes), or Bloomers (for a flower shop).

Clearly, whether a trademark is distinctive will depend on both its components and the context in which these components are used. Here we describe the sorts of marks that are routinely considered by the courts to be inherently distinctive and therefore legally strong. These, therefore, are the kinds of marks we advise you to use, taking into account the marketing considerations outlined later in this chapter.

Marks Using Coined Terms

Coined terms (also known as coined marks and fanciful marks), such as Exxon, Pepsi, and Kodak, are wholly new, made-up words with no meaning or connotation other than the one you will create for it with your advertising and other marketing activities. A coined term can also be made up of parts of different words, such as Velcro (combining velvet and crochet). The key to a coined mark is making it pronounceable and appealing to both eye and ear, or at least suitable to the image you want to project for your product or service. To avoid coined terms that evoke unintended images, run your choices by a variety of people and note their responses to the sound and appearance of the mark. (Save your customer surveys until marks have passed the legal availability test.)

Despite their legal strength, most coined words require extensive and costly marketing efforts to become established as product or service identifiers in the first place. More than any other kind of mark, coined words require lots of initial advertising, because coined words don't mean anything to the general public without explanation. That's a major drawback for a small business with limited start-up capital.

Opting for a coined term as your trademark has a second drawback. With over 200,000 new trademarks being federally registered each year, the well of coinable words is fast being drained. Despite our rich Celtic, Anglo-Saxon, Norman, and Latin linguistic heritage, new combinations that sound good and look appropriate—that is, ones that are marketable and not already in use—are becoming harder to develop.

Marks That Suggest but Don't Outright Describe the Product or Service

A mark is usually considered suggestive when you need to take at least one more mental step to figure out what is being suggested. Suggestive marks—such as Sharp's Nonalcoholic Beer or Intuit Software—are favored by marketing folks because they operate to evoke an image or idea to customers who associate it with the product or service being marketed. "Obsession," for example, creates the aura of irresistibility, certainly a desirable attribute for a perfume. This kind of mark is especially effective for the sorts of services or products that sell by affecting one's self-image, like beauty services, clothing, jewelry, sports businesses, or even cars. Again, test your ideas out on a number of people to see if they are getting the message you hope to send.

Though suggestive marks may also require marketing to become broadly identified with a product, they are usually easier to promote than coined ones because they connote something about the product or service. Some name consultants argue that suggestive names are the most useful, because of their comparative legal strength (customers remember them), and because the images they evoke make them very effective marketing tools. On the other hand, it takes lots of thought to come up with a suggestive mark that's appropriately evocative, suits your customer base, and hasn't been taken.

Marks That Use Fanciful Terms in the Context of Their Use

Fanciful marks—such as Double Rainbow Ice Cream, Yahoo! Internet Services, and Penguin Books—are fun to invent, because you can use any term or combination of terms that does not in fact describe your service or product in any way. The trick is to think up a term that is interesting, memorable, and somehow appropriate without literally describing some aspect of your service or product. For example, "Guess?"

works for youthful sportswear—it carries the idea of a company and products that are innovative, unusual, and related to adventure. Of course, clothes by themselves have none of these attributes, but that doesn't matter. Also, being the first to use such an original mark (a verb with a question mark) makes the company seem innovative. A company that comes along later and names its products "Why?" would only seem imitative.

Clearly, consumer responses to these types of marks are subjective and intuitive, and the creator of a fanciful mark must therefore try to consider all the possible evocations that a mark might have and make the most of them.

Marks That Use Arbitrary Terms in the Context of Their Use

Words that are descriptive or ordinary when associated with one product or service (and thus, unprotectable altogether) can be very strong for another. These are called arbitrary marks because they have nothing to do with the product or service being offered. For example, the trademark Apple is distinctive and therefore strong because apples have nothing to do with computers, whereas the trademark Green Apple for applesauce is weak because it literally describes the product. Similarly, the word Cherokee works well as a trademark on a four-wheel drive utility vehicle and on women's apparel, because in each case the word is arbitrary in the context—that is, it doesn't describe any aspect of the underlying products. But Cherokee wouldn't work well as a trademark on Native American crafts, because in that context, it simply describes the expected origin of the goods. Finally, Jellibeans is a distinctive name for a skating rink, but is mundane (and probably generic) as the name of a line of oval, colored, chewy candies.

Common Terms in Uncommon Arrangements

As mentioned earlier, the individual terms that make up strong marks do not need not to be inherently distinctive by themselves. So far, we have focused primarily on what are essentially one-word trademarks—such as Yahoo!, Exxon, and Apple. However, the distinctiveness of a trademark can also reside in a phrase, or in several words put together in an unusual way. Their common characteristic is that taken together they are somehow different from everyday words and names. For example, Taco John's has weak components—taco is a common food item, and there are millions of Johns in the world—but the way the two words combine make the whole trademark distinctive and therefore protectable.

When evaluating a phrase to see if it's a strong or weak trademark, it is the overall impression that counts. If the phrase as a whole has an original ring to it, the fact that some of its elements are ordinary won't matter. For example, Speedy Turtle Delivery Service is memorable for the contrast of speed and turtle. This makes it distinctive, despite the fact that Speedy Delivery Service without the "Turtle" would be purely descriptive and therefore weak.

Ordinary Terms Combined With Novel Designs

Distinctive design elements can add distinctiveness to an otherwise trite name. Toys Я Us (with a backwards "R") is one example of a trademark where the words themselves incorporate a design that lends the name originality. More often, the words have a conventional design, but they are portrayed as part of a distinct design or type style that accompanies them. One example is the bell inside a circle that indicates one of the "Baby Bell" telephone companies. Others are the profiled eagle with red and blue bands signifying the U.S. Postal Service, the script letters "G" and "E" inside a circle indicating General Electric, the red Texaco star, or the face of an Eskimo on the tail of Alaska Airlines planes.

Sources of Marks That You Might Not Think Of

Though it might seem that all the good marks have been taken, there is, in fact, a virtually inexhaustible supply. But, like diamonds, they usually aren't just lying on the ground for the taking; a little mining must take place, and like the diamond in the rough, some cutting and polishing might be required to make them shine. Some of the sources for finding a distinctive name for a trademark are:

- new combinations of existing words (Palmolive, Diehard)
- combinations of word roots (Navistar, Soloflex)
- distinctive foreign words (Sirocco car, Soleil watches), and
- abandoned marks that are no longer in use but that were once famous. (These marks might bring a certain cachet to your product or service, if their former image corresponds to the one you now want to project.)

If you do discover a mark you know has been in use at one time, you should find out if it is now available for your use by doing the sort of searches we describe in Chapter 4.

Again, remember that what counts in evaluating a trademark's strength is the overall impression that the trademark creates in the mind of the consumer, rather than the impact of any single word or design element.

Names to Avoid

Now that we've suggested what types of words make distinctive marks, it helps to describe the types of words that cut against distinctiveness (unless they obtain secondary meaning through use over time).

Personal Names, Including Nicknames, First Names, Surnames, and Initials

Probably the most common type of name trademark used for a business is one that carries the owner's first or last name. Mary's Pizza (yes, it is owned by Mary), Thurlow's Web Designs, and Brian Loman Electronics are examples. For the most part, these personal name trademarks are legally weak and not much good for customer recognition outside the business's locale. But combined with a non-name term, such as Taco John's or Trader Joe's, a mark built around a personal name can be quite distinctive. And if you have a name like Orville Redenbacher, you have no distinctiveness worries at all.

Practical Pointers on the Use of Personal Names as Trademarks

Now that you have a general idea of how personal names fit into the general rules regarding strong and weak marks, here are some pointers on using specific types of personal names.

Surnames. Using your surname (last name) as a trademark has a few drawbacks you might want to consider. You might want to sell the business someday, and it will be necessary, as a practical matter, to sell the name with it. This means a stranger will be operating under your name. And perhaps worst of all, the sale of your business could prevent your children or other relatives from capitalizing on the family expertise by opening their own similar businesses under their own name. Finally, as we saw, marks that are "primarily surnames" do not qualify for federal registration, absent a showing of secondary meaning or perhaps an association with another term that makes the combination inherently distinctive as a whole—such as Warner's Wasteland for a line of stores specializing in recycled products.

First Names and Nicknames. First names are generally even weaker as trademarks than surnames, because most are so much more common. But, for the same reasons, they have fewer of the disadvantages that go with selling a business. And, as we have seen, they can also become unusual simply with the addition of an unusual modifier, like Trader Vic's or Aca Joe.

As with surnames, anyone can use his or her first name or nickname on a business unless it's too close to a famous one. For example, "Sony" Florendo can't call her restaurant Sony's, and Mayo Priebe can't call her drugstore Mayo's Drugs. Sony Corp. and the Mayo Clinic objected to these uses and won, even though there was little likelihood of confusion between the local businesses and their more famous namesakes. Perhaps the judge felt that these were really attempts to capitalize on the more famous trademarks or that the second uses diluted the original marks.

But one is tempted to conclude that the size and wealth of the complaining parties were significant factors.

Initials. A trademark consisting completely of letters that aren't a person's initials is not inherently weak. Rather, its trademark strength depends on the strength of the words the initials represent. If the initials do not stand for anything and are an uncommon arrangement of letters, the mark can be distinctive from the outset. For instance, ABC is not considered distinctive because this combination of letters is in such common use as a mark (except, of course, in the media world, where the television network's initials have acquired secondary meaning). However, a mark consisting of XQE might be.

When Can You Use Your Own Name as a Trademark?

One of the reasons that personal names are not protectable is the idea that no one should have a monopoly on a personal name. Unless the name has already come to mean a particular service or product through the secondary meaning rule, it isn't fair for one Jones to prevent all the other Joneses from using their family name. For this reason, the courts used to say that everyone had an absolute right to use his or her own name to identify a product or service.

That's been qualified over the years. Now, individuals still have the right to use their own names, but not if it will confuse consumers or smack of an unfair attempt to ride on the coattails of their famous namesakes. Generally, that means you can use your own name but not in the same line of work as a trademark owner of the same name. So, for example, Prosper Champion (unrelated to the original spark plug Champion) was not allowed to make and market spark plugs under his name. Nor would anyone named Marriott be permitted to open a hotel under that name. For the same reasons, a person who sells his or her name as the mark for a business can't later go into the same field using that name again. Finally, you won't be able to use your own name as an Internet domain name if somebody else has beaten you to it (unless you have been using your name as a trademark and can establish bad faith on the part of the domain name registrant). For information about domain names and trademark law, see Chapter 2, "Trademarks, Domain Names, and the Internet."

Marks That Describe Attributes of the Service or Product or Its Geographic Location

The main reason to avoid these marks is that they are legally weak and therefore not extensively protectable until they have been in use long enough that they have become easily recognized by your customers. However, many business owners believe that if they use some words in their trademarks that either describe the types of businesses or some positive characteristics of the businesses, they will benefit far more by the marketing payoff than they risk from would-be copiers. (See Chapter 9, "Evaluating Trademark Strength," for more on these marks.)

Names With Bad Translations, Unfortunate Homonyms (Sound-Alikes), or Unintended Connotations

These you should avoid because they can easily backfire as advertising tools. A famous example is the French soft drink called Pschitt, which had to be renamed for sale in this country. Also the Chevy Nova is an unwise trademark for a car in Spanish-speaking countries (including perhaps our own because of the high proportion of Spanish speakers) because the mark means "it does not run" in Spanish.

Names That Closely Resemble Well-Known Marks

If you definitely want to avoid being sued for trademark infringement, avoid using famous marks or obvious variations of them. Whether they succeed or not, claims of trademark infringement and dilution are commonly brought by owners of famous marks in order to clear the field. McDonald's regularly sues companies that use the "Mc" prefix or yellow arches. Often they succeed—preventing the use of "McSleep" for motels and yellow arches for a computer company. (See Chapter 11, "When Someone Infringes Your Mark.")

Be Careful About Deception When Using Geographic Marks

Earlier, we warned about using deceptive or misleading marks. This warning is especially appropriate for geographic terms that are used fancifully. There are really two types of possible deception in the use of geographic marks:

- actual deception in which a customer is induced to buy a product in the belief that the item comes from the region on the label, and
- deceptive misdescription in which the public might make a false geographic connection but wouldn't particularly rely on the geographic factor in buying the service or product.

For instance, a deceptive trademark would be the mark Limoges for china that was neither made in France nor of French clay; or American System, for clothing made in Italy. A deceptive trademark is not protectable and can never become so, even if it acquires secondary meaning. Further, using a deceptive mark may subject you to legal liability for false advertising.

On the other hand, using a mark like Neapolitan (especially with an Italian flag on the label) for Italian sausages made in Florida is seen as merely "deceptively misdescriptive." That is, some people might be confused into thinking the sausages come from Naples, but that's either unlikely or not the main reason they would buy the sausages. Another example is calling a chewing tobacco Durango even though it is not from the noted tobacco growing region of Durango, Mexico. Such marks are not protectable until they have developed secondary meaning. Once the mark has secondary meaning, the potential for confusing the public is lessened, because presumably the public knows the product for what it is and doesn't care where it comes from.

Obviously, the trademark implications of geographic terms can get a little muddy. We suggest this general rule: Don't use a geographical term if a reasonable consumer might think that the place named has something to do with the origin of the product. If you decide that you absolutely have to use a geographic trademark, either make sure your mark has only a vague suggestive connection to your product or service (like Sedona, for a Portland, Maine, restaurant) or try combining it with other more inherently distinctive terms that make the trademark protectable from the outset, like The Abilene Albatross for a bar.

Marketing Considerations When Choosing a Name

Now that we have dissected what makes a mark distinctive, here are a few practical pointers that combine the legal information just discussed with some marketing savvy that is part of picking the "right" name for your business, service, or product.

General Advice

George Eastman, founder of Kodak and a man with an eye for a good trademark, suggested that trademarks should:
- be short
- be vigorous
- be easily spelled, and
- mean nothing.

Though this advice certainly worked for him, it may not apply to your situation. If not, heed the advice of other trademark experts who recommend that name marks be:
- pronounceable
- memorable
- graphically attractive (for instance, no hyphens), and
- legally available.

Whether your mark meets the other criteria discussed in this section is a more subjective decision that you will have to make yourself. However, these lists of desirable trademark characteristics omit an important point: Your mark must also be tailored to meet the needs of your business and your customers.

How to Come Up With a Good Name

Like most business decisions, your choice of how to select a good name mark will reflect your own personal style of decision making. Here are some alternative methods:
- Delegate the job to a committee.

- Throw a name-brainstorming party and invite all your friends.
- Make lists yourself.
- Devise a contest to generate a name.
- Use all of the above methods.
- Hire a professional name consultant.

Whatever method you use, you will probably want to develop a long list and a short list. The long list would consist of likely possibilities that meet the criteria we discuss below for tailoring your mark to your needs. Then you can use any of the above methods again to narrow the list to five or ten of the most likely.

When you have your short list, you must find out how to tell which of your possibilities can also be used as an Internet domain name (Chapter 2), and then turn to Chapters 4 through 6 to discover which possibilities meet the all-important criterion of legal availability. Once you have searched and cleared each name for possible conflicts with existing marks and Internet domain names (if you plan to use the Internet for marketing purposes), you can make a final decision based on aesthetics or marketability or whatever you decide is your ultimate criterion.

Useful Concepts in Creating a Name Mark for Your Product or Service

The most useful concepts in creating a name mark are the same ones you or your advertising consultant would think about in devising a marketing scheme. Your mark is, after all, the most important aspect of your advertising plan. What will help you invent your mark are basic commonsense conclusions about what kinds of advertising will work best with your product or service, based on what you know about your customers.

Use the following questions to develop criteria that are specific to your needs and that you can use, along with the suggestions above, to develop a list of potential marks. If you already have developed these criteria, this section tells you how to apply them to trademarks. And if you haven't, you might as well figure this stuff out now:

- What is your customer base (current or projected)? Is it a broad economic group, within a small region? Or is it a select group of professionals scattered nationwide? This is the most important factor, as it affects all of the other criteria below.
- What are your customers' demographics and income and educational level? This will inform the tone and style of your advertising, as well as the sort of words to use in your mark—for example, whether to use words that are young and hip, older and more traditional, funny or serious, highly literate or simple.
- What are your customers' buying habits? Are purchases typically made in a hurry or more carefully considered? If your customers tend to buy in a rushed manner, then your trademark needs to be simple with a high visual impact. If they tend to buy in a more considered manner, then your mark can be more subtle and complex.
- What aspect of your service or product will appeal to your potential customer base? This affects the image you want to project—if the main appeal of your service is convenience, then the trademark should evoke that idea.
- Can you distill the essence of your product or service into a word or phrase? If a dominant idea is connected with your service or product, a mark that incorporates or reflects that idea will help you promote it and make it easy for your customers to remember it.
- What image do you want to associate with your service or product? If the image you have is not exactly the one you want, you can try to develop a mark that better reflects your vision of your service or product. Keep your audience in mind: A mark incorporating symbols popular with teenagers might not help you if you seek to appeal to stable young families.
- How is your service or product different from those of the competition? Perhaps the main thing about your service or product is that it is unique—the mark should help identify that characteristic—or that it's cheaper, or fancier, or whatever sets you apart in the marketplace.

- How will the mark be advertised—in what media and with what level of visibility? This affects whether you need both a logo and a name, whether a short word is essential or a longer phrase will do, or whether you want to focus on trade dress (creative packaging, and so on). Also, how broadly and where you will advertise your mark—on business cards, letterhead, pamphlets, a storefront, signs, packaging, radio ads—affects what sort of mark to use. That's because a complicated logo might translate well to business cards, but you might not be able to clearly see it on a storefront.

The answers to some of these questions will also help you figure out what sources to use to create your mark, and what attributes the mark should have. For example, if your customer base is gourmet coffee drinkers, you could consider using foreign words, mythological names, or literary references in creating a mark that evokes sophistication and good taste. But if your customers comprise a broad section of the population whose main concerns are value and convenience, you might want a more straightforward simple name using American roots or references.

Using a Professional Name Consultant

Most name consulting firms cater to large corporations and are not likely to meet the needs or the budgets of small businesses. To find one that will help you on a smaller scale, take the advice of Ira Bachrach of Namelab (www.namelab.com), a corporate name consulting firm in San Francisco. He recommends calling a small to medium-sized ad agency and asking them to help you create a name as a discrete, time-limited project for a fixed fee. He advises you to specify what you expect them to produce for that fee and to propose paying when you get the result, or paying half in advance, half at the end.

Where to Find More on Trademark Strength

Now that we have taken a closer look at what makes an effective trademark, you might want to go on to Chapter 9, "Evaluating Trademark Strength." That chapter teaches you how to classify your (or another's) mark in terms of its legal strength. It discusses in much greater detail the varieties of distinctive and ordinary trademarks, including coined, fanciful, and suggestive categories of distinctive marks, and descriptive, geographic, personal name, and initial types of ordinary marks.

 FREQUENTLY ASKED QUESTION

Creating a trademark based on PERL programming

"I want to create a trademark called AlchemicPerl. Perl is a programming language and the Perl Foundation, which owns the registered trademark, has told me that I cannot use the word Perl. Does AlchemicPerl violate their trademark? AlchemicPerl will be used to market software and consulting services related to the Perl programming language. I know there is also a trademark called ActiveStatePerl which seems not to have a problem, but I just wanted to be more certain."

The short answer is that we're not sure what will happen if you proceed, but we have a feeling it's not going to be good. The Perl Foundation does have a federal registration for the word PERL combined with the image of an onion. The registration is for computer software (among other things), and the Perl Foundation warns others against using the word, Perl, as part of a software product (and even counsels against using an onion, the Perl mascot). The foundation's desire to protect this mark has something to do with its intention to maintain the Perl language as an authenticated open source language without worrying about commercial interlopers preventing others from using the name—a tactic that can have unexpected publicity consequences for those seeking open source freedom. You have a series of challenges ahead of you—for example, a trademark examiner could object to your use based upon the existing registrations; or the Perl Foundation might oppose the registrations as being likely to confuse consumers. For these reasons, we'd probably back off the choice of AlchemicPerl.

Trademark Searches—What They Are and Why You Should Do One

I n this chapter, we introduce you to the process of finding out whether your choice for a mark is already being used by someone else—a task commonly referred to as a trademark search. Then, in Chapter 5, we walk you through how to perform your own search. If your search turns up an existing mark that is the same as or similar to your proposed mark, you will then want to proceed to Chapter 6, "How to Evaluate the Results of Your Trademark Search," which helps you decide whether the existing mark legally conflicts with yours.

What Is a Trademark Search?

A trademark search is a systematic hunt for the existence of any registered or unregistered trademark or service mark that:

- is the same as or similar to a mark proposed for use by the searcher
- is being used anywhere in the country (or world, if the proposed mark is to be used internationally), and
- is being used in a context that would likely result in customer confusion if the proposed mark is put into use.

Why Do a Trademark Search?

There are two good reasons to search for potentially conflicting marks. First, if you are not the first user of the mark for the goods or services in the marketplace, you might be infringing on someone else's trademark rights. This means you might have to change your mark and, in some cases, pay damages to the first user if a judge concludes that your use creates a likelihood of customer confusion. Second, if you are planning to apply for federal registration of the mark, you will save time and money by discovering whether your proposed mark is already registered for similar goods and services.

Resources You Can Use in a Trademark Search

A trademark search can involve some or all of these resources, depending on the scope of the search:

- **The federal trademark register:** a list of all trademarks and service marks that have been authorized for federal trademark registration with the USPTO.
- **Pending trademark applications:** a list of all trademarks and service marks for which federal registration applications have been filed with the USPTO.
- **State trademark registrations:** a list of all trademarks and service marks that have been registered at the state level (usually with a state's secretary of state).
- **Publications containing relevant product and service names:** trade magazines, print directories of commercial names, yellow pages, and electronic databases containing product and service names that are in use in the United States generally, or with respect to specific fields, for example, computers, biotechnology, or bicycles.
- **The Internet:** domain names, Internet sites, and goods and services being offered on the Internet.

Where Are Trademark Search Resources Located?

Many of the resources used in a typical trademark search are available online for free. Others are available only through proprietary databases that any member of the public can access for a fee directly or over the Internet. Still other resources can be accessed for free using workstations and print collections found in special public libraries, known as Patent and Trademark Resource Centers (PTRCs). You can find a list of locations in your state at the USPTO's website: Go to www.uspto.gov/learning-resources and select "Support Centers," followed by "Patent and Trademark Resource Centers (PTRCs)."

Trademarks on the Federal Trademark Register and in Pending Applications

Perhaps the most important resource for a trademark search is the Trademark Electronic Search System (TESS). This search engine allows you to search the USPTO's database of registered trademarks and prior pending applications. Although the database doesn't include nonfederally registered trademarks—which may cause trouble down the road if you don't know about them in advance—a search of the USPTO database is a necessary first step.

It's also possible to search the USPTO trademark database at sites like Trademarkia (www.trademarkia.com), which offer additional benefits, such as simplified logo searching. Other Internet resources include Trademark.com (www.trademark.com) and SERION, a division of Compumark (www.compumark.com). Our recommendation is that you first use TESS to search the federal trademark register for marks that are the same as or very similar to yours.

Trademarks Registered With State Agencies

Many trademark owners who use their trademarks solely within particular states register the marks with those states' trademark agencies. Because such a registration might block the use of a later proposed mark within that state, the owner of the proposed mark will often search for instances of state registration. You can do this yourself by using the TrademarkScan State Database, available through SAEGIS, or by calling the secretary of state's offices for the states you are interested in. (For a list of state trademark agencies and statutes, go to www.ggmark.com and select your state under "U.S. State Trademark Laws and Databases.")

Unregistered Trademarks and Service Marks

Because trademark ownership is based on who uses the mark first, it is important to search for marks in actual use, even if they aren't registered. To do this, you must hunt for the use of your proposed mark (or something very similar) on products and services that are similar to the products or services you plan to use the mark with. While this hunt will undoubtedly produce many marks that appear on the federal trademark register, it will also turn up marks that aren't on the list.

You can use one or more of several approaches to performing this type of search (called a "common law search" because the importance of unregistered marks stems from court decisions, which are called the common law):

- Use an Internet search engine, such as Google, to search for use of your proposed mark on the Internet and as a domain name.
- Use SAEGIS on SERION to search its common law database on the Internet and all domain name registries for a modest fee.
- Use SuperPages (www.SuperPages.com) or the Thomas Register of Products and Services (www.thomasregister.com) to search for trade and corporate names for free on the Internet.
- Use the print resources in a PTRC or a large public library that contain listings of product and service names.
- Use PROQUEST (www.proquest.com) to access a number of databases listing product and service names in use around the country (this service can be costly, and involves a learning curve).

Different Levels of Trademark Searches

Three different levels of trademark searches are available to you:

- direct-hit searches
- analytical searches, and
- comprehensive searches.

Direct-Hit Searches

This type of search looks for marks on the federal trademark register that are the same as or very similar to the mark you propose to use. It is, in essence, the starting place for any trademark search. Its purpose is to get a quick fix on the marks that are most likely to cause your proposed mark trouble in the future. If you adopt and use a mark that clearly conflicts with one already on the federal trademark register, whether you actually know of it or not, you will be considered a willful infringer of that mark and may be sued for substantial money damages. The obviousness of your infringement will greatly reduce your ability to negotiate an acceptable settlement with the existing mark's owner. A direct-hit search that steers you away from using your proposed mark prevents this sort of difficulty.

In addition, a direct-hit search tells you whether it's worthwhile to apply for federal trademark registration. Your trademark won't qualify for placement on the federal register if the USPTO thinks customers are likely to confuse it with a mark already on the register. This means that a direct-hit search can expose marks that might conflict with yours and tell you whether an examiner is likely to approve your application.

A direct-hit search will tell you if your proposed mark has been registered for so many goods or services within the same class or classes as your mark that it would receive little protection under the federal trademark laws. You might want to use the mark anyway, but at least you'll have a better idea of its relative strength. (See Chapter 6 for more on classifying goods and services.)

Practically speaking, a direct-hit search is especially helpful when you have several choices of potential trademarks and you wish to narrow the field by eliminating obviously unavailable marks.

Direct-hit searches are quick and easy to do. All it takes is entering your mark into the search box in the USPTO's TESS database and seeing what comes up. In addition, you can browse the registered marks that come before and after your proposed name alphabetically.

(We tell you how to do all this in Chapter 5, "How to Do Your Own Trademark Search.") By using TESS, you will save approximately $30 to $50 per mark searched, the amount it typically costs to get a direct-hit search from a professional search service.

Analytical Searches

For most businesses, especially those that plan to operate regionally or nationally, direct-hit searching is only the first step to clearing a name. Especially when the proposed name is distinctive, a more thorough search will be in order. On the other hand, if you already know that your proposed name is legally weak, or your business is small and local and you can tolerate some risk that an undiscovered prior user will pop up at a later time, the direct-hit search is really all the searching for registered marks that you'll need to do.

Depending on the type and complexity of your mark, the analytical search compares your mark with all federally registered and pending marks that sound or look like your mark, plus all marks that mean the same thing or in some other way might lead to customer confusion. An analytical search frequently involves searching for homonyms, synonyms, phonetic equivalents, alternative spellings, anagrams (words with the same letters rearranged), marks with similar components, and marks that start or end the same, or that have any other similarity. This type of search is more thorough, or "deeper," than a direct-hit search, and consequently more expensive and time-consuming. However, it permits you to uncover more potential conflicts.

For example, an analytical search for the mark Bioscan might reasonably include a look at all the marks that immediately surround Bioscan alphabetically, and then look up all marks including "bio" or "scan," then all marks with the sounds -io or -osc in the middle. Next, you would search for all synonyms you could think of. Then, you might want to check for anagrams (scaniob) and alternative spellings (bayouskan). This degree of complexity might not be called for in the case of a more straightforward mark, such as Fish Head Graphics.

An analytical search is essential for any business that wants to make sure its proposed mark isn't likely to be challenged on the grounds it is confusingly similar to, or evocative of, an existing federally registered mark. For instance, assume the manufacturer of certain gas barbecue components wants to use the mark Flamethrower. Because the components will all be stamped with this mark, the manufacturer wants to make sure that no existing mark has priority. To do this, an analytical search would look for all marks with the word "flame," all marks with the word "thrower," and all marks with words that sound like or mean the same thing as either of these.

It is especially wise to do this level of search if your prospective mark is distinctive. Because a distinctive mark can be protected to a much greater degree than a mark that lacks distinctiveness, it's worth making sure the distinctive mark is clear of all conflicts. For instance, the makers of Raintree shampoos would want to do an analytical search before marketing product regionally, as would the operator of an 800-number information service that had a distinctive name. For a company that expects to expand its use of a particular mark in the future, an analytical search reduces the likelihood of eventual problems due to customer confusion caused by marks that are not identical but are reminiscent of each other.

The USPTO's TESS database is ideal for doing analytical searches. However, doing a competent analytical search involves a moderate learning curve. (We give you the basics in Chapter 5, "How to Do Your Own Trademark Search.") TESS provides good online support, but you should plan on spending at least half an hour familiarizing yourself with the system before launching a search. By using TESS, you will save approximately $100 per mark searched, the amount it typically costs to get an analytical search from a professional search service.

In some ways, the SAEGIS on SERION search engine (which uses the proprietary Thompson CompuMark database) is even better than TESS in that it automatically provides an analytical search. However, it takes some time to learn how to use SAEGIS and could end up costing you as much as a professional search service. Of course, the better you get at doing a SAEGIS search, the more efficient your search will be and the less it will cost.

Comprehensive Trademark Searches

A comprehensive trademark search includes both direct-hit and analytical searches of the federal trademark register and examines other resources where unregistered marks and state registered marks might be found, such as proprietary online databases, hard-copy and electronic telephone directories (yellow pages), trade directories, the Internet, product catalogs, business ratings services, and so on. The goal is to discover any actual use of your proposed mark, whether or not it is officially registered. As mentioned, the reason for this is that most disputes between marks are resolved in favor of the first to actually use the mark.

For local businesses, a comprehensive search should, at a minimum, consist of checking the relevant yellow pages, newspapers, trade and product journals, and any other resource that might show a possibly conflicting locally used mark. For businesses that have broader horizons in mind, including Internet start-ups and e-commerce enterprises, this type of search can involve many different hard-copy and online resources and can therefore become costly.

So far, we have suggested that you can do direct-hit and analytical searches yourself. The same is true with comprehensive searching. However, currently you won't be able to search state registered trademark databases on the Internet unless you are willing to pay a fee to use SAEGIS. If you are planning on sinking a lot of money into your new business or website that will carry your proposed mark, and your mark is inherently distinctive, you might do well to hire a professional search service to cover all the bases for you. Comprehensive searches run between $300 and $600 per mark searched.

Because of this price tag, you can save yourself a lot of money by using TESS to perform direct-hit and analytical searches as a screening mechanism. That is, once you decide to spring for a comprehensive search, you should first assure yourself that your proposed mark does not legally conflict with registered or pending marks on the federal or state trademark registers. This will prevent you from paying for a comprehensive search for a mark that you most likely would decide not to use.

Planning Your Trademark Search

Now that you have a good idea of what is involved in a trademark search, you need to decide on the appropriate search for you and your particular situation.

The Trademark Uncertainty Principle

Let us start by saying that if time and money are no problem, you will be well advised to do a comprehensive trademark search for every mark you plan to use. You can only gain from being as careful and conscientious about clearing your mark as possible. But two warnings apply here.

Your Results Will Be Incomplete No Matter How Thorough Your Search

No search is going to uncover every possible conflict in the United States and certainly not internationally. It's just too difficult to know for sure whether a prior unregistered user of a similar mark is in North Carolina when you are in South Dakota. The best you can do is to make sure that your proposed mark doesn't obviously conflict either with registered marks or with any unregistered marks you can find by systematically examining pertinent sources of trademarks, service marks, or trade names.

This means no matter how thoroughly you search, you will have to live with a small degree of uncertainty that someone else began using your mark first. What does it mean, legally, if someone did? Nothing, if the other user doesn't object to your use. Even if the other user does object and sues you in court to force you to stop using the mark, you probably would be allowed to continue to use the mark in your present marketing territory (unless both marks are used to market related or competing goods or services on the Internet). However, a judge could prevent you from acquiring the nationwide exclusive rights to your mark that otherwise would be available to you by being the first to register it.

Your Search Results Will Be Legally Uncertain

As you are undoubtedly tired of hearing by now, trademark law has no absolute answers. Even the most extensive search will probably not end your uncertainty, because it will likely uncover at least a few marks that are somewhat similar and used on products that are at least vaguely related to yours. Whether such a trademark definitively infringes on the other is a decision that only a judge or jury can make when the dispute comes before them. In other words, it's only after you have been sued and a ruling has been made that you will know with some certainty whether your mark infringes on another. In many real-world situations, you can be sure that the other user is unlikely to sue. But a thorough search will give you as much assurance as possible under the circumstances.

Planning the Scope of Your Search

Because the best you can do is weigh factors and estimate probabilities, it's important for you to decide what level of risk is acceptable to you now. That way, you can tailor your search to minimize the risk associated with your decision. Below we set out some general rules to follow when planning the scope of your trademark search.

Rule 1: Always check the federal trademark register.

All searches should check the federal trademark register first for the same or a very similar mark as the one you propose to use. As mentioned, it is relatively easy to do, it's free, and it is the best way to uncover conflicts that necessarily require you to pick another mark.

Rule 2: A big advertising budget warrants a more extensive search.

Because comprehensive searches can cost time and money, it might not make sense for a small business to check for every possible conflict. Whether you should do an extensive search depends on the size of your business, your future goals, your mark, and how you plan to use it. A good general rule is that if you plan to spend a fair proportion of your budget on promoting your mark, you should first spend whatever it takes (perhaps hundreds of dollars) making sure the name is safe for you to use. Otherwise you risk wasting your advertising dollars if you have to change the mark later. On the other hand, if your advertising budget is small, it could make more sense to accept a more limited search as sufficient.

Rule 3: A strong mark requires a thorough search.

How extensive your search should be will depend on how much protection you need or can get for your mark. With a strong mark, you have more to protect, and a thorough search process is a better investment than in the case of a weak mark, where the extent of your rights is likely to be more limited anyway. The more distinctive, and therefore the stronger, the mark, the greater degree of assurance you need that no one else is using a similar mark elsewhere. If you have a strong mark and your goal is to be able to use your mark exclusively regionally, nationwide, or even worldwide, that will entail a comprehensive search.

One important reason you need a comprehensive search to protect a proposed strong mark is that the existence of similar marks could prove that your chosen mark is not as strong as you originally thought. Remember that marks are distinctive either because they are inherently distinctive (fanciful, suggestive, or coined), or because they become well known to the public through widespread use over time. If existing marks sound or mean the same thing as your proposed mark, or look like it while sounding different, or have elements in common with it, your proposed mark might not be as legally strong as you had hoped.

Rule 4: Think long term.

In determining your trademark search goals, consider the future. For example, if your local engineering consulting service is limited to one city now, but you might want to expand later—perhaps through the Internet or franchising—you'll want to conduct a more extensive search than might otherwise be appropriate for a firm of your current size. Rather than risking the possibility of having to change your mark later, conduct a thorough trademark search with those long-term goals in mind. This involves doing both direct-hit and analytical trademark searches, as well as thorough common law searches (to search for unregistered marks). By contrast, if you run a local hobby or kitchenware shop and plan to stay small, a direct-hit search coupled with a local or statewide common law search should prove sufficient (unless, again, you plan to market on the Web).

Rule 5: The geographic scope of the use affects the size of the search.
Where you will use your mark will determine what kind of a search you need to perform. This makes each case a fact-specific determination. Nevertheless, the following general guides are reliable:

- **For a mark used only in one region of one state, and for which there is no expectation of expansion:** Generally speaking, the smaller the geographic area in which you market your goods or services, the less extensive the search needs to be. If you check federal and state registered trademarks for direct hits and then do a thorough common law search for your area and type of business, you should be relatively well protected. That's because if another similar mark is not registered federally or with the state, and is not in use in your geographic area or line of business, you will not likely cause customer confusion. The only potential concern you could have is dilution. However, if the other mark is not famous enough for you to run across it through these searches, then it is probably not famous enough to get relief under the theory of dilution.

- **For a mark in use in two or more states:** Suppose you are clearing a mark for your new computer program, gardening supply catalog, or 800-number phone service. You can clear such a mark only with a comprehensive search. That ideally should include a federal analytic search, an analytic search in all states, and a thorough common law search. This more extensive search is necessary because other businesses might have rights through registration in marks that are not yet being used in your particular region. In addition, because such marks are marketed nationally, they will face a greater array of potentially conflicting marks and thus a greater potential for infringement claims.

Remember that the Internet is rapidly eliminating the very concept of local marketing territories, and if you expect to do business on the Web some day, you'll want to do your search just as if you planned to do business on a national level.

Rule 6: Marketing channels affect the size of the search.

- **For a mark used in a narrow niche of the market:** Your mark could be cleared with a search that is limited to direct hits on similar names used on related and competing goods. That's because with a narrow circle of competitors and limited marketing avenues, you can minimize the chances of a confusingly similar mark hurting your sales by looking only at similar marks in the same market. For example, a mark used only on industrial ball bearings probably need only clear conflicts within industries related to machinery and steel, along with the recommended direct-hit search of the federal trademark register.

- **For a mark used by one owner on a wide variety of goods or services:** If you plan to use one mark on several different services or products, then you must be careful to find all other marks that are even vaguely similar. That's because your investment in such a mark will be high, and because you will need to be sure it evokes no other connection than the one to your business. For example, if you intended to develop a mark for use on clothes, shoes, luggage, jewelry, and cosmetics, you would conduct the most thorough search possible.

Using a Professional Search Service

Before you decide whether to do your own searching or farm it out, consider that a combination of approaches could give you the best legal protection for your time and money. For example, using your computer to access the TESS database on the trademark section of the USPTO's Internet site (www.uspto.gov) can be quick and easy and provide good preliminary information. And if you are willing to pay the fees and spend the time learning the system, SAEGIS on SERION gives you access to the state trademark databases and a good search of the Internet and domain name registries. But unless you have the opportunity to practice, you probably should not attempt a comprehensive search on your own. For that, you should pay someone who knows what he or she is doing. In Appendix C, we provide portions of a comprehensive search that Nolo commissioned from Thomson CompuMark, a professional search service, in 2007. Although a dozen years have passed since we commissioned this search, it still accurately reflects the organization and structure of a professional search. Feel free to take a look, but don't get stuck there. The example assumes that you are familiar with the material in this chapter and Chapter 5.

Why Use a Search Service?

Next to hiring a trademark attorney, paying a trademark search firm is the most expensive means of clearing your mark. However, except for a direct-hit search—which you can reliably do yourself—a search service is likely to provide more reliable results than you will produce on your own, for several reasons. Most important, analytical and comprehensive searches come with considerable learning curves, regardless of which database or resources the searcher is using. Searching for possible conflicts is a kind of art form that involves a lot more than typing in a word or phrase and asking whether it appears on the source being searched. An additional benefit of search services is that they have access to databases that are not yet available to the public for free, such as proprietary (private) databases the service will use in a common law search.

What Trademark Search Services Cost

The services provided by various trademark search firms, and the fees they charge for different types of searches, vary considerably. Often, the cost of the service will depend on how much analysis the service will do with the raw information before the service delivers a report to you. Generally, the more unanalyzed the data you receive, the cheaper it will be. Only attorneys are allowed to offer opinions about potential trademark conflicts, and as a result, trademark search services offered by attorneys tend to cost the most because they come with legal advice.

What do search services charge? Firms that search (but do not give legal advice) generally charge as follows:

- direct-hit federally registered trademark search (for identical marks)—from $50 to $150 per mark searched
- analytical federally registered trademark search (for similar or related marks) from $100 to $300 per mark searched
- common law search only—from $100 to $200 per mark searched, or
- comprehensive search (combining analytical federal, state, common law, and domain name searches)—between $200 and $500 per mark searched.

The difference in rates might reflect variations in the coverage of the search, the sort of report you get, the experience of the searchers, or simply economies of scale. On the other hand, some firms advertise an unusually low price to draw in customers, but then add on charges that end up exceeding another firm's total price (a professional version of bait and switch). To evaluate the true cost of each service, you should ask, for example, whether a stated fee covers the whole report, or whether the cost will be determined on a per-page basis? Obviously, to sensibly shop you need to know the total cost of each service.

The Role of Attorneys in Trademark Searches

If you decide to hire a trademark attorney to advise you on the selection and registration of a trademark or service mark, the attorney will be able to arrange for the trademark search. Some attorneys do it themselves, but most farm the search out to a search firm. Once the report comes back from the search firm, the attorney will interpret it for you and advise you on whether to go ahead with your proposed mark. Although you are getting considerably more in this attorney package than you'll get from a search service alone, it will cost you.

How to Find and Use a Trademark Search Service

Type "trademark search services" into your search engine and a lengthy list of companies and law firms will be displayed. The most popular choice among legal professionals is Thomson CompuMark (www.trademarks.thomsonreuters.com), the company that helped to design the USPTO's trademark database. Like all search services, rates vary depending on the type of search and how soon you need the results. Another company that's been in business for decades is Trademark Express (www.tmexpress.com), which offers a full choice of trademark searches. By the way, trademark search firms will not interpret their search results; that task is left to you. In Chapter 6, "How to Evaluate the Results of Your Trademark Search," we take you step by step through a sample search report.

Some trademark search services will try to convince you that you are making a mistake if you don't search every corner of the globe for possible conflicts. Before taking the bait, review our remarks in "Different Levels of Trademark Searches," above, about the different levels of searching, and make an independent decision about the scope of search that is appropriate for you. Also, some search services provide additional services, such as preparing applications for federal and state trademark registrations. As with trademark lawyers, these businesses have a vested interest in convincing you that you will be better served by paying them to handle the tasks in question than by doing them yourself. If you feel that this point of view—which could in some cases be perfectly reasonable—is being too aggressively pushed in your situation, get a firm hold on your wallet and consider finding another service.

Using a Patent and Trademark Resource Center to Do Your Own Search

Using a Patent and Trademark Resource Center (PTRC) to do your federal trademark search is less expensive than hiring a search service, but it will cost you in time and transportation expenses—unless you live or work close to a PTRC. Most PTRCs offer free access to the CASSIS DVD-ROM. The CASSIS trademark list is a good way to search for direct hits. You can also use CASSIS to do an analytical trademark search, but the results will likely not be as reliable as a TESS database search.

Every PTRC has print materials that you can use to search the federal trademark register database. You might want to head for these hard copies if you are computer challenged or the wait to use the PTRC CASSIS workstation is too long.

Whether using a PTRC is cost-effective for you will depend on factors such as:

- how many potential marks you need to search
- how far you are from the nearest PTRC
- whether you have the time to visit a PTRC during regular working hours, and
- the time it takes you to learn the CASSIS system (library staff can provide help).

If you opt to visit a PTRC, see Chapter 5 for instructions on how to conduct a PTRC trademark search.

Does Your Failure to Search Mean You Acted in Bad Faith?

In 1998, designer Tommy Hilfiger was found to have acted in bad faith when adopting the mark "Star Class" for nautical sportswear. (*SCYRA v. Tommy Hilfiger, U.S.A., Inc.*, 80 F.3d 749 (2d Cir. 1996).) Mr. Hilfiger's attorney performed a search of federally registered marks and found no conflicts, but Mr. Hilfiger disregarded his attorney's advice to obtain a complete trademark search for state and common law trademarks, which would have revealed an unregistered trademark for Star Class owned by an international yachting organization. The court ruled Mr. Hilfiger should have been aware of the need for a full search, because star class was a common term in yachting. As a result, the court assessed special damages against Mr. Hilfiger for acting in bad faith. In other words, Mr. Hilfiger had to pay more than usual for infringing a trademark because of his failure to search.

In a subsequent case, a map company adopted the mark Streetsmart, without conducting a formal trademark search. A court of appeals ruled this was not bad faith because the company had not disregarded its attorney's advice, had previously used similar marks with the suffix "smart," and was aware of the conflicting mark, Streetwise, but believed the two terms were not confusing. (*Streetwise Maps, Inc. v. Vandam, Inc.*, 159 F.3d 739 (2d Cir. 1998).)

In another case, a court summarized the standard by stating that a failure to search equals bad faith only if either of the following is true:

- The trademark owner had reason to believe it was infringing another mark.
- The trademark owner's attorney advised it to perform a more complete search.

How to Do Your Own Trademark Search

S earching for registered or pending trademarks on your own by using the USPTO's online search system is easy. A typical direct-hit search takes only about 15 minutes. An analytical search using TESS takes longer but still can be accomplished in well under an hour once you have learned the basics. And if you learn to use SAEGIS (officially known as SAEGIS on SERION, www.serioninfo.com), an analytical search will be even faster but will involve costs that depend on the number of search results you wish to review (usually, $2.50 per mark displayed).

Both the USPTO and SAEGIS searches allow you to compare your proposed mark with registered trademarks and trademarks that are pending registration with the USPTO. The results you come up with will include a list of the trademarks that meet your search parameters and the names, addresses, and contact information for the owners of those trademarks. You'll also learn how the trademark is being used (on what products or for what services) and what international class (category of goods or services) the mark has been assigned to by the trademark owner or applicant. This information is key in deciding whether you can go ahead and use the name without creating the likelihood of customer confusion. (See Chapter 6 for more on evaluating the results of your trademark search.)

Meet TESS—The Trademark Electronic Search System

TESS is an acronym for Trademark Electronic Search System, the search system that the USPTO has made available to the public for free on the USPTO's website. It is about as good a system as you can find anywhere and is roughly equivalent to the USPTO's internal trademark search system known as X-Search. It's updated every day, has enormous flexibility in terms of the type of search that you can perform, and all in all, is a most valuable gift from the federal government. TESS comes with its own comprehensive help file, and if you are doing your own trademark search, you would be wise to study it before beginning your search.

The USPTO's Three Ts: TESS, TEAS, and TSDR

The USPTO provides three powerful databases at its site, TESS, TEAS, and TSDR. These databases are distinguished as follows:

- **TESS (Trademark Electronic Search System).** Use TESS when searching through federal trademark registrations and pending applications.
- **TEAS (Trademark Electronic Application System).** Use TEAS when applying for a trademark, collective mark, certification mark, or filing a Statement of Use/Amendment to Allege Use, or other application and postregistration forms.
- **TSDR (Trademark Status and Document Retrieval).** The TSDR combined two preexisting databases, TARR (for checking status of active applications) and TDR (for retrieving trademark documents and correspondence). The TSDR allows you to search by serial number or registration number and to review and download any of the millions of relevant documents and correspondence for trademarks (whether "live" or "dead").

Getting Started With TESS

The first step is to go to the USPTO's website (www.uspto.gov). Click "Trademarks" at the top of the screen. Under "Application Process," select "Searching Trademarks." Then, under "Search Trademark Database," click the box, "Search Our Trademark Database (TESS)." You'll encounter the choices set out below.

Choose the Type of Search

TESS offers five basic approaches to searching:

- Basic Word Mark Search (New User)
- Word and/or Design Mark Search (Structured)

- Word and/or Design Mark Search (Free Form)
- Browse Dictionary (Browse Dictionary), or
- Search OG Publication Date or Registration Date (Search OG).

Select A Search Option
▶ **Basic Word Mark Search (New User)** This option cannot be used to search design marks.
▶ **Word and/or Design Mark Search (Structured)** This option is used to search word and/or design marks. **NOTE:** You must first use the Design Search Code Manual to look up the relevant Design Codes.
▶ **Word and/or Design Mark Search (Free Form)** This option allows you to construct word and/or design searches using Boolean logic and multiple search fields. **NOTE:** You must first use the Design Search Code Manual to look up the relevant Design Codes.

Additional Search Options
▶ **Browse Dictionary (Browse Dictionary)** This option browses all fields in the database unless you limit to a particular field. Results are returned in a dictionary-style (alphabetic) format.
▶ **Search OG Publication Date or Registration Date (Search OG)** This option searches the Official Gazette for marks published or registered on a particular date.
Logout   *Please logout when you are done to release system resources allocated for you.*

The first two, Basic Word Mark Search (New User) and Word and/or Design Mark Search (Structured), are similar. The main difference is that a structured search allows for a more flexible search. In this chapter, we take you through the structured search, but by all means use the New User Search if you want a milder learning curve. As you become more skilled at using TESS, you might want the even greater flexibility offered with the third option, Word and/or Design Mark Search (Free Form). Regardless of which of the first three approaches you take, you'll also want to do a quick browse through the dictionary.

The USPTO also offers the ability to search the USPTO's *Official Gazette*, the electronic publication in which trademarks are published for public comments or opposition. The *OG* also includes notices regarding other interoffice trademark activity. As a final searching tool, you can check your search terms within the *OG* to avoid any last-minute surprises.

Browse the Dictionary

The dictionary is an alphabetical listing of all the marks that appear in the TESS database. If you wish to search for the mark "Domain Name King," for example, simply click the "Browse Dictionary" link and enter the name "domainnameking" as one word in the search box. Click the "Browse" button, and you'll see the page set out below.

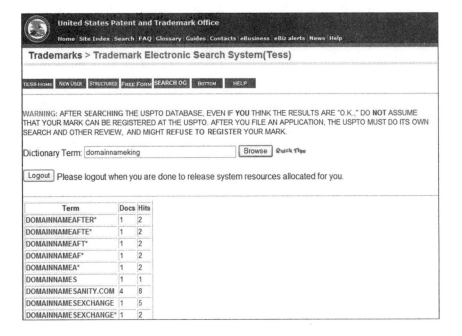

By obtaining a listing of marks that alphabetically precede and follow the name you're searching, you can get a quick overview of marks that are alphabetically close to yours.

Sometimes you will encounter a list of marks in the dictionary that starts with the full word and then shows the same word several times with a decreasing number of letters at the end. For example, browsing for the word "domain" also shows domainalyzer, domainalyzer*, domainalyze*, Domainalyz*, and domainaly*. The terms with the asterisks in this example are not registered marks but rather are roots of the term "domainalyzer" and show up in the index for search purposes only.

Understand the TESS Word and/or Design Mark Search (Structured)

First, let's look at the Word and/or Design Mark Search, which we'll refer to as the structured search page (see below).

Search History

The first active link is titled View Search History and is designed to keep track of your searches so you can easily go back over ground that you covered before. Each previous query is identified with a number, as in s1, s2, and so on. You can reproduce the search by simply entering the search number into the first Search Term box. But beware. The system will kick you off after 15 minutes of inaction, and when you are kicked off, your search history goes away. Unfortunately, you cannot save your search history from one session to another.

United States Patent and Trademark Office

Home | Site Index | Search | FAQ | Glossary | Guides | Contacts | eBusiness | eBiz alerts | News | Help

Trademarks > Trademark Electronic Search System(Tess)

TESS HOME | NEW USER | FREE FORM | BROWSE DICT | SEARCH OG | BOTTOM | HELP

WARNING: AFTER SEARCHING THE USPTO DATABASE, EVEN IF YOU THINK THE RESULTS ARE "O.K.," DO NOT ASSUME THAT YOUR MARK CAN BE REGISTERED AT THE USPTO. AFTER YOU FILE AN APPLICATION, THE USPTO MUST DO ITS OWN SEARCH AND OTHER REVIEW, AND MIGHT REFUSE TO REGISTER YOUR MARK.

View Search History:

Records Returned: 100   Plurals: No   Quick Tips

Search Term: Field: ALL   Operator OR

Search Term: Field: ALL

Submit Query   Clear Query

Logout | Please logout when you are done to release system resources allocated for you.

TESS HOME | NEW USER | FREE FORM | BROWSE DICT | SEARCH OG | TOP | HELP

| HOME | SITE INDEX | SEARCH | eBUSINESS | HELP | PRIVACY POLICY

Records Returned

This drop-down menu gives you the option of returning 50, 100, or 200 records as a result of your search. The default is 100, and there is little reason to change it unless your search results indicated a larger number of records meet your search specifications.

Plurals

This drop-down menu allows you to automatically retrieve the plural as well as singular forms of words that you enter into the Search Term boxes. Choose "No," if you don't want plurals, "Yes," if you do.

Search Terms

The Structured Form Search lets you search for one or two terms. The terms can be individual words, or they can be phrases. You might need to search for only one term. For instance, if your proposed mark is Mandalay, initially to be used with your famous lemon pies, you might want to search only for the word "Mandalay," the distinctive element of your name. If so, you would enter that word in the top search box and then click "Submit Query." Or, if you want to see if there are any marks containing the phrase "lemon pie" in connection with Mandalay, you could enter "lemon pie" surrounded by quotation marks in the top search box and Mandalay in the bottom box. (You'll need to use an operator; see below for instructions.)

Incidentally, because you might want to expand the use of Mandalay to other types of pies or baked goods, the most appropriate search in this context would be Mandalay in Class 30 (baked goods). (See Chapter 6 for more on the trademark classification system.)

Field

This drop-down menu lets you specify which fields of the TESS database records you want to search. Every trademark record has a number of fields, including the trademark's owner, its registration date, its registration number, the description of goods or services that the mark is used to market, and the classification assigned to the mark by the USPTO. If you want to focus on records that show your search terms in the marks themselves, then you should choose the Basic Index field. However, if you wish to produce every record that contains your search terms regardless of which field they occur in, select the ALL fields option.

If you are searching for two terms, you can choose separate fields for each term. For instance, you might want to use the Description of Mark field for the term in the top box and the Basic Index field for the term in the lower box.

Logical Operators

If you enter terms in both the top and bottom Search Term boxes, you'll need to pick what's called an "operator" to connect them. You can use the drop-down menu to choose among the available operators.

The AND Operator

If you select AND from the pull-down menu of operators, you are telling TESS to pull up all trademark records that contain both of the search terms entered in the Search Term boxes. For example, the search query "mandalay AND lemon pie" will produce every record that contains both "mandalay" and "lemon pie." It will not produce a record that doesn't have both. The advantage of using AND is that you can narrow your search to only those marks that have both terms. The disadvantage to AND is that you won't get any marks that don't have both terms as you have entered them in the Search Term box, which means you might miss marks that you should know about. For example, if you require the search results to contain both "mandalay" and "lemon pie," you would miss all marks that contain "mandalay" but not "lemon pie" and likewise all marks that contain "lemon pie" but not "mandalay."

The OR Operator

If you enter these same search terms but select the OR operator—making your query "mandalay OR lemon pie"—your search will produce a list of all trademarks with the term "lemon pie," all trademarks with the term "mandalay," and all trademarks with both terms. Needless to say, that list would be very long, because so many trademarks are likely to have either term in them.

However, this approach can be very useful if your proposed mark contains two distinctive words and you want to review every trademark that has either word. For instance, suppose you're considering the mark AnalogAstromaps for a website featuring a series of star charts. You would most likely want to use the OR operator to search for any trademarks containing either "analog" or "astromaps." Any trademark with either term might knock out your proposed mark if the context showed a likelihood of customer confusion.

Although the OR operator has the advantage of inclusiveness—that is, you are less likely to miss a relevant mark than when you are using the AND operator—it can have the disadvantage of producing much too long a list of marks to intelligently assess. The more common the terms being searched, the greater the risk of an unwieldy list of results. Probably the best approach is to initially use the OR operator and see what turns up. If the resulting list is too long, you can retreat to the more restrictive AND operator.

The NOT Operator

A third operator—NOT—can be used to exclude from the search results any term you enter in the lower Search Term box. For instance, you might decide that you want to see every trademark with the term "astromap" but no trademark with the term "starchart." This search query would look like this: astromap NOT starchart.

The XOR Operator

A fourth operator—XOR—lets you search for any trademark that has either the first Search Term or the second Search Term, but not both. For example, if you searched for "analog XOR astromap," your search would turn up trademarks with either "analog" or "astromap," but not trademarks that contain both terms. Because there is seldom a reason to exclude a combination of two terms, you probably won't need to use the XOR operator much.

Additional Operators

TESS provides additional operators that are most appropriate for searching fields in the trademark records that contain whole sentences or paragraphs. For instance, you can specify that the two terms you enter in the boxes be in the same sentence (WITH) or paragraph (SAME), or within a certain proximity of each other (for instance, within two words of each other in any order (NEAR), or in the order specified (ADJ)). You will find these operators most helpful if you want to search the "Goods and Services" or "Description of Mark" fields. For most trademark searching purposes, however, the AND, OR, and NOT operators should be sufficient.

Tips on Using the Word and/or Design Mark Search (Structured)

The tips we outline here are intended for basic trademark searching. As you get more familiar with TESS, you should feel free to experiment with the many options it offers.

Focus on the Most Distinctive Part of the Mark You're Searching

You should focus on the part of your mark that is most distinctive because it is that part of your mark that would most likely cause customers to confuse your name with an existing trademark using that same term. For instance, if your proposed mark is Zoroaster Designs, the word to use in your search is "Zoroaster," because it is by far the more distinctive of the two words. "Designs" is a generic word that can be used in a lot of different trademarks without creating customer confusion. So, although you might wish to search for any mark that contains either "designs" or "Zoroaster"— just to see what's out there—you are primarily interested in "Zoroaster."

Search for Distinctive Syllables

It is wise to go a step further and search for marks that contain one or more of the distinctive syllables in your name. For example, if your proposed mark is Bioscan, you should search for trademarks that contain either "bio" or "scan," because you might turn up something similar like "biosearch" or "cellscan." But it wouldn't make much sense to search for marks containing syllables that wouldn't likely be used. For example, the syllables "ga," "zoon," and "tite" (as in the website gazoontite.com) are not nearly as likely to be used in existing marks as are "bio" or "scan."

Don't Use the .com in Your Search

You are probably searching for conflicts for your proposed domain name for one of two reasons. First, you might be seeking to federally register your domain name. Or, you could be trying to learn whether your proposed domain name (regardless of whether you will federally register it) will conflict with a registered trademark. In either case, when checking for trademark conflicts with domain names, the best approach is to separate the domain name into its various components and search only for the distinctive components.

For instance, if your domain name were zoroasterdesigns.com, you would start your search with "Zoroaster." That search would turn up all federally registered Zoroaster marks (including those with the .com or any other top-level domain name suffix such as .org or .net). This is especially important when choosing a domain name, because the owner of a federally registered mark can stop you from using a similar mark as your domain name if you are offering similar products or services. For example, the owner of the federally registered mark Zoroaster Furniture might be able to stop your use of zoroasterdesigns.com if your website offered furniture or similar goods.

Keep in mind that even though a large number of domain names are registered as marks, for example, priceline.com, it is the portion of the name to the left of the dot that will create the trademark conflict.

The USPTO requires that the registrant disclaim the ".com" portion of the mark because it is a generic term. This is true for all top-level domains such as .org, .net, and the new top-level domains, such as .biz, .info, and .name. (For more information on registering domain names as trademarks, see Chapter 7.)

Searching for Phrases

As we saw with the lemon pie example, you can use two or more words as a single search term by enclosing them in quotation marks. For example, a sensible search for "Big Daddy's Sweet Tooth Donuts" would include a search for the phrase "Big Daddy's" and the phrase "Sweet Tooth." You would do this by entering:

- "Big Daddy" in quotation marks in the upper Search Term box and
- "Sweet Tooth" in quotation marks in the lower Search Term box.

If you want to search for only a single phrase, as in "Sweet Tooth Munchies," simply enter the phrase in quotation marks in the top Search Term box and run the search.

Use the Truncation Feature Where Appropriate

When you search for a particular term, it's useful to also search for slight variations of the term—for instance, if you are searching for the word "saber," you'll want to know about trademarks using the British spelling, "sabre." The computer won't find these variants for you without special instructions. Fortunately, it's easy to locate slight variations in TESS by using the truncation feature.

Right Truncation

One of the options offered by TESS is what's called word truncation, which can be right truncation and left truncation. Right truncation allows you to chop off as much of the right-hand (ending) portion of a word as you wish and have the computer search for all words that start with what remains. For instance, instead of wondering whether to search for "sabre" or "saber," you could search for all trademarks that contain the root segment "sab." This would pull up both variations of "saber" but would also produce unrelated terms, such as "sabbath." To create this truncation effect, simply put an asterisk at the end of the string of letters that you want to search, as in "sab*."

If you are using right truncation, turn off the plural function (if you don't, the search engine will become confused). You can avoid the confusion by choosing "No" from the drop-down menu above the Field box. In addition, you cannot use the truncation feature when enclosing a phrase in quotation marks. For example, the TESS system will not retrieve truncations for the phrase "Big Daddy*" when it is enclosed in quotation marks.

Left Truncation

If you use left truncation, for example "*time," the search results will produce all marks that have words to the left of "time," for example Drive Time, Doubletime, Bed Time Stories, and Comfy Time. Unlike right truncation, the plural function works fine with left truncation.

Using Both Left and Right Truncation

TESS allows you to search for words that have both left truncations and right truncations. For instance, if you want to use the word "Geezer" in your mark, you might want to do a search for all marks that contain the "eez" portion of the word, because all marks with those three letters will resemble each other at least a little bit. You would get this result by truncating "eez" with an asterisk on both sides, as in *eez*. Again, remember to turn off the plural function.

Wildcards

TESS also allows you to substitute "wildcard" characters for specific letters in a word. For instance, if you want to search for all occurrences of women or woman, you should enter the search term wom?n, which would retrieve both words because the question mark stands for any character in that particular position.

TESS comes with an entire set of wildcards, such as characters that stand for vowels, consonants, and the like. As you become more familiar with trademark searching in the TESS system, you'll pick these up.

Search for Sound-Alikes

In addition to searching for names that are similar to yours in appearance, it is also important to search for words that sound alike. For example, gazoontite.com and gesundheit.com don't look that much alike, but they sound identical and might well confuse customers. The best approach to searching for sound-alikes is to focus on the most distinctive syllables in the proposed mark and search for these by themselves. You might pull up a longer list of marks than you want to deal with, but if you do find a mark that sounds like yours and is in use with goods or services that are commercially related to yours, you would do well to choose another mark.

If you are using the TrademarkScan Autoquery search that is available through SAEGIS, you will find that the search automatically searches for sound-alikes.

Search for Foreign Translations

If your mark has exactly the same meaning as another mark in a different language, the owner of the other mark can challenge your mark if it can be shown that customers would likely be confused. For instance, if you wanted to name your restaurant The Milkhouse and somebody already had a mark for Casa de Leche, you have the potential for a trademark infringement charge. The bad news is that there is no do-it-yourself trademark search system that pulls up translations. The good news is that these types of conflicts are relatively rare. If you are using distinctive terms in your mark that have an independent meaning (which would be the case with arbitrary or suggestive marks), consider using a foreign language dictionary to find translations and then search for those as well as your proposed mark.

Trademark Searching With TESS: An Example

Here we provide an example of a typical search using TESS. In this case we are searching for the term "Hooky Wooky" for use as a trademark for crafts products, specifically crocheted clothing and accessories.

We start by using the Structured Form Search and enter "Hooky" in the top Search Term box and "Wooky" in the lower Search Term box. We choose "Yes" for plurals, choose "AND" from the pull-down menu of operators, and change the drop-down menu for both fields to "Basic Index." The search results show no registered trademarks using the combination of terms.

We perform another search, this time using "Hooky" in the top search term box and leaving the lower search term box blank. This time the search turns up 27 items that use the word "Hooky" or a sound-alike such as "hookee."

| | TESS HOME | NEW USER | STRUCTURED | FREE FORM | BROWSE DICT | SEARCH OG | PREV LIST | NEXT LIST | IMAGE LIST |

Logout | *Please logout when you are done to release system resources allocated f*

Start List At: [   ] OR Jump to record: [   ] **27 Records(s) found**

Refine Search (Hooky)[Bl] [   ] Submit

Current Search: **(Hooky)[Fl]** docs: 27 occ: 33

	Serial Number	Reg. Number	Word Mark	Check Status	Live/Dead
1	88108061		PLAYING HOOKY	TSDR	LIVE
2	88208771		PLAYIN HOOKEY CHARTERS	TSDR	LIVE
3	88202607		DU-HOOKY	TSDR	LIVE
4	87593148	5593256	GYM HOOKY	TSDR	LIVE
5	87528640		HOOKY BREWING	TSDR	DEAD
6	86680418		HANDY HOOKY	TSDR	DEAD
7	86158435		HOOKY	TSDR	DEAD
8	86234772		PLAY'N HOOK'E	TSDR	DEAD
9	85086412	3973158	HOOKIES	TSDR	DEAD
10	85782687		HOOKY BALLS	TSDR	DEAD
11	85857368	4410766	PLAYIN HOOKY OFFSHORE	TSDR	LIVE
12	85795104	4379414	PLAYIN' HOOKY DESIGNS	TSDR	LIVE
13	78657928		PLAYING HOOKY	TSDR	DEAD
14	78387207		LETS PLAY HOOKY	TSDR	DEAD
15	77826811	3901606	OFFICE HOOKY	TSDR	DEAD
16	77539648		HOOKY DAY	TSDR	DEAD
17	77341860		HOOKIES HEALTHY COOKIES	TSDR	DEAD
18	76698507		HOOKEEZ	TSDR	DEAD
19	76522831	2960373	HOOKIES	TSDR	DEAD
20	76406134	2784876	HOOKY	TSDR	LIVE
21	76381978	2706635	WALLHOOKY.COM	TSDR	LIVE
22	74045098	1631736	PLAYN HOOKY	TSDR	DEAD
23	73650429	1460223	HOOKY	TSDR	DEAD
24	73368437	1251682	HOOKY!	TSDR	DEAD
25	73219313	1161650	HOOKY	TSDR	DEAD
26	73178028	1162760	TIGER HOOKIES	TSDR	DEAD
27	72157481	0766990	HOOKY	TSDR	DEAD

Of the 27 entries that appeared (at the time we did the search), eight are listed as "live" and 19 are listed as "dead." Live means that the mark is either registered or pending registration, while dead means that the mark used to be in the system as a registered or pending mark but has since been canceled or abandoned.

The classes of goods listed for the eight live trademarks are: clothing (Playing Hooky and Playin Hooky Offshore), fishing charter services (Playin Hookey Charters), hand hooks (Du-Hooky), fitness training services (Gym Hooky), downloadable crochet patterns (Playin' Hooky Designs), spiral binding equipment (Hooky), and indoor and outdoor action games (Wallhooky.com).

Except for "Playin' Hooky Designs" for downloadable crochet patterns, the other uses of "hooky" do not conflict with our intended use because they are for different goods. "Playin' Hooky Designs" is a red flag because it is for crochet-related products. The question in making a final decision is whether consumers would be likely to distinguish "Playin' Hooky Designs" from "Hooky Wooky." Both trademarks conjure up the tools of knitting and crocheting (hooks), but even though the products and services are related, it seems unlikely that consumers would be confused by these different sounding marks. Therefore, we don't think that our search has found anything that would prevent our proposed use.

Next, we perform a search just for "Wooky" and obtain one relevant live entry, a registration by LG Electronics for a design (a whimsical faceless character with a knit cap) combined with the word "Wooky" in several classes, including clothing. This is another red flag. Further online research shows that "Wooky" is a character widget used in LG smartphone applications. Although LG Electronics would make a formidable opponent in court, our mark seems distinguishable by the average consumer who is unlikely to conclude that handmade crochet items come from LG Electronics.

Finally, although it doesn't necessarily reflect on federal registration, we check with Register.com (www.register.com) and find that the domain name hookywooky.com is available for domain name registration.

Timed Out by TESS

To maintain its system resources, the TESS program will terminate your searching session after 15 minutes of inactivity. All searches and results will be lost, and you will receive a message: "This search session has expired. Please start a search session again by clicking on the TRADEMARK icon, if you wish to continue." You must exit and reenter TESS to continue searching. If you wish to save searches, you can use the "save" feature of your browser and save the results in an HTML file.

Understanding the TESS Word and/or Design Mark Search (Free Form)

The TESS Word and/or Design Mark Search (we'll refer to it as "Free Form" to distinguish it from the Structured Search) lacks the ease of the Structured Form Search but adds some flexibility.

The Free Form Search page resembles the Structured Form Search page, with two major differences:

- Instead of separate Search Term boxes, the page provides one box that permits the construction of complex search queries.
- The bottom of the page sets out the various fields that are available for searching and provides hypertext links to descriptions of these fields.

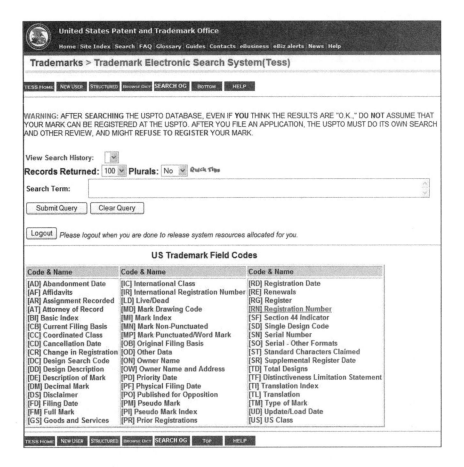

Using the Free Form Search Box

Probably the most important feature of the Free Form Search option is that you can combine operators (unlike the Structured Form Search that only gives you one operator for your entire query). For example, suppose your proposed domain name is MiracleMediations.com. You might have started out with the Structured Form Search entering "mirac*" in the top Search Term box and the term "mediat*" in the bottom box. You chose the AND operator to search for trademarks that contain both terms.

This search is a good start, but as you review your search results, you realize that you want to search for trademarks that contain the word "arbitration" as well. To do this, you use the Free Form Search to create a new search query that looks like this:

"mirac* [bi]" AND "mediat* [bi]" OR

"arbitrat* [bi]"

This search expression tells the computer that you want all trademarks that appear in the Basic Index and that contain a variant of the truncated term "mirac*" and either the term "mediat*" or the term "arbitrat*."

How to Use the Field Codes

The [bi] that follows the truncated terms is what's known as a field code. The Free Form Search requires that you use these field codes if you want anything other than an "all fields" search. For instance, if you want to search for all marks owned by a particular company, you can use the field code [on] in connection with the company's name. Similarly, use of the field code [gs] lets you search for all marks that are used on goods or services containing the terms you use in your search query.

You aren't limited to one field code. You may search in as many fields as you wish. For instance, you will get a deeper search by combining the [bi] and [ti] fields. (The "ti" field contains English equivalents to foreign words or characters used in a trademark.) You combine fields for each term by separating the fields with a comma, as in geezer [bi,ti]. In fact, in the help file it provides for TESS, the USPTO seems to suggest that when you are using the Free Form Search to find occurrences of a term in a trademark (as opposed to one of the other types of fields in a trademark record), you should search both the "bi" and "ti" fields.

For more on field codes, use the table that appears on the Free Form Search page and click whatever field code you wish to know more about.

Understanding the Results of Your Search

It's one thing to search for marks using TESS; it's another to understand what the system reports back. The screen shot below indicates one of the reported items from our Hooky Wooky search.

Understanding the Report Returned by a TESS Search

Let's take a few moments to interpret the various lines of information on the screen shot below, which shows the item page for Hooky.

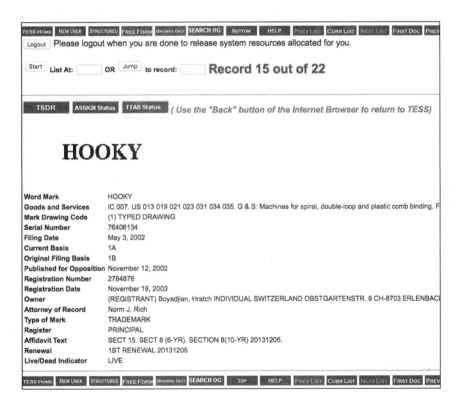

Word Mark: This shows the mark as registered (or as shown in the trademark application if the mark is pending).

Goods and Services: This line identifies the international classifications (the IC class) under which the mark is registered and provides brief descriptions of the underlying goods and/or services. In this case, the mark is registered under International Classification 007. The U.S. classifications following the international classification are artifacts of an earlier time when the United States had its own classification system. (See Chapter 6 for the importance of classes in deciding whether there is a likelihood of customer confusion.)

Mark Drawing Code: If the mark consists of words only (even when they are imaginatively arranged or come with stylistic fonts), this line says "Typed Drawing." However, if your mark consists of a logo with graphical elements, this line will show a set of six numeric characters that reflect how the USPTO has classified the logo.

Serial Number: This is the number that is assigned to the trademark application by the USPTO.

Filing Date: This is the date that the application for registration was filed.

Current Basis and **Original Filing Basis:** If, as here, the application was originally filed on an intent-to-use basis (1B), that fact will be indicated here. If the application was filed on an actual use basis (1A), that will be indicated as it is here for the "Current Basis."

Published for Opposition: This line indicates the date the USPTO published the trademark application to give the public a chance to oppose the mark (usually on grounds that someone thinks the proposed registration legally conflicts with his or her trademark).

Registration Number: This line will appear only if the mark has, in fact, been registered. Pending marks, for instance, do not have a registration number.

Registration Date: This line will appear only if the mark has been registered.

Owner: This line identifies the person or entity that was named as owner of the trademark in the application and also provides the owner's address.

Attorney of Record: This line indicates the name of the attorney, if any, managing the application.

Type of Mark: This line identifies the label given the mark by the USPTO. For most purposes, this label makes little difference. However, if two potentially conflicting marks are very similar, but one is a service mark while the other is a trademark, the type of mark could make a difference as to whether a legal conflict exists.

Register: This line designates whether the mark has been registered on the Principal Register or the Supplemental Register. Marks on the Principal Register get more protection, and marks on the Supplemental Register are deemed by the USPTO to be too descriptive to be placed on the Principal Register—which means that the likelihood of a successful infringement action being brought on behalf of that mark is small.

Affidavit Text: This line indicates whether any affidavits have been filed on behalf of the mark—for example, an Affidavit of Use (see Chapter 8).

Renewal: This line indicates whether the registration has been timely renewed.

Live/Dead Indicator: This line indicates whether the mark is registered or pending, or whether it has been canceled (because of the owner's failure to renew or file statements of continued use) or abandoned in the course of the application.

CAUTION
Even though a mark is labeled as dead, it might in fact be very much alive in the world of commerce and can spell trouble for you if you adopt a legally conflicting mark. The dead/live label only refers to the mark's registration status with the USPTO, not to whether it is or isn't in actual use in the economy.

Determining a Mark's Status

Each item page has a link to the USPTO's Trademark Status and Document Retrieval database (known as TSDR). This database shows the status of the mark (registered, pending, canceled, published for opposition, and so on). When we clicked the TSDR link on the Hooky item page, we got the status report shown below.

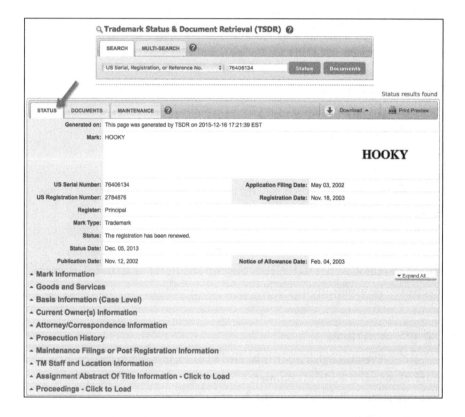

The status report has some of the same information as the item page and also provides a chronological history of the mark's journey through the USPTO. This status report is most helpful when you discover a pending mark and want to know where it is in the process.

The TSDR page provides more than a status report. It also includes access to all of the documents and correspondence filed in that case. If you click the "Documents" tab, as shown in the image below, you will find a list of all of the documents filed with the USPTO relating to that trademark application. It also shows you what format the document is in (for example, XML, JPG, or TIFF), and permits you to click the link to download the document.

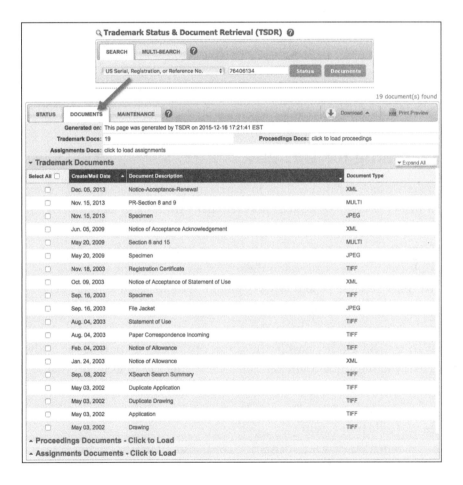

The newest feature of the TSDR system is the "Maintenance" tab, which lists the documents that have been filed in order to maintain the registration, as well as the dates when future filings are due.

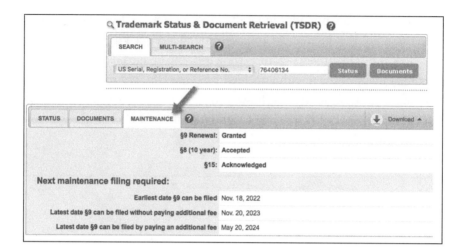

Searching for Designs

So far, we have focused on how to search the USPTO trademark database for marks made up of words. However, many trademarks consist of or contain graphic elements that word searches don't accommodate. Design marks, as these types of trademarks are referred to, must be searched by using a set of codes assigned to them by the USPTO upon registration. The codes describe various types of graphical elements and are publicly available in a publication known as the *Design Search Code Manual*, available on the USPTO's website.

To search for other possible instances of a design mark that you wish to use, you must first figure out the code for the design elements that your mark incorporates, and then enter this code in the search box (for either the Structured or Free Form Search) and select the Design Search Code field (DC).

Trademarkia (www.trademarkia.com) also offers a method of searching the USPTO database for logos. The interface is more intuitive than TESS, and it can locate logos by identifying the elements (dog, tree, house) or the words used with the logo.

Searching State-Registered Trademarks

To search for trademarks on state trademark registers, you must check the registers for each state. (For information about determining how many state registers to search, see Chapter 4.) Usually, you will search only in your own state. But if you plan to operate in several states, you would want to check each. If you decide to search in more than a few states, it would be smarter to have your trademark search done by a professional or to search state trademark databases by computer.

The method for doing a search for state-registered trademarks varies from state to state. Many states will do a preapplication search for you by phone, either for free or for a small charge. In other states, you must request a search by mail. In still others, the USPTO will not search for you but will let you peruse the microfiche or loose-leaf lists of registered trademarks in person. The state agency in charge of trademarks is generally within the department of state, the department of corporations, or the department of revenue.

Regardless of who does it or how the search is performed, state trademark agencies provide limited types of search services—most commonly marks can be searched only in alphabetical order. Sometimes they are broken down by classes of goods or services. If so, you will need to specify which class to search.

The main drawback to state searches is that state laws vary somewhat as to what constitutes a conflict with a registered trademark. This means the criteria a state uses to conduct its search might not be the same as federal or common law criteria. As a result, while obtaining a state clearance probably means there are no directly identical marks in your class, it might not give you any assurance that your trademark does not legally conflict with other marks in that state. When searching state trademarks, the same principles apply as when searching the federal trademark register—look for synonyms, homonyms, phonetic equivalents, and so on, both in your class and in as many other classes as might be relevant.

Searching for Trade Names and Unregistered Marks

The goal here is to make sure your mark won't conflict with a trade name or corporate name in use in your state. Although trade names, used solely to identify businesses, do not have all the same kinds of rights attached to trademarks (for instance, unlike trademarks, they cannot be registered), they can be protected by unfair competition law. For example, a company can sue you if you use their trade name as a mark in a way that causes the public (or suppliers) to confuse you with them. Also, if the trade name is being used as a mark but is not registered as such, a search of one of the trade name indexes we describe below could result in discovering a mark that no other search method would have brought to your attention. In short, you will need to make sure your mark is not going to conflict with a registered corporate name or unregistered trade name by searching all sources of trade names that you can reasonably find.

One good way to search for a trade name conflict is to make sure no corporation registered in your state already uses the name. You can do this via a phone call or letter to the agency in charge of corporations, usually the department of corporations or the secretary of state. (See Chapter 1 for more about corporate names.)

Even if you have already incorporated and wish to use your corporate name as your mark, you should not skip a trade name search. When you incorporated, your proposed corporate name was checked against other corporate names, not against trademarks or any other trade names. So you still need to check how it compares to marks, other trade names, and perhaps even corporate names in other states if your mark will have a presence in those states.

Google

Google is an invaluable tool when searching for common law marks. When performing searches with Google, here are some tips and tricks to keep in mind:

- **Google ignores many common words and characters.** Google disregards words such as "where," "the," "how," "why," and some single digits and letters. (Google believes these slow down your search without improving the results.) You can see which words are ignored on the search results page—for example, if you search "Who is the owner of the Shasta trademark?" Google will tell you that the words "who is the" were not included in your results. So if the mark you are searching for contains a common word such as "the," "what," and so on, put a "+" sign in front of it. For example, if you were searching for Lover of Salsa, type "Lover +of Salsa." (Be sure to include a space before the "+" sign.)

- **You can make Google search for synonyms.** If you want to search not only for your search term but also for its synonyms, place the tilde sign ("~") immediately in front of the search term. For example, if searching for "Lover of Salsa" and you wanted to find similar or related products, you might type, "Lover +of ~Salsa"

- **You can search for a range of numbers.** If you want to obtain results within a numerical range—for example, you want to use *10 Decibels* as the name of your record company, but you want to check any other uses of numbers with the word "decibel," just include the range of numbers, separated by two periods, with no spaces, into the search box along with your search terms. For example, type, "decibels 1..1000."

- **Use quotation marks for phrases.** Often you'll want results that include an exact phrase. In this case, put quotation marks around your search terms—for example, "Independence starts with I."

- **Get rid of multimeaning terminology.** If your search term has more than one meaning, you can focus your search by putting a minus sign ("–") in front of words related to the meaning you want to avoid. (Be sure to include a space before the minus sign.) For example, let's say you're searching for "Pot Luck" but want to avoid common results such as cooking pot, coffee pots, or melting pot. You would type "pot luck –cooking –coffee –melting" and it would eliminate many unnecessary common results.

How to Evaluate the Results of Your Trademark Search

This chapter explains how to evaluate the results of your trademark search. It's one thing to search for marks that are the same as or similar to the mark you propose to use for your own business, goods, or services. It's quite another to decide how to proceed once you have the results of the search in your hands.

What's Involved in Evaluating Trademark Search Results?

If you are choosing a mark, evaluating your trademark search results is essentially a preventive study. You are trying to make sure that your proposed mark qualifies for registration (if you choose to register it) and will be secure against attacks by other trademark owners. If the USPTO decides that your mark is confusingly similar to an already-registered mark, registration will be denied. And even if your mark is registered, a trademark owner who used the mark before you, can successfully sue you in the future if it discovers your mark and convinces a judge that the use of your mark creates a likelihood of customer confusion with its own mark.

If you already have a mark but are involved in an infringement dispute, you can use the material in this chapter to help you sort out whether there is a likelihood of customer confusion caused by the use of the two marks.

The Importance of Avoiding Customer Confusion in Trademark Law

As you probably gathered by now, the core decision you'll need to make here is whether the simultaneous commercial use of your mark and any marks that your search turns up would likely create customer confusion as to the underlying goods or services or their source. If you conclude that customer confusion would be likely, you'll want to pick another mark. If no customer confusion is likely, then you can feel reasonably confident about using the mark—unless it happens to be identical or very similar to a mark that the courts would consider famous (in which case the owner might have a claim for dilution).

Likelihood of Customer Confusion Is a Slippery Concept

Being able to assess whether customer confusion is likely in a particular situation is a skill that depends as much on experience and intuition as it does on any hard-and-fast principles. Though we can and do explain how the courts generally go about assessing the likelihood of confusion, each case is inevitably unique in some particular. Predicting the future outcome of any case is definitely an art rather than a science. If you are uncertain about the correct course of action after applying our guidelines to your situation, you should consult with an experienced trademark lawyer. (See Chapter 14, "Help Beyond This Book.")

Even a Lawyer's Opinion Can't Give You Certainty

Even if you consult with a lawyer, remember that trademark lawyers are subject to the same limitation as the authors of this book—that is, there is no firm way to predict the outcome of a trademark dispute, should one erupt over your choice of a mark. All a trademark lawyer can do is offer a professional opinion. But if that opinion turns out to be wrong, it is you and not the lawyer who will face the consequences, with one important exception. A lawyer's written opinion that your mark doesn't conflict with a mark on the federal trademark register might save you from a stiff damage award if you go ahead and use the mark and are later sued for infringement.

Knowing that they aren't likely to get in trouble if they act conservatively, most lawyers won't give you the go-ahead if there is much of a chance of a trademark dispute in the future. In short, the lawyer's advice might be both a disservice (because it might be overly cautious) and an important service (you'll feel more confident about your choice if it passes the lawyer test).

> CAUTION
> **The discussion in this chapter assumes that any mark you come across in a trademark search is currently being used** and was either put into use, or the subject of an intent-to-use application, before you started using your mark. In these instances, if you conclude that confusion is likely, you're going to have a hard time overcoming an infringement lawsuit. If, however, you started using the mark first, or the would-be registrant fails to follow up on an intent-to-use application, the results might be quite different. In this chapter, we primarily explore how the courts determine the likelihood of confusion. (In Chapter 10, we help you assess the legalities of any trademark disputes that might arise.)

What Is the Likelihood of Customer Confusion?

Suppose you do a trademark search and the results indicate that the same or a similar mark is already being used by another business. Whether you should go ahead with your mark depends on whether your use would create a likelihood of customer confusion.

Understanding the Likelihood of Confusion Test

First let's look at the term "likelihood." In the trademark context, likelihood means that confusion is probable—not necessarily that it has happened, or that it will happen, but that it is more likely than not that a reasonable customer will be confused by the simultaneous use of the two marks.

Confusion in this context can mean two different things. Most commonly, it means that the goods or services a customer buys are different than what the customer intended to buy. For instance, if a consumer wants to purchase the services of ABC Emergency Care on the basis of a friend's recommendation, but he ends up going to ABD Emergency Room by mistake because of the similarity of the two names, you have an example of customer confusion between the two services.

The other situation that creates customer confusion is where a misleading mark causes the customer to believe—wrongly—that a product or service is sponsored by, approved by, or somehow connected with a business that the customer already frequents or knows about. In other words, the customer is confused about the source of the product or service. This would be the case, for example, if a customer took a TV to a repair shop called LG Electronics because she thought that LG somehow sponsored the business.

Do the Hypothetically Confused Customers Have to Be Reasonable Customers?

Before we go on to discuss all the factors that can help you assess a likelihood of confusion, let's take a moment to examine who these hypothetically confused customers really are. The law imagines a "reasonable" customer who exercises ordinary care to distinguish among the products or services being purchased. This reasonable customer is neither someone who confuses two products as a result of bizarre reasoning, nor someone who obsessively checks all references before buying a product or service, but rather, someone in between.

Courts recognize that a reasonable consumer will often make a snap judgment. If, after only a hurried glance, Mrs. Serrano is confused between Heartbeat and Heartlite cooking oils, then the marks are too similar. However, the law would surely not find it reasonable if a customer confused Heartbeat cooking oil with Esther's Cooking Oil because her Aunt Esther had recently died of a heart attack. Nor would a customer be reasonable in confusing Heartbeat with Esther's because of similar packaging, so long as the very different names are prominently displayed on the packaging.

The law says that in cases of conflicting trademarks, the challenger must show that a reasonable customer might be confused. How is this done? Typically, the challenger must somehow prove that a significant percentage of customers would likely be confused—anywhere between 5% and 50%, depending on the situation. We can't give you a more exact number, because the number varies from one court decision to the next.

An Overview of How Courts Evaluate Marks for Their Potential to Cause Customer Confusion

Court decisions have produced a number of criteria to apply when determining whether there's a likelihood of confusion between two marks. As would a judge, you will want to ask the following questions:

Question 1: Are the goods and services represented by the marks related—that is, are they sold in the same marketing channels to the same general group of customers?

Question 2: Do the goods or services compete—that is, will the decision by customers to buy one business's product or service be made at the expense of the other business?

Question 3: How similar are the marks in sound, appearance, and meaning?

Question 4: How strong is each mark? (Is the mark in question very distinctive when compared to a competing mark?)

Question 5: How much do the underlying goods or services cost? (How carefully does the public usually decide whether to buy the goods or services offered by the two businesses?)

Question 6: Do the two marks share the same customer base?

Question 7: Does one owner use the mark on several different products or services, or is the owner likely to do so in the future?

Whether use of a trademark is likely to cause customer confusion depends on the exact facts of the case, how the judge weighs the criteria listed above in light of the facts, and the judge's subjective perceptions of the evidence.

The three most important criteria to examine in deciding how likely it is that the use of a mark will cause customer confusion are the first three on our list.

Criterion 1: How closely related are the goods and services?

Two similar services or products with the same or similar names that are distributed in the same markets are far more likely to confuse the public than if very similar names were to grace dissimilar products. In this latter case, the confusion is more likely to come from confusion about the source of the products than from confusing one product with another.

Criterion 2: Do the goods or services compete?

If the underlying goods or services directly compete with each other, then the use of the same or similar marks on both is likely to cause the type of confusion that will lead to the customer purchasing the wrong product.

Criterion 3: How similar are the marks in terms of their appearance, meaning, or sound?

The more similarities two marks share, the more likely it is that they will confuse someone. This is known as the "sight, sound, and meaning" test for customer confusion.

When evaluating your mark, first apply these three factors to your situation. In a borderline case, consider the four additional factors that we discuss later in this chapter. Or, you can pick some of all seven factors that seem most relevant to your situation, and use them selectively to determine whether your mark may cause a likelihood of confusion with another.

To see how judges apply this likelihood-of-confusion standard, let's examine a hypothetical conflict between two uses of very similar trademarks.

> **EXAMPLE:** Ethereal Fragrance Company produces a line of products, including perfume, carrying the distinctive and therefore strong registered trademark Ekbara Scents. These products are marketed in boutiques throughout California and several other western states primarily to women in the middle- and upper-income brackets. The Ekbara mark has been used in this manner by Ethereal for two years when Rubin Santiago of Oakland, California, opens a small printing company specializing in business cards, which he calls Ekbara Cards. The cards are marketed to small businesses in the San Francisco Bay Area. Ethereal claims infringement and demands that Rubin stop using the Ekbara mark on his cards. When Rubin refuses, Ethereal files a trademark infringement lawsuit and seeks a preliminary injunction (an order to bar Rubin from further using the Ekbara mark). The key point for the judge to decide in this example is, simply, whether Rubin's use of the Ekbara mark creates a likelihood of customer confusion—thereby entitling Ethereal to a court order stopping Santiago's use of the mark.

In deciding this question, a knowledgeable judge would probably engage in something like the following analysis:

"It is not likely that purchasers of business cards will think a fragrance company is involved in the printing business. Neither business is likely to go into competition with the other. The purchasers of the two products as well as the distribution channels are likely to be quite different. There is no similarity between the two goods in terms of what they accomplish. Ethereal's customers are unlikely to care who manufactures or distributes business cards. There is no indication Rubin Santiago intended to get a free marketing ride on Ethereal's mark. By contrast, the only factor supporting Ethereal's claim of infringement is the strength of the word Ekbara as a mark (it suggests the Middle East, which itself is suggestive of fragrances). This is simply not enough to overcome all the other factors that lean against the likelihood of customer confusion."

> EXAMPLE: Now suppose Rubin Santiago creates a line of enamel earrings, calls them Ekbara Designs, and franchises them for sale in shopping malls that also feature boutiques that carry Ethereal's products.

In this case, the judge's decision would be different. The likelihood of confusion is much higher due to the fact that the two marks are used on goods distributed in the same channels, the same consumers are exposed to both marks, and the underlying goods might actually compete with each other in the sense that customers searching for impulse gifts might buy the earrings instead of the fragrance, and vice versa.

CAUTION

Before you conclude that you are safe in going ahead with your chosen mark, look at the final three factors in the section "Final Factors," below. They do not predict a likelihood of confusion so much as a likelihood of success in a lawsuit, which may be a more practical determination anyway.

How Closely Related Are the Goods and Services?

A good place to start when deciding whether one mark conflicts with another is to ask if the goods and services that the two marks promote are related—in a commercial sense. That's because when products or services are considered to be totally unrelated, the courts will generally find that there is no likelihood of customer confusion and thus no infringement—unless the existing mark qualifies for special protection under the dilution doctrine.

If, on the other hand, a court finds the products or services to be related, it is also likely to find that a likelihood of customer confusion exists and to issue judgment for the owner of the existing mark in an infringement lawsuit. This is because when similar marks are used on related goods or services, the risk of consumer confusion is high. You can determine whether the potentially conflicting marks are used on related goods or services by asking either of two questions:

- Do the goods or services belong to the same international "class" of goods or services?
- Are the goods or services distributed through the same marketing channels?

We discuss these two questions in further detail below.

An Overview of the International Trademark Classification System

International classes are descriptive categories of goods or services used by the U.S. Patent and Trademark Office to help keep track of the many thousands of new marks that it registers every year. The system has 45 classes in all, 34 for products and 11 for services. Appendix A contains a complete list of all 45 classes.

The purpose of the International Classification of Goods and Services is to group together goods or services that are offered through the same channels of trade and to the same general types of consumers. The International Classification helps the USPTO determine whether the specific goods or services associated with conflicting marks are so closely related to each other, for example, that they are likely to be marketed in the same channels and sold to the same consumer.

> EXAMPLE: Mark is a jeweler with a line of handmade jewelry (necklaces, bracelets, and earrings) that feature small, black, rubber parts with an industrial look. He calls this special line of jewelry The Rub. Jackie's Tool Shop, Inc., has designed and manufactured a line of hand tools with rubber handles for three years and has a registered trademark for the name of the line, The Rub, under Class 8, for hand tools. Mark would like to register the mark, The Rub, for his line of jewelry. Can he still do so, even though Jackie's has already registered it?
>
> Mark will likely succeed in registering his mark if Jackie's mark is the only obstacle to registration. Mark's line of jewelry would be registered under Class 14, for jewelry. The fact that Jackie's mark is registered under Class 8, for hand tools, indicates that these goods are not marketed in the same channels and to the same consumers. Jackie's hand tools are marketed to hardware stores, home improvement stores, and the hardware section of department stores. Mark's jewelry is marketed to jewelry and clothing boutiques. Because the marketing contexts do not overlap, consumers would not likely be confused by the use of the same mark on both goods.

CAUTION

Even if your proposed mark falls into a different class than another mark, we recommend that you not use your mark if it is very similar to the other mark and would appear in the same marketing channels. Keep in mind that the prohibitive cost of litigation usually makes all borderline decisions too risky. (See "Marketing Channels," below, for more information.)

If and when you search the list of registered trademarks to see whether someone else got to your mark ahead of you (see Chapters 4 and 5), the search results will indicate the class for each similar mark that the search turns up. If your mark belongs in the same class as one or more of the existing marks, this is a good indication that the underlying products or services will be considered related. And if your search comes up with unregistered marks, you will want to try to assign a class to them, and then compare those classes with the probable class that your mark fits under.

Here are some examples to help familiarize you with how this classification system works:

- **CLASS 1 (Chemicals).** Chemicals used in industry, science, and photography, as well as in agriculture, horticulture, and forestry; unprocessed artificial resins, unprocessed plastics; manures; fire extinguishing compositions; tempering and soldering preparations; chemical substances for preserving foodstuffs; tanning substances; adhesives used in industry

- **CLASS 3 (Cosmetics and cleaning preparations).** Bleaching preparations and other substances for laundry use; cleaning, polishing, scouring, and abrasive preparations; soaps; perfumery, essential oils, cosmetics, hair lotions; dentifrices

- **CLASS 5 (Pharmaceuticals).** Pharmaceutical, veterinary, and sanitary preparations; dietetic substances adapted for medical use, food for babies; plasters, materials for dressings; material for stopping teeth, dental wax; disinfectants; preparations for destroying vermin; fungicides, herbicides

- **CLASS 14 (Jewelry).** Precious metals and their alloys and goods in precious metals or coated therewith, not included in other classes; jewelry, precious stones; horological and chronometric instruments

- **CLASS 16 (Paper goods and printed matter).** Paper, cardboard, and goods made from these materials, not included in other classes; printed matter; bookbinding material; photographs; stationery; adhesives for stationery or household purposes; artists' materials; paintbrushes; typewriters and office requisites (except furniture); instructional and teaching material (except apparatus); plastic materials for packaging (not included in other classes); playing cards; printers' type; printing blocks

- **CLASS 35 (Advertising and business).** Advertising; business management; business administration; office functions.

Fitting Your Goods and Services Into the Appropriate Class

You might need to spend a little time and effort to determine the class to which a product or service fits best. For instance, does a belt made of woven cord belong under Class 22, which includes cordage and fibers? As it turns out, the answer is "no," because the cord is made into clothing, which belongs in Class 25. Similarly, when a mark represents a new type of service or product, it might be difficult to decide how to categorize it. For example, if you are running an Internet-based store-to-home grocery-ordering and delivery service, you might wish to register in a variety of classes, including International Classes 29 (meats and processed foods), 35 (advertising and business), 9 (electrical and scientific apparatus), and 39 (transportation and storage).

Because goods or services in the same class are usually considered related or competing, the use of the same or similar marks within the same class has a high potential for customer confusion. For example, the owner of Titan brand cigarettes was able to stop a cigar maker from using the Titan mark. Cigars and cigarettes are in the same USPTO class, Class 34, which also encompasses "tobacco, raw or manufactured, smoker's articles, and matches."

Coordinated Classes

The USPTO has grouped the various international classifications into what it calls "coordinated classes." If you search for a mark and designate a particular class for it, the search will return marks in the coordinated class group. For instance, if you designate the international class for software when you are performing your search, your results will also include marks in Classes 10, 16, 28, 35, 38, and 42. Although the USPTO considers these classes "related" for the purpose of trademark searching, the goods and services described by the related classes are not necessarily related for the purpose of determining the likelihood of customer confusion.

On the other hand, the owner of Titan cigarettes probably couldn't stop a maker of biodegradable soap, which is in Class 3, from using the same mark. That is because cigarettes and soap do not compete in any way; they are not considered related goods; and the Titan mark could be used on both without creating the likelihood of customer confusion.

It's important to understand that by itself, the fact that two products or services are in the same or different classes does not conclusively establish that the two marks are legally in conflict. Because the international classification system has packed all goods and services into only 45 classes, combining, for example, abrasive cleansers and cosmetics, products within the same class might be marketed in totally different ways, thus avoiding customer confusion. So, in evaluating a conflict, you could at least argue that a trademark for a scouring powder that is similar to a trademark for lipstick won't confuse customers. But then again, as we've pointed out, even when two goods or services are in separate classes, the actual means used to market them could create a likelihood of customer confusion. Simply put, use the classification system as an indicator of possible confusion, rather than a way to definitely determine its likelihood.

To place a product or service within its appropriate class, follow these steps:

Step 1: Study the list of classes in Appendix A. See whether the goods or services for which your mark will be (or is being) used naturally fits into one of the groupings.

Step 2: If you are unsure, study the list in Appendix A that provides examples of goods and services for each class. Does that help?

Step 3: If you are still not sure, use the *Acceptable Identification of Goods and Services Manual* (see below).

The *Acceptable Identification of Goods and Services Manual*

Probably the best source for finding the right class or classes for your goods or services is the *Acceptable Identification of Goods and Services Manual* (also known as the *ID Manual*). The *ID Manual* is a database of approved classes and descriptions prepared by the USPTO in conjunction with the Nice Agreement—the international agreement for classifying trademarked goods and services. The manual is actually an interactive database that you can search at the USPTO's website.

To search the manual:

Step 1: Go to the USPTO website (www.uspto.gov). On the menu bar, click "Trademarks," then click, "Guides, Manuals and Resources," and then choose "Acceptable Identification of Goods and Services Manual (ID Manual) Next Generation."

U.S. Acceptable Identification of Goods and Services Manual (ID Manual)
[Reflects Nice Agreement 10th Ed., 2015 Version]

NEW - The USPTO encourages you to try a newly available "Beta" version of Trademark Next Generation Application Trademark ID Manual that features more advanced searching and browsing capacities, and provide comments and suggestions at your option. Please see the "Beta" version for details.

The ID Manual contains a listing of acceptable identifications of goods and services. Any entry you choose must accurately describe your goods and/or services. Failure to list the goods and/or services accurately with which you are using or intend to use your mark could prevent you from registering your mark.

Need more information on how to identify your goods and services? Watch the Trademark Information "how-to" video on "Goods and Services." Or need more information on how use in commerce and intent to use differ? Watch the "Filing Basis" video.

Please see below for updated Quick Tips or click on "Searching the ID Manual" for detailed information on searching and use of the ID Manual features.

Please click on the "Guidance for Users" link below for information about the ID Manual's features, general identification and classification notices, and for guidance on identifying and/or classifying specific goods and services. For information about USPTO policy on identification and classification of goods and services, please also consult Chapter 1400 of the Trademark Manual of Examining Procedure (TMEP).

Searching the ID Manual | Guidance for Users | Browse Entire Content | To suggest additions to the Trademark ID Manual click here.

Search Manual

Choose Field Basic Fields ▾   **Enter Search Terms** |

(If choosing a field other than "Basic Fields," all status checkboxes must be unchecked.)

Return results with status: ☑A - Added   ☑M - Modified   ☑X - Examples   ☐D - Deleted

Click here for more information about ID Manual entry statuses and using the status checkboxes.

Submit   Reset

Step 2: Enter a word or words in the "Enter Search Terms" box that you would use to identify your product or service—for example, "wrench," "accounting," or "telephone"—using the appropriate logical operator. (A reminder: The "AND" operator searches for listings in the manual that contain all of the words you type in; the "OR" operator searches for listings that contain any one of the words you type in, but not necessarily all of them together.)

Step 3: After you click the search icon (the magnifying glass) or tap "return," the search engine will return a list of class and description information for the product or service you entered. For example, if you wanted to find the correct classification for your website design and hosting service, you could use the search words "website and design." The results you would find are shown below. The appropriate class is Class 42.

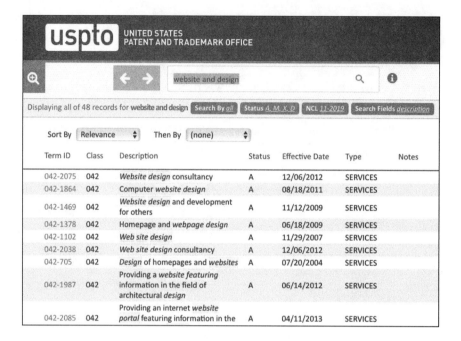

Suppose, as another example, that you have created a line of paper coffee filters for use in automatic drip coffee makers. Your filter paper is printed with retro, playful, and unique designs to make your coffee filters more interesting to look at and fun to use. You want to register the mark for your line of paper coffee filters, Zoo Filters. To find out what class the USPTO deems correct for this product, and what description to use for your application, you could simply do a search using the words "coffee and filter." Your search would produce the results shown below. From this line item, you can see that the USPTO considers Class 16 as the appropriate class for paper coffee filters.

You can also access an Advanced Search option on the search results page by clicking on the magnifying glass with the "+" sign. The most useful Advanced Search feature is the ability to limit your search results to certain classes.

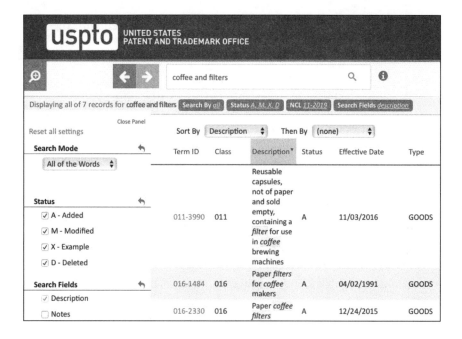

Search for Classes Used by Competitors

If the U.S. Patent and Trademark Office *Acceptable Identification of Goods and Services Manual* doesn't do the trick for you, you might consider examining the database of marks registered with the USPTO to find out what classes have been assigned to the marks registered by your competitors. Also, once you conduct a trademark search in the course of adopting your mark, the report generated by that search might provide some good tips as to the class that you should use.

You can do this search for free using the TESS database at the website of the USPTO. (Chapter 5 explains how to access and use TESS.) For this type of search use the Free Form Search. Enter some terms that best describe the goods or services you and your competitors are offering the public, and put "gs" in brackets after each of the terms ("gs" means "goods and services"). For instance, if you want to start a delivery system that operates from an Internet website, enter "delivery [gs] and Internet [gs]" and click "Submit Query." This will produce a long list of marks that are used on goods or services that have been described with the terms "delivery" and "Internet."

Related Goods and Product Expansion

Each trademark has a net of protection defined by its channels of commerce and class of goods. In some cases, this net may be very broad if a court determines that the owner of the mark is likely to expand into new markets. For example, in the case of a famous mark, the net is very wide because the owner of a famous mark is likely to expand into many product areas. In other cases, the net is not too wide because a smaller company is not likely to move into other areas. For example, it is possible that the owners of the Gallo trademark (for wine) will expand into the sale of cheese, which the consuming public identifies with wine. However, the net of protection might not extend to cheese for a lesser-known wine trademark.

There is no simple method of predicting how either the USPTO or the courts will evaluate the strength of the net of related goods. Sometimes product expansion can be determined by the actions of the company (for example, evidence that the company is considering new products), and sometimes it is determined by marketplace factors (for example, record companies often expand into producing films). To help them reach a decision regarding a new product's registration, attorneys and judges study decisions reached by appellate courts in cases with similar facts.

Another approach is to enter one or more terms that a competitor is using in its trademark and then examine the registrations to see the classes that have been assigned to that mark.

EXAMPLE: You have created a new kind of coloring crayon that makes the colors brighter when applied to any type of paper or poster board. You know that Crayola has been making crayons for decades. You type in the word "Crayola" in the search box and click on the search button. You will get a long list of all the registered trademarks containing the term "Crayola." If you look at Registration Number 1279429–Crayola, you will learn that crayons have been assigned to Class 16.

Trademark Assistance Center

If, after reading this section, you are still in doubt about the proper class or classes for your product or service, you can call the USPTO (800-786-9199), describe the product or service, and ask them which class or classes might be involved. The trademark information specialist will answer your question and normally give you sound advice. Unfortunately, you don't have the legal right to rely on this opinion. For instance, if you later decide to register your mark, and you apply for registration in the class recommended by the Trademark Assistance Center, the person who eventually examines your application may disagree with the answer you were given. No big deal. You'll just have to assign a different class to the product or service—one that's acceptable to the examiner.

Marketing Channels

In addition to using the classification system for determining whether two marks are related and thus might confuse customers in the marketplace, you should look at the marketing channels through which the goods or services reach the public.

Goods and services are considered related when they are sold in similar outlets, marketed in similar media, placed near each other in stores, and generally considered alike by the consumer. If they are marketed quite differently, then no likelihood of confusion can exist, regardless of the class they are in for registration purposes.

For example, you should determine whether the same sorts of information sources (billboards, websites, television, newspapers, magazines, and radio) carry ads bearing both marks. Would both marks appear in ads in the same trade journals? Might the products or services be displayed or sold in the same store or catalog, or under the same heading in a trade directory? Will they both target the same customer base? Do both marks advertise on the same types of websites? In any of these cases, it's fair to say that the marks are being used in the same marketing channels, which increases the likelihood of customer confusion.

> **CAUTION**
>
> **To some extent, the Internet is one large marketing channel, and all goods and services moving through it are related to a degree.** This is partially because of the way people search out information by using a search engine to locate sites containing a set of words they have chosen. Unfortunately, cases dealing with the issue have not yet made their way up to the appellate level where law is made, so we can't be more specific about marketing channels on the Internet. In coming years, we will learn whether the courts view the Internet as one large channel (that is, the equivalent of a Wal-Mart on the Net) or a series of smaller channels (like specialty shops at a mall).

Do the Goods or Services Compete?

Goods and services directly compete if the purchase of one negatively affects the purchase of the other. Two brands of bacon sitting side by side in a grocery display compete. So do airlines, fast food restaurants, personal computers, mobile telephones, and computer game stations.

How Similar Are the Marks?

The third factor in determining whether a likelihood of confusion exists is how similar the marks are. Do they sound or look alike, and if so, how much? Do they convey the same meaning? The closer two marks are in sight, sound, and meaning, the more likely it is that a legal problem will arise.

In comparing marks, remember that variations in spelling or punctuation do not make marks different if they sound the same. Thus, Phansee-pants is the same as Fancy Pants, and Duncan Doughnuts duplicates Dunkin Donuts. Even using foreign language equivalents can't make a mark different enough, if most of the public could tell they mean the same. So La Petite Boulangerie would infringe on The Little Bakery, and El Sombrero Blanco probably infringes on The White Hat.

Even marks with more definitive differences may be confusingly similar, in the same market. For example, courts have found Quirst is too close to Squirt, Sarnoff too much like Smirnoff, and Lorraine too reminiscent of La Touraine. Each of these pairs of marks was used on nearly identical goods. Probably the use of such duplicate marks would have passed legal muster if they had been on very different kinds of products. Again, that's because the more competitive the marks are in a class or market channels, the less similar the marks have to be to cause confusion.

Are Two Marks Confusing? Use the Golden Rule and Get Some Feedback!

Telling whether the simultaneous use of two marks risks customer confusion can be a very subjective exercise, heavily influenced by the experience and mind-set of the person doing the analysis. Nevertheless, there are two ways to get a handle on the question of potential confusion. First, ask yourself how you would feel if you were out there using your proposed mark and the other business came along with theirs. If you think you'd become energized to take some action, you have your answer. Second, if you are able to arrange for several objective friends or relatives to eyeball the two marks and give their honest impression of how they would react as customers, you'll probably have a good idea of how a judge would react. If even one of your friends or relatives thinks he or she might be confused by the marks, then chances are a judge would reach the same conclusion as to hypothetical customers. Because this is a risk you don't want to take, chances are you'll want to pick another name.

Additional Factors

The next four factors from our list also affect whether likelihood of customer confusion exists between the members of any pair of marks.

How Strong Is Each Mark?

A strong mark is generally given a wider range of protection than a weak one. As we explained in Chapter 2, a court would consider a mark to be strong if either of the following is true:

- The words, phrases, or symbols it consists of are distinctive (arbitrary, coined, or suggestive).
- Long and continuous use has made the public recognize it as the symbol of a particular product or service (the secondary meaning rule).

The point is, the stronger the original mark, the more likely it is that the second mark will be found to be confusingly similar if it has any similarities to the original mark at all. Conversely, the weaker a mark is, the less legal protection it is given and the more likely it is that a second mark will be found to not be confusingly similar, even if it has many similarities. This means you are safer in using a mark that is similar to an existing weak mark than one that is similar to an existing strong mark.

How Much Do the Goods or Services Cost?

Cost will also affect the likelihood of customer confusion. Because customers tend to take their time and consider carefully when buying an expensive item, the more expensive the item, the less chance of confusing customers. Conversely, an item that is cheap or subject to impulse buying is more likely to result in customer confusion when it is sold with a mark that is similar to another on goods that are even slightly related.

Are the Two Marks Directed Toward the Same Customers?

Two businesses that use similar marks to sell to the same customers are highly likely to cause customer confusion. Conversely, if businesses have separate customer bases, then the use of similar marks is unlikely to confuse anyone. For example, the market for replacement wood windows is likely to be limited to contractors and homeowners. As a result, a window manufacturer who uses the mark Walls of Light in its advertising probably won't confuse the customers of a magician who calls his show the Wall of Lights, because the two groups of customers won't often overlap.

It's useful to look at the size of the market sector that uses your product or service. If a small sector of the market knows and purchases a service, a similar mark used by a different small group is unlikely to confuse the two sets of consumers. But if a large segment of the public knows one mark, using a similar mark is more likely to cause customer confusion, even when aimed at a slightly different market, because of the greater potential for overlap between the two groups.

Does One Owner Use the Mark on Several Different Products or Services?

A red flag should go up when you see a potentially conflicting mark that has already been used on a variety of products or services by the same mark owner, even if you wish to use it on a product that is unrelated to any of these uses. The problem is that because the first mark owner has already begun to use the mark on several products or services, it has asserted what is called in legal lingo the "right of expansion." Some examples of businesses that do this are Calvin Klein or Pierre Cardin (although the dilution rule would also keep anyone from using an identical mark or marks—see Chapter 1).

When the owner of a mark has asserted this right of expansion (by using the mark on a number of different products), a court will assume that the first user might wish to expand its use further. The court will protect this right of expansion by permitting very few other uses of the same mark. So a second user seeking to use such a mark even on greatly dissimilar products will have less luck than if the mark were being used in a more limited fashion. By the same token, the public, having seen the mark on a variety of goods by the same owner, is more likely to assume that any new uses also belong to that owner, and thus are likely to be confused. Thus, the public would expect the mark Yamaha, which already appears on motorcycles, lawnmowers, and guitars, to represent the same company if it also appeared on computers or musical recordings.

Final Factors

After you have determined whether there is a likelihood of customer confusion between the marks you are evaluating, look at the following additional factors. They will help you determine the likelihood of getting into a lawsuit or of prevailing if you are mired in one. Then you will have a very clear idea of whether it's wise to use a particular mark.

History of Trademark Infringement Lawsuits

Knowing whether the owner of a similar mark has a history of initiating trademark disputes is the most revealing factor in predicting the likelihood of a lawsuit. It makes sense to assume that the owner will act similarly when made aware of your mark, vigorously challenging any uses that are potentially confusing—and perhaps even some that clearly are not. Even if you eventually win such a suit, the cost of defending against it, averaging $100,000, is rarely worth it in the long run. For example, anyone who follows these matters knows that McDonald's vigorously protects its golden arches and the prefix "Mc" when it comes to any type of fast, efficient, and low-cost service business. For this reason, you should stay away from using anything that might get up the ire of McDonald's.

One way to discover a company's litigation history is to look up some of the secondary sources of trademark law listed in Chapter 14. Those books have tables in the back that list cases by the names of the litigants (parties to a lawsuit). If you don't find the name of the business with which you may have a conflict, the records of the county and federal courthouses nearest their corporate headquarters will probably list cases in which they have been litigants (not all of which will be trademark cases). Or, you can consult an attorney, who will search for the company name on one of several comprehensive legal databases that list all cases in a given field. Consulting an attorney is likely to be the most expensive method, but also the most effective.

How Long the Allegedly Infringing Use Has Been Going On

If your business has used a mark for a long time without complaint from the owner, the inactivity on the part of the other owner may establish two things:

- It makes it look as though the alleged infringement has not harmed the complaining owner very much. This is known in legalese as "sleeping on your rights," and a court is less likely to give the owner any relief if it has not taken action to protect its rights despite another's use of the same mark for a long time.
- You have established some rights in the mark that may be superior to the true owner's rights, if only in the geographic area in which you have been using it. (See Chapter 10, "Sorting Out Trademark Disputes," for more on legal priorities in such situations.)

The Intent Behind Adopting and Using the Mark in Question

The intent of the alleged infringer is also relevant. If it appears probable to the court that your business chose its mark only in order to take advantage of its similarity to the other mark, then the court is very likely to find that you infringed against the original mark. If, for example, a successful and well-known marketer of French bread uses Staff of Life as a trademark, and a new rival calls its product Stuff of Life, the court will be very suspicious about the intent of the rival—and it might be hard to persuade the judge or jury that the owner of the Stuff of Life mark did not intentionally copy the first mark.

How to Read a Trademark Search Report

In previous sections, we advised you what to look for when evaluating the results of your trademark search. In this section, we'll walk you through a typical search report, and we'll answer some common questions. Appendix C to this book includes relevant sections from a search report generated by Thomson CompuMark. We requested the Thomson CompuMark search for the name Incorporator Pro, which Nolo (the publisher of this book) had intended to use as the name for a software program that helps users form a corporation.

The Thomson CompuMark search is the broadest type of search report, in which a searcher wades through through three groups of trademarks—those that are federally registered, those registered with state governments, and those that are not registered (common law). The major search report companies generate similarly comprehensive searches.

> ⚠ **CAUTION**
>
> **No guarantees.** Trademark searchers and database inputters make mistakes. But don't be deterred from getting a report just because search companies won't guarantee their results. These reports are still the established legal standard for prejudging a trademark choice.

Jump Right In

Before starting a search, you must know what you're seeking. In our case, we're looking for marks that are:

- identical to Incorporator Pro on similar or related goods or services
- similar to Incorporator Pro on similar or related goods or services, or
- famous and similar to Incorporator Pro.

The easiest way to start is to pick up the report and start reading. This task might seem overwhelming, considering the bewildering number of entries. Don't worry. For now, you can disregard the information about search strategies, databases, or other explanatory text and just look at the actual entries. You'll notice that each section usually starts with a list of possible matches, followed by individual analysis of each relevant entry.

Page through the report and make a cursory review. We did this with the report in Appendix C. (Not all of the report is reproduced in the appendix. We included just those portions that are relevant to our discussion.) Initially, we noted that no marks—federal, state, or common law—are identical to our proposed mark, Incorporator Pro. We saw, however, one abandoned application for Incorporator Pro. That application was filed in 2004 by Nolo, the publisher of this book, and later abandoned for business reasons. We saw no marks that included both the words "Pro" and "Incorporator," such as "Legal Pro Incorporator." We also didn't recognize any of the marks in the report as being famous. We made a table as shown below.

Standard	Mark
Identical to Incorporator Pro (on similar or related goods or services)	Incorporator Pro (previously filed and abandoned by Nolo)
Similar to Incorporator Pro (on similar or related goods or services)	Internet Incorporators Incorporators USA Incorporate Corpro The Incorporator Pros Incorporated California Incorporators Pro Incorporated
Famous and similar to Incorporator Pro	None

After completing this first pass, we took a second tour of the search report, examining more of the search details.

Federal Trademark Search

Search reports are usually divided into tabbed sections for federal, state, and common law. As noted, each section usually starts with a list of entries, followed by details relevant to each entry. These individual entries provide the most helpful decision-making data—for example, whether the mark is live or dead, the type of goods, the class of goods, the owners, and the length of registration. The federal trademark search portion is always first.

Below we provide some questions and answers that describe how this data affects your trademark decisions:

- **Am I free to use dead (cancelled or abandoned) marks?** Trademark search reports always indicate whether a mark is live (active and currently registered) or dead (abandoned by the owner or canceled by the USPTO). For example, the search report provides information about the mark Pros Incorporated. An application was filed for this mark in May 1997 on the Supplemental Register, but the application was abandoned in March 2000. An applicant might abandon an application for various reasons—for example, the applicant might believe that registration is unlikely, or perhaps the applicant decided to discontinue the product or service because of the marketplace. If a similar mark shows up as being abandoned during the application process, it often pays to dig deeper in the application file to find out if the reason was due to an examiner objection. That may foretell what's in store for your application.

```
PROS                    PROS| INCORPORATED
INCORPORATED
                        Status:    ABANDONED
                                   SUPPLEMENTAL REGISTER
                                   AMENDED TO USE APPLICATION

                                   USPTO Status: ABANDONED-FAILURE TO RESPOND
                                   USPTO Status Date: MAR 28, 2000
                        Goods/Services:
                                   International Class 35:  PROVIDING BUSINESS AGENT SERVICES
                                   FOR PROFESSIONAL ATHLETES AND OTHER CELEBRITIES
                                   First Used: MAR 02, 1973  (INTL. CL. 35)
                                   In Commerce: APR 01, 1973
                        Last Reported Owner:
                                   PROS INCORPORATED
                                   VIRGINIA CORPORATION
                                   9 SOUTH 12TH STREET
                                   P.O. BOX 673
                                   RICHMOND, VIRGINIA 23218

                        Chronology:
                                   Filed: MAY 08, 1997       Serial Number: 75-288,910
                                   Abandoned: MAR 28, 2000

                        Ownership Details:
                        Applicant:
                                   PROS INCORPORATED
                                   VIRGINIA CORPORATION
                                   9 SOUTH 12TH STREET
                                   P.O. BOX 673
                                   RICHMOND, VIRGINIA 23218
```

A different type of abandonment applies when a mark has been registered but later abandoned or canceled. For example, the mark Capro Incorporated was cancelled because the owner failed to file a Section 8 affidavit (a statement of continued use, which is necessary to maintain a trademark registration). In this case, the owner likely used the mark on goods and services and then later, for one reason or another, failed to file the affidavit .

Keep in mind that when a mark shows up as "dead" like this on the Federal Register, it's possible that the mark is still being used, albeit in an unregistered status. As long as the mark is still in use, no one else can use it (in a way that would create the likelihood of customer confusion) without infringing it.

There are many ways to determine if a trademark is no longer being used. The simplest method is to call the company and ask if the product can be purchased. If the response is something like, "No, we haven't sold that product in years," there is a chance that the trademark is truly abandoned. A presumption of abandonment arises after three years. For example, a company that owned the trademark registration for Android Data (for e-commerce software) went out of business in 2002 and failed to use the mark for a period of three years, thereby opening the door for Google's use of the Android mark. (*Specht v. Google, Inc.,* 758 F.Supp.2d 570 (N.D. Ill., 2010).)

If you can afford the additional expense, consider hiring a professional investigator who can help you determine the extent of the company's use. If you believe that a mark has been abandoned, even if it is showing up as live on the search report, you may file a Petition for Cancellation based upon abandonment with the USPTO.

- **What importance should I place on trademarks on the Supplemental Register?** The answer depends on the similarity of the marks and how long the mark has been on the Supplemental Register. As you may remember from Chapter 1, the Supplemental Register registers weak or descriptive marks. These marks get very limited rights. After five years on the Supplemental Register, however,

the mark becomes eligible for the Principal Register. Consider the trademark Internet Incorporators: The services are similar to those for Incorporator Pro. The names are similar, though perhaps not confusingly similar. The mark is registered on the Supplemental Register, not the Principal Register, and the five-year period has passed. We need to perform more research, if possible, to find out if the product is still available, and if possible, whether the trademark will move to the Principal Register. Because marks registered on the Supplemental Register are, by their nature, too weak to be registered on the Principal Register, we also realize that it's possible that our proposed mark Incorporator Pro might also be considered to be weak by the USPTO.

- **What if the report indicates that the trademark owner has disclaimed some portion of the trademark? Does that mean I'm free to use it?**
  Yes and no. You're free to use the disclaimed terms without infringing, but if you attempt to register your mark, you'll

probably have to disclaim the same terms. In other words, you won't be able to stop anyone else from using those terms either. As explained in Chapter 7, a disclaimer is a statement that a trademark owner asserts no exclusive right in a specific portion of a mark, apart from its use within the mark. Disclaimers are required by USPTO examiners as a condition of registration. For example, in the Incorporator Pro search in Appendix C, you will note Disclaimer Statements for terms such as "Nationwide Incorporators" and "Internet Incorporators." You might wonder, how can the owner of the Internet Incorporators trademark claim any trademark rights, if its whole name has been disclaimed? In the case of this and many other marks, the owner claims limited rights to the stylized appearance of the mark and the accompanying graphics. By reading disclaimers, you will learn what will have to be disclaimed when applying for your trademark.

- **What if a mark is pending but has not yet been registered?** The trademark search report always informs you as to the status of the mark, whether it's presently registered, or is a pending application. As explained in Chapter 7, pending applications, including intent-to-use applications (assuming they later issue as registrations), will have priority over owners who commence use after the earlier application filing date. So, if a pending mark is similar and will be used on similar goods, that's an important strike against your proposed use.

- **What if the search report indicates that a company has assigned the mark to another business? Should that affect my determination?** No, the assignee (the company that has purchased the mark) acquires all of the rights of the original owner and can enforce those rights to stop you from using a similar mark.

- **What matters more, whether the mark is used on similar goods or in the same class?** Generally, your first concern should be whether the goods and services are similar. This is especially true in crowded classes like Class 9, in which the Incorporator Pro trademark will be registered. That's because Class 9 is the class for most scientific, technical, computer, and Internet marks, and it's the class in which 20% of all trademark applications are filed. In Class 9, for example, it's possible for similar marks to be registered for different goods, say, video games or nautical equipment. For our purposes, therefore, we're much more concerned with companies that offer similar goods (whether books or software) or similar services. (This distinction between goods and classes may not be as dramatic in less crowded classes.)

State Registration Search

If you are paying for a trademark search, it's always a good idea to have the search firm include a search of the state trademark registration database. The state search report section, like the federal search section, starts with a list of state registered marks, followed by details on each relevant listing. Almost all such reports, regardless of the searching company, are performed using the TrademarkScan database owned by Thomson CompuMark.

How do you quantify the effect of a state trademark registration versus a federal registration? A federal registration creates a presumption of national priority. Not so with a state registration or a common law mark. The impact of these types of marks is quite often local. Nonetheless, a local user can obstruct you if you attempt to sell goods or services in their geographic area. For that reason, you need to determine the extent of the use. Ask yourself—are the products distributed or services offered over a wide geographic area? Does the company's trademark have an Internet presence? In a nutshell, the smaller the Internet presence and the more localized the use, the less of a threat to your proposed use.

It's important to keep in mind that those who have claimed state and common law rights did not encounter the same standardized scrutiny as did federal registration applicants. Consider the data provided for the state registration for "California Incorporators The Professional Solution" in the Incorporator Pro search. The "Goods/Services" are vaguely described as "new business in California," even though the mark was first used in 1996. Because many state trademark offices simply rubber-stamp applications without a thorough analysis, these marks are sometimes more susceptible to challenges on the basis of descriptiveness or genericness.

Common Law Report

The common law trademarks section includes trademarks that aren't registered anywhere, as well as company names and other names that might not actually be used as trademarks. The search companies wade through many sources, including public databases, product announcements, business products databases, and proprietary database records. The rules for state registrations apply for common law marks: If you are concerned about an identical or similar mark, do more research to determine whether the name is actually (and currently) used as a trademark.

CALIFORNIA INCORPORATORS THE PROFESSIONAL SOLUTION

State:	CALIFORNIA
Status:	REGISTERED
Date Registered:	MAR 20, 1997
Registration No.:	47569

Goods/Services: International Class: 42
NEW BUSINESS IN CALIFORNIA
State Class: 42

First Use In State:	First Use Anywhere:
FEB, 1996	FEB, 1996

Design Phrase: THE WORDS "CALIFORNIA INCORPORATORS" WITH THE FIRST LETTERS OF EACH NAME IN A DROP CAP STYLE, THE NAME IS ACCOMPANIED WITH A LOGO IN THE STYLE OF TWO CRESCENTS FACING EACH OTHER (LOCATED ABOVE THE NAME) AND THE WORDS "THE PROFESSIONAL SOLUTION" (LOCATED BELOW THE NAME)

Registrant:
CALIFORNIA INCORPORATORS
CALIFORNIA CORPORATION
15928 VENTURA BOULEVARD, SUITE 108
ENCINO, CALIFORNIA 91436

We Have Located Other Marks With This Owner

NATIONWIDE INCORPO RATORS THE INCORPO RATION PROFESSIONALS	USPTO	Page 19

Manner Of Display:
USED ON ADVERTISING BROCHURES, ON ADVERTISING LEAFLETS, ON BUSINESS CARDS, ON LETTERHEADS.

Our Conclusions

We made two conclusions after reviewing the Incorporator Pro search. First, we did not find any marks so similar in appearance or phonetics to merit serious concern of infringement. In other words, the coast was clear. The reason that the coast was clear, however, led to our second conclusion that terms such as "Incorporator" or "Incorporate" and "Pro" might be considered descriptive and might have to be disclaimed; or, they might require registration on the Supplemental Register. In short, even though Nolo is free to use the term, it could run into problems if the company attempts to register it on the Principal Register.

Your trademark search results, obviously, will differ. If in doubt about your conclusions or the search report data, your best course of action would be to consult with a trademark attorney for help.

Federal Trademark Registration

This chapter helps you register your trademark with the U.S. Patent and Trademark Office (USPTO). Registration is optional, but it provides a number of significant advantages to the trademark owner. Registration on the Principal Register provides you with exclusive nationwide ownership of the mark (except where the mark is already being used by prior users who haven't registered the mark) and official notice to all would-be later users that the mark is unavailable. In addition, registration provides a legal presumption that you are the owner of the mark, which means it's easier for you to prove ownership if a dispute over the mark ends up in court.

Taken together, these benefits make it more likely that you will win an infringement lawsuit and collect damages. That could mean more money to pay the attorneys, which often makes it worthwhile to bring the lawsuit in the first place.

To make the most of this chapter, you should first have a basic understanding of:

- how trademark law works on and off the Internet (Chapter 1)
- how to choose a legally strong trademark (Chapter 3)
- how to find out whether other marks exist that might conflict with yours (Chapters 4 and 5), and
- how to tell whether your mark is confusingly similar to another (Chapter 6).

Brief Overview of Federal Registration

If you are already using the mark, here are the four steps required for federal registration:

1. Gather the necessary information, such as the date you first started using the mark anywhere, the date you first used it in commerce that Congress may regulate (for example, shipping products across state lines), and an example showing how the mark is actually being used (called a "specimen").
2. Complete an application—either online or on hard copy.

3. File the application with the USPTO—either online or by mail—accompanied by a specimen of how your mark is being used and a fee of (a) $400 per class for a regular electronic TEAS application, (b) $275 per class for an electronic TEAS RF application, (c) $225 per class for an electronic TEAS Plus application, or (d) $600 per class for a paper application.

4. If required, modify the application in response to the trademark examiner's comments.

If you are not using the mark but wish to reserve it for future use, you should apply on an intent-to-use basis. You will not have to supply a specimen, but once you start using the mark you'll have to:

- file an additional form notifying the USPTO that you are now using the mark
- provide a specimen of the use, and
- pay an additional $100.

More fees and forms are required if you don't use the mark within six months after the USPTO approves the mark for registration.

What Marks Qualify for Federal Registration

Now that you have an overview of the trademark registration process, let's start by examining the basic qualifications for placement of a mark on the federal trademark register. The USPTO maintains, in fact, two trademark registers—the Principal Register and the Supplemental Register. Your goal is to get your mark placed on the Principal Register, because it provides most of the benefits of federal registration. However, if your mark doesn't qualify for the Principal Register, you might be able to place it on the Supplemental Register—which does provide a few benefits. (See Chapter 1 for more on the Supplemental Register.) From this point on, when we speak of federal registration, we are referring to registration on the Principal Register.

In Chapter 1, we described qualifications for federal trademark registration. To review, a mark qualifies for placement on the Principal Register if:

- The USPTO considers the mark distinctive, either inherently so or because it has obtained a secondary meaning through use over time.
- The mark does not legally conflict with an existing registered mark.
- The mark is in actual use.
- Its use is in commerce that Congress may regulate (that is, it moves across state, territorial, or international borders, or affects commerce across these borders).
- The mark is not scandalous, immoral, or deceptive.

The first two qualifications—distinctiveness and nonconflicting marks—have been explained in Chapters 3 and 6, respectively. Now we will cover the last three.

Is the Mark in Actual Use?

A mark must be in actual use before it can be placed on the Federal Register. This doesn't mean that you have to be using the mark when you apply for registration (see below, on intent-to-use applications) but only that the mark will not be registered until you notify the USPTO that the mark has been put into actual use, provide a sample, and pay an extra fee.

What constitutes actual use? As a general rule, "in use" means that you have placed the mark in the marketplace to identify your goods or services. The criteria used by the examiners to determine whether a trademark is in use vary, depending on whether the trademark is being used for a product or a service.

For products (tangible goods), your mark is in use if the mark appears on the goods or on labels or tags attached to them, and the goods have either been sold or shipped to a store for resale purchase. A token sale made only for the purpose of getting your mark "in use" doesn't count. The following examples show legitimate uses of the marks for purposes of registration.

> **EXAMPLE 1:** Ben sent a sample of his No-Knees pants to a department store that will resell them.

> **EXAMPLE 2:** Emily's earrings were shipped in a box carrying the label All Ears, for resale by a local street vendor.

> **EXAMPLE 3:** Peter developed software for recording podcasts, and he sold four copies of his software online. He used the mark Bearware prominently on his website and on the software.

For services, your mark is in use if the services are actually being marketed under the mark and you can legitimately deliver the services to customers.

> **EXAMPLE 1:** Toby purchased a 900 number phone line for providing sports trivia under the name Sportorific. As soon as his lines were up and running and he had advertised his services under the name Sportorific, his mark was in use.

> **EXAMPLE 2:** Helen decided to call her housecleaning service Mistress Tidy. When she first advertised her services under that name on a bulletin board at a local market, she put her mark into use.

> **EXAMPLE 3:** Alice started her own Internet service provider business under the mark CosmoNet. She set up her system and prepared all of the equipment she would need to offer her services. The day she first started advertising her services under her mark and with all of her systems in place and ready to go, she put her mark into use.

Are You Using the Mark in Commerce That Congress May Regulate?

Even if the mark is in actual use, it won't qualify for federal registration unless it is in use "in commerce that Congress may regulate." To satisfy this requirement, you must do one or more of the following:

- ship a product to which the mark is attached across a state line (most manufacturers, wholesalers, and mail-order businesses do this regularly)
- ship a product to which the mark is attached between a state and a territory or between a territory and another territory (for instance, between New York and Puerto Rico, or between Puerto Rico and the Virgin Islands)
- ship a product to which the mark is attached between a state or territory and another country (for instance, between California and Hong Kong, or between Puerto Rico and Cuba)
- use the mark in advertising in which your business offers its services to those outside the state (many businesses that have sites on the Internet and other businesses, such as Disneyland, do this regularly) provided that you can provide those services at the time of the advertisement
- use the mark in the course of conducting a service business across a state line (such as most trucking operations, many 900 numbers, and, increasingly, businesses that offer e-commerce over the Internet)
- use the mark to identify a service business in more than one state (such as McDonald's, Holiday Inn, or Hilton Hotels) or across international or territorial borders
- use the mark in the course of operating a business that caters to interstate or international travelers (such as a hotel, restaurant, tour guide service, or ski resort), or
- use the mark in a business that is regulated by the federal government.

The basic reason for this commerce requirement is that the federal government has no constitutional authority to regulate marks that are used only within one state's borders.

Here are examples of marks used in commerce that Congress may regulate:

- **Goods**
  - Alan's mousetrap is sold in three states under the mark MiceNoMore, and the mark appears on the packaging.
  - Rosebud, Inc., distributes a computer program called Rosecare to nurseries throughout the country. The mark appears on the packaging and opening screen of the software.
  - Ruth lives in White River Junction, Vermont, a town just across the river from Hanover, New Hampshire, where Dartmouth University is located. She sells a brand of baked goods in both towns—under the label Ruth's Bakery Delights.
  - Travelers come to Point Reyes Station, California, from around the world to buy bread at Brickmaiden Breads. The bakery draws national and international trade under the trademark, Brickmaiden Breads.

- **Services**
  - Etta's computer consulting services markets their service by telephone and direct mail to potential customers in Canada, California, and Nevada under the mark Quick-Bytes.
  - Toby Drysdale markets its 900 phone number for sports trivia, Sportorific, through ads on national radio and television networks and is also available to purchasers in Puerto Rico and Mexico.
  - Rose syndicated her newspaper advice column in three Northeastern states under the name Rosie to the Rescue.
  - Doug markets his mail-order shoe repair service under the name Sole Security via ads in national magazines and newspapers.
  - Ninth Wave Surfing provides lessons in Hawaii to vacationers from all over the world.

This last example shows the effect that a business can have on interstate commerce. Though the effect may also qualify a mark for federal registration, it is not as clear-cut a case as when the mark actually appears in more than one state—for instance, in advertising or mail-order catalogs.

CAUTION
As a general rule, the USPTO trademark examiners do not investigate whether the mark for which registration is being sought is being used in "commerce that Congress may regulate." Nor is there any place in the application to describe exactly where, geographically, the mark is being used. Although few applications are rejected because the commerce requirement hasn't been satisfied, it does happen. For example, in 2016, the USPTO refused to register the trademark for a cannabis vaporizer because cannabis distribution is unlawful commerce under federal law. However, if you ever have to defend your registration—in court or before the USPTO—you might be required to prove that the mark was in fact being used in commerce at the time of its registration.

Is Your Mark Immoral, Deceptive, or Scandalous?

You may not register a mark if it:
- contains "immoral," "deceptive," or "scandalous" matter (for example, a mark resembling a sex organ would be considered immoral; a mark suggesting miracle properties in a product that are not substantiated would be deceptive; and a mark showing a mutilated corpse would be scandalous)
- falsely suggests a connection with persons (living or dead), institutions, beliefs, or national symbols (for example, a baseball-related mark falsely suggesting a connection with Babe Ruth)
- includes the flag or coat of arms or other insignia of the United States, any state or municipality, or any foreign nation; or includes any simulation of such flag or insignia
- consists of or contains a name, portrait, or signature of a particular living individual (except with that person's written consent), or the name, signature, or portrait of a deceased president of the United States during the life of his spouse, if any (except with the written consent of the widow)

- is already taken by an organization that has been granted the exclusive right by statute to use the marks or symbol (such organizations include the Boy Scouts, the U.S. Olympic Committee, and the Department of the Interior for the character name Smokey the Bear)
- is misleading or just plain false (such as a trademark that suggests chocolate in a product that contains no chocolate), or
- is primarily a geographic name or a surname (see Chapter 3 for a discussion of these types of names and when they are and are not considered distinctive).

Prior to 2017, the Lanham Act prohibited registration of marks that "disparaged" persons, institutions, or beliefs (examples include a mark showing the president standing on the American flag, and a mark used by a Greyhound competitor showing a defecating dog). But in a unanimous 2017 decision, the Supreme Court held that the "disparagement" clause of the Lanham Act violated the First Amendment's free speech clause. The USPTO had denied an Asian-American band's registration for SLANTS on the basis that the term was disparaging to persons of Asian descent. Acknowledging that speech that demeans on the basis of race is hateful, Justice Alito wrote that "the proudest boast of our free speech jurisprudence is that we protect the freedom to express 'the thought that we hate.'" (*Matal v. Tam*, 582 U.S. _____, (2017); 2017 WL2621315).

If You Haven't Started Using Your Mark, Should You File an Intent-to-Use Application?

If you are not yet using your mark, you can wait until you put it into use before filing a trademark application, or you can file an application on the grounds that you intend to use it within six months of the date the USPTO approves the mark for registration . If you are unable to put the mark into use within that period, you can purchase additional six-month extensions, one at a time, until three years have passed, if you are able to convince the USPTO that the reasons for the delays are legitimate.

The advantage of filing an intent-to-use application is that your filing date will serve as the date of your first use of the mark—assuming you go on to put the mark in actual use and take the other steps necessary to get the mark placed on the federal trademark register. This first-use date can be very important in the event a conflict develops with another mark. (See Chapter 1 for the importance of the date of first use.) Once you decide to file on this basis, you should do so as quickly as possible, to obtain the earliest possible date of first use.

As mentioned, the intent-to-use approach is more expensive than filing an actual use application—at least $100 more expensive, plus $125 for each additional six-month extension that you need. Therefore, it is most appropriate to use the intent-to-use application when you have come up with a truly distinctive mark (see Chapter 3, "How to Choose a Good Name for Your Business, Product, or Service"), or you plan to spend big bucks "tooling up" to use the mark and you don't want to lay out the cash until you know that the mark will be yours.

If your mark is legally weak—for instance, it uses common words in a common way or is descriptive of the products or services—you will have little choice but to wait until you have put the mark into use and can demonstrate that the public associates the mark with your product or service. This is because the USPTO will only issue a Notice of Allowance—an official response approving an intent-to-use application—for marks that are distinctive, either inherently or under the secondary meaning rule.

Examples of Your Mark to Submit With Your Application?

SKIP AHEAD

If you are filing an intent-to-use application, you won't have specimens yet and don't need to deal with this information at this time; you should skip ahead to the next section. However, if and when you put the mark into use and file the proper documents necessary to complete the registration process, you will need the information in this section.

When applying for federal registration on an actual-use basis, you must submit an example of how you are using your mark in commerce, known as a specimen. If you plan to apply for registration under more than one trademark class, you will need to submit a separate specimen showing use for each class.

Most likely, you will be filing online using TEAS. In that case, you will need to submit the specimen as a JPEG file that can be attached to your online application. Prepare this photographic or graphic file before beginning the application process. Its file size must be under two megabytes and it should be scanned at 300 DPI or higher.

If you are using the printed forms, you will need to include a physical specimen in your mailing to the USPTO. The specimen may not exceed 8½ inches (21.6 cm) wide and 13 inches (33 cm) long, and it must be flat. There is no minimum size. As we emphasize later, the specimen must portray the exact same mark that appears in the drawing you will be submitting with the application. The drawing is a clear image of the mark by itself, either in "standard characters" (for a word mark with no design elements) or "special form" (for a mark with stylized lettering or design elements).

Specimens for Marks on Goods (Trademarks)

Specimens must show a very close association between the mark and the goods. Acceptable specimens usually include labels, tags, or containers showing the mark.

Displays as Specimens for Goods

Displays, such as banners and window displays, may also be used, but with caution. The display must be meant to catch the buyer's attention where the item is for sale (for instance, at the store), and the mark must be prominent and clearly connected to the goods. For example, a window sign in a drugstore that reads "See our All Ears earrings special!" would probably qualify as an appropriate specimen. However, the line between displays and advertising can be fuzzy, and advertising is not sufficient for specimens of marks used for goods. If you have a choice, use another type of specimen.

Marks on Goods as Specimens

If you place your mark on your goods by using a rubber stamp or stencil, you may submit a specimen of an impression of the stamp or stencil on a piece of paper.

Photographing Your Specimens

If your *Solve-it Solvent* mark is used in connection with 55-gallon drums of solvent and printed only on the drums, you can submit a photograph (in JPEG format, when filing electronically) of a drum or drums clearly showing the whole mark. The photograph must show the whole item, or enough of it so the examiner can clearly see what is shown in the picture, and all writing on the item must be legible. If a photograph of the whole item does not show the mark in enough detail, send one photo of the whole item and another close-up photo of the writing including the mark (the two photos together would constitute one specimen). If one side has more writing than the other, either send more than one photo or place several items in one photo so they show all sides of the item on which writing appears.

> EXAMPLE: Suppose your mark Solve-it Solvent appears on the front and back of the drum in large type, surrounded by other writing describing the contents. Your first photo should portray three or four drums, each showing a different part of all the writing (Solve-it Solvent and the description). You should then take a few more photos, from a closer range, so that the examiner can see all the writing that appears on a typical drum. (Again, all the photos together would constitute one specimen.) If the writing is not legible for some reason (maybe it's too small to photograph well), submit a separate piece of paper including all text on the drum.

The reason all the writing has to be visible is that the USPTO wants to see the context in which your mark is used to be sure it is consistent with the class under which you are registering the mark.

Unacceptable Specimens for Marks on Goods

The following are *unacceptable* specimens for marks on goods:

- advertising material, including anything that is produced for the sole purpose of notifying potential buyers about your product, even if you package it with the goods (such as cards packaged with a new pen telling how wonderful it is and what it's made of)
- price lists, catalogs, trade directories, and publicity releases
- instruction sheets
- internal company documents, including invoices and memos sent within the company
- specimens showing the mark with the ® symbol—it is illegal to use the ® symbol until after your mark is officially registered with the USPTO (specimens with a TM next to the mark are okay; see Chapter 8), and
- any use of the mark merely to identify your business (not in direct connection with particular goods), including letterhead stationery, labels carrying only a company name and return address, and bags and boxes used at store cash registers to carry sold merchandise.

Specimens for Marks Used for Services (Service Marks)

When you are offering a service, you have no product to which you can affix a label. Because of this, acceptable specimens for services include a variety of materials that can't be used for product marks. Acceptable specimens include scanned copies of advertising and marketing materials, such as newspaper and magazine ads, brochures, billboards, direct mail pieces, and menus (for restaurants).

Letterhead stationery and business cards showing the mark may also be used if the services are plainly reflected on them, because the name or symbol being claimed as a mark is being used to identify the services in that context—that is, it's being used as a mark rather than as a trade name (remember, trade names may not be registered—see "Trade Names," below).

EXAMPLE 1: Etta's business cards for her personal computer consulting services include her mark Quick-Bytes and the text, "consulting services for the PC user." The USPTO would accept the cards as a specimen.

EXAMPLE 2: When Toby's sports trivia 900 line grew, he had stationery printed, including the line, "Sportorific Gives You The Latest Sports Trivia 24 Hours A Day." The stationery is an acceptable specimen.

A letter on stationery will also be accepted as a specimen for a service mark if the mark appears in the letterhead and the services are described in the letter. For example, assume Toby's letterhead only said "Gen-X Sports" and gave the address and phone number. He could submit a copy of a letter sent to a national sports magazine asking that his 900 number be listed in its directory, as long as the letter described the services.

Gen-X Sports
555 First Street, West
Sonoma, CA 95476

Dear Sir or Madam:

As you may know, our sports trivia line, *Sportorific*, 900-555-7777, has been providing customers with sports trivia 24 hours a day for the past year. We would be honored if you would consider listing our line in your directory.

Audio

Most marks appear in writing. But if your service mark appears only in radio ads or in some other audio form, you may submit a sound file of the audio. You can do so through the TEAS application. You can send the sound mark specimen, consisting of a WAV file or an MP3 file, as an email attachment directly to the TEAS Support Team, at teas@uspto.gov. However, because the TEAS form will require a JPEG attachment for the specimen, you will still need to create a JPEG file for this purpose. The JPEG can consist merely of a statement such as: "A WAV file (or MP3 file) has been sent directly to the TEAS Support Team for processing." For easier association of the WAV (or MP3) file with the proper application, you should submit the actual application first and then send an email to the TEAS Support Team, referencing the assigned serial number and an indication that this is a "new application." Handle all other filings (for example, required maintenance filings; see Chapter 8) in the same manner, with the serial number or registration number referenced in the email and a clear indication of the type of filing.

Internet Pages

A screen shot of the full webpage should also suffice. You can take a screen shot by using the screen capture feature on your computer and pasting the screen shot into a graphics program file, or by using a software program such as *Snag-It*. If your home page prominently displays the mark, so much the better.

If I Registered My Trademark, Do I Need to Register My Trademark.com?

Let's say you have been using the name Loudness as a trademark for a line of menswear. You registered Loudness with the USPTO. Now you're selling the same menswear online using the domain name Loudness.com. Do you need to register Loudness.com with the USPTO?

In this case, there's little to be gained from registering Loudness.com with the USPTO because you already have the ability to stop anyone from using Loudness for menswear, whether they are selling it online or off. Another reason not to bother is that you cannot claim any separate trademark rights in ".com," because the USPTO considers top-level domain terms such as ".com," ".org," and ".edu" unprotectable.

You should, however, consider registering Loudness.com if you will be establishing some services or products unique to your Internet business. For example, if you are establishing an online store that will offer a fashion newsletter as well as your menswear, you should consider registering Loudness.com.

Domain Name Specimens

If you are registering your entire domain name, the specimen should be a JPEG picture of your webpage showing your domain name. You can take a photo using the screen capture feature that comes with your computer or by using a software program such as *Snag-It*. If you are just registering the unique part of your domain name (without the .com), your specimen may be an advertisement of your services. Either way, make sure your specimen shows your name exactly as you portray it in the "mark drawing" box in the application.

Your domain name specimen must show two things:

- **You are using your domain name as a trademark.** A specimen that shows your website and the domain name typed into the address line of your browser is not sufficient. Your domain name should be a prominent part of the design of your home page. Ideally, it should be at the very top of the page, easy to spot and easy to read, and it should dominate the quadrant of the page in which it is located.
- **The services being offered on your website match the description of the services in your application.** If you are providing financial information as your service, for example, make sure your specimen shows that you are doing so.

Unacceptable Specimens for Services

The following are unacceptable specimens for service marks:
- news releases or articles based on news releases
- documents showing use of the mark in connection with goods rather than services
- invoices and similar documents such as packing slips, and
- specimens showing trade name usage only (use of the mark to identify a company, such as on letterhead). As discussed earlier, one exception to this is if the letterhead or the text of the letter identifies the services represented by the mark.

Trade Names

A trade name is the name of a company and is not registrable as a trademark or service mark unless it is used for more than identification purposes. To be registrable, the trade name must also be used to identify goods the company sells (trademark) or to market or promote services (service mark). However, it is common for a company's trade name and the trademark used in providing the company's services to be the same, which makes the trade name registrable in its capacity as a mark.

Which International Class Is the Best Fit for Your Product or Service?

Part of the trademark registration process involves assigning your product or service to one or more international classes. A full list of these classes is in Appendix A. We explained the classification system in Chapter 6.

If you've read the material in Chapter 6 and are still in doubt about the proper class or classes for your product or service, you can always call the Applications section of the USPTO at 800-786-9199 and ask which class or classes might be appropriate for you. You can also email the section at trademarkassistancecenter@uspto.gov. The clerk will answer your question and normally give you sound advice. Unfortunately, you don't have the legal right to rely on this opinion. If the person who eventually examines your application in the USPTO disagrees with the answer you got over the phone or in an email, you will have to assign a different class to the product or service.

You can apply for registration of a mark under more than one class. The reason you would do this is to broaden the scope of protection you receive.

EXAMPLE: Etta, who both sells computer software and offers consulting services under the mark Quick-Bytes, registers the mark under Class 9 (electrical and scientific apparatus). This registration should go far to protect Etta against the same or similar marks used on computer software and other related products. But it might not protect her against uses of the mark in connection with computer consulting services. She would also need to register the Quick-Bytes mark under the appropriate service class (Class 35 or Class 41) in order to obtain the maximum possible protection of her mark.

CAUTION

The classification system is designed more for the convenience of the USPTO when making registration decisions than as a means for the courts to determine whether infringement exists. Quite simply, courts may find a likelihood of customer confusion (and thus infringement) where two marks are in different classes and find no likelihood of customer confusion where two marks are within the same class. Still, the more classes a mark is registered in, the wider the protection the courts are likely to give its owner.

The number of classes you should include in your initial application depends on your circumstances. The downside of registering under more than one class is that you must pay an additional application fee (currently $225 to $400, if filing electronically) for each additional class. For this reason, applicants sometimes apply under one class and then wait to see if the mark (and their business) is successful enough to warrant applying under other classes as well.

Some applicants who can afford the fees register under several classes in their initial application, thinking that multiple registrations will preserve future rights in those classes and broaden the scope of protection by the courts. But the classes you can register under are restricted to those that encompass the goods or services you are already offering (as shown by the specimens you submit) or that you plan to offer (if you are registering on an intent-to-use basis).

Deciding How Many Marks You Want to Register

So far, we have assumed that you have one mark to register—typically a business or product name. However, what might seem like only one mark could in fact be considered several different marks. The most common examples of this are marks that combine graphic designs or distinctive typefaces with a business or product name, and marks that combine a business or product name with a slogan. In these situations, the name can be one mark while the combination of a graphic design or a slogan with the name may be a separate and distinct mark. For example, on the front, back cover, and spine of this printed book you will find several manifestations of the word "Nolo"—including Nolo with the scales of justice, or Nolo in connection with the website nolo.com. Each of these manifestations using the word Nolo is really a separate mark.

Even if you might technically be dealing with more than one mark, you don't have to register more than one mark.

After all, the registration fee for each mark is $225 to $400 when filing electronically, and funds may be too scarce to accomplish all possible registrations. Also, if you want to register a mark in more than one class, the combination of multiple marks and multiple classes can make it prohibitively expensive to cover all bases. Below, we suggest some ways to think about this issue for the most common multiple mark situations.

Name Marks Combined With Unusual Typefaces

If your name mark uses an unusual typeface (the Nolo example described above), your mark has two important aspects—the words that constitute the name and the look and feel of the typeface. If money is no object, register both separately. But if funds are short—as they usually are—

you probably will want to choose one or the other. As a general rule, you will be better off registering the unadorned name. This gives you the flexibility of using the name in many different configurations in the future without having to pay for new registrations.

Name Marks Combined With Graphic Designs

If you use your name with a graphic image—for example, the word Nolo with an image of the scales of justice—you will have several choices when it's time to register:

- Register the name alone.
- Register the combined name and graphic image.
- Register both the name alone and the combination of the name and graphic image.

Again, if money is no object, the last option is the best. But if every dollar counts, you should probably start with the combination name/ graphic image, assuming the graphic image is distinctive. If the graphics are not particularly distinctive, however, register the name by itself. The idea is to get the most mileage for your initial registration, and if you are limited to one mark, it is wise to register the mark that has the most distinctive elements.

Applying for Registration Online

Filling out and filing a trademark application for your mark with the USPTO is a snap. The USPTO website offers TEAS, an acronym for Trademark Electronic Application System. The TEAS program lets you complete and file the application online. According to the USPTO, it shouldn't take more than 20 minutes to complete the application, assuming you have the necessary information at your fingertips.

Although it's easy and quick to apply for trademark registration, the overworked and understaffed USPTO can take a year or more to process your application. In the meantime, your actual or intended mark will appear (a few months after the filing date) in the USPTO's trademark database as a pending registration. This means that anyone doing a trademark search will likely find your mark and know that you are claiming it as yours. This in itself gives you a lot of protection because it will scare off potential copiers.

But Wait ... There's More

Created in 1997, TEAS really provided only one service during the first four years of its existence—the ability to automate the preparation of a trademark application for the Principal Register. But gradually, the USPTO rolled out more online services and now offers a wide range of automated forms, including a Preliminary Amendment, Allegation of Use, Request for an Extension of Time, Request to Divide, Certification Mark applications, Collective Trademark/Service Mark applications, Collective Membership Mark applications, and an application for filing on the Supplemental Register.

CAUTION
Once you decide to register your mark with the USPTO, get it done quickly. If the USPTO receives two or more applications for the same mark, the one filed first will be examined (reviewed by the USPTO) and published for opposition first. All conflicting applications will wait in line until the outcome of the first application is known. Also, if you are filing an intent-to-use application (and you follow up by putting the mark into actual use and

getting it placed on the federal trademark register), your date of filing will be the date of first use of your mark, which could prove very important in the event of a later conflict. Though it's impossible to say whether a particular filing will make a difference in your situation, yours might be the one case in a thousand where a day's difference in filing will mean that your rights are senior to another filer's.

The USPTO Disfavors Paper Applications

For a variety of reasons, some people will prefer to work strictly with print copies of the trademark application and file them by mail. That is, instead of filling out an application on your computer, you might wish to complete the application by hand or by typing in the details. Unfortunately, the USPTO no longer provides blank downloadable application forms. The USPTO's reluctance to supply blank forms is part of its attempt to make the TEAS program the standardized format for filing. We support the use of TEAS instead of paper, because the online filing procedure is less likely to result in errors, particularly for first-time filers.

How to Use TEAS to Register Online

Using TEAS can be a pleasant experience. Just follow along with our step-by-step instructions below. If you need additional help, the USPTO provides its own help system.

First, go to the USPTO's website (www.uspto.gov). On the home page, click "Trademarks" and from the dropdown menu, choose "Apply Online" (see Figure 1 below).

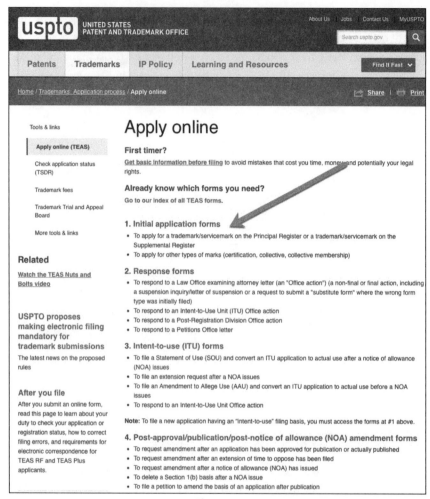

Figure 1

Next, choose "1. Initial Application Forms." This will take you to the "Trademark initial application forms" page (Figure 2):

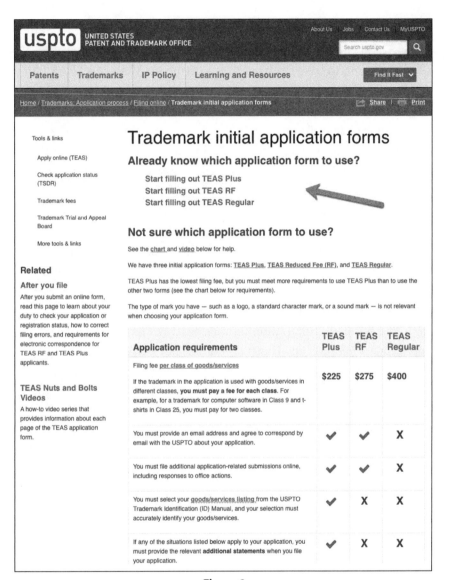

Figure 2

TEAS Plus Application. This is the least expensive option, with a filing fee of $225 per class of goods or services. The USPTO also considers this application to have the strictest requirements. With the TEAS Plus Application you must:

- pay the filing fee for all classes listed in the application at the time of submission
- identify the goods or services using descriptions taken directly from the USPTO Trademark ID Manual, and
- authorize the USPTO to communicate with you electronically.

If you use TEAS Plus, you must pay an additional fee of $125 per class if, at any time during the examination of the application, the USPTO decides you did not meet any of the above requirements.

TEAS Reduced Fee Application (TEAS RF). The TEAS RF application is a new filing option with a fee of $275 per class. As with the TEAS Plus application, a TEAS RF applicant must pay the filing fee for all classes up front and authorize email communications. However, unlike TEAS Plus applicants, TEAS RF applicants do not need to select an identification of goods or services from the Trademark ID Manual. Instead, applicants can use their own wording to describe the goods and services. This can be helpful if the applicant doesn't feel that the preset descriptions are accurate enough. However, like TEAS Plus, an applicant who files a TEAS RF application but does not satisfy the relevant requirements will be required to submit an additional processing fee of $125 per class of goods or services.

TEAS Regular Application. The TEAS Regular filing option has a filing fee of $400 per class. TEAS Regular applicants have the same requirements as TEAS RF, except they don't have to communicate electronically with the USPTO and don't have to pay an additional $125 per class if the application does not satisfy the relevant filing requirements.

The idea behind TEAS Plus is to get you to use preset choices instead of free-form text entries when describing your goods and services. If you are able to use the preset choices, try the TEAS Plus application as your first choice for filing. It's the least expensive filing option and the easiest to navigate.

We'll proceed through the rest of this section as if you were filing a typical TEAS Plus application form (the TEAS Regular, TEAS Plus, and TEAS RF applications are nearly identical). Choose the TEAS Plus form by clicking "Start filling out TEAS Plus." This will take you to a page entitled "Trademark/Service Mark Application, Principal Register," which provides filing instructions (see Figure 3, below).

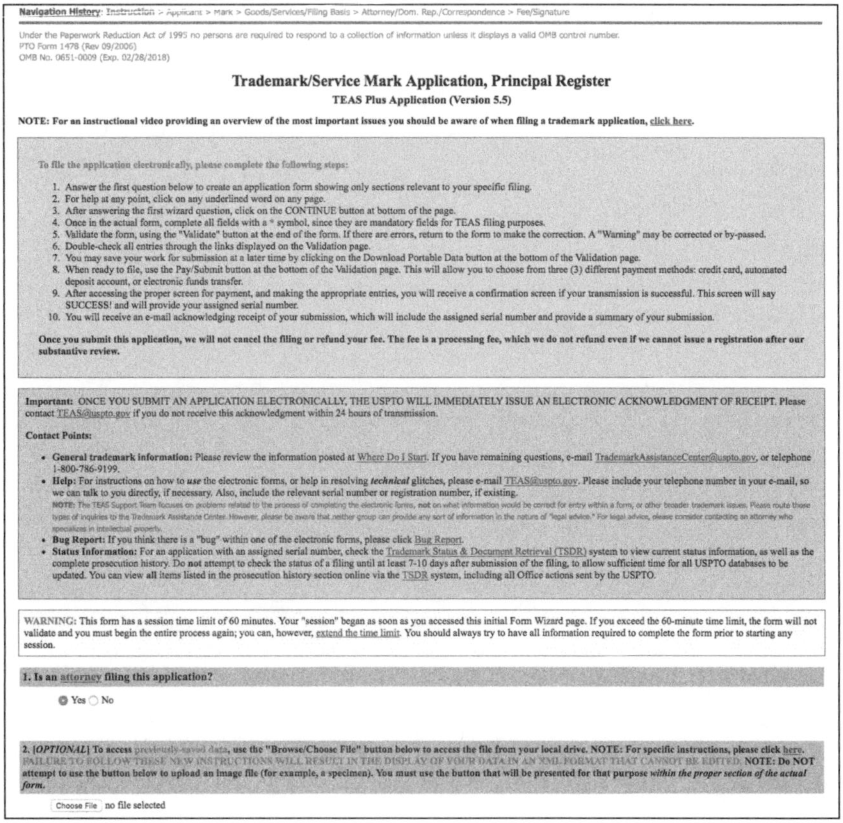

Navigation History: Instruction > Applicant > Mark > Goods/Services/Filing Basis > Attorney/Dom. Rep./Correspondence > Fee/Signature

Under the Paperwork Reduction Act of 1995 no persons are required to respond to a collection of information unless it displays a valid OMB control number.
PTO Form 1478 (Rev 09/2006)
OMB No. 0651-0009 (Exp. 02/28/2018)

Trademark/Service Mark Application, Principal Register

TEAS Plus Application (Version 5.5)

NOTE: For an instructional video providing an overview of the most important issues you should be aware of when filing a trademark application, click here.

To file the application electronically, please complete the following steps:

1. Answer the first question below to create an application form showing only sections relevant to your specific filing.
2. For help at any point, click on any underlined word on any page.
3. After answering the first wizard question, click on the CONTINUE button at bottom of the page.
4. Once in the actual form, complete all fields with a * symbol, since they are mandatory fields for TEAS filing purposes.
5. Validate the form, using the "Validate" button at the end of the form. If there are errors, return to the form to make the correction. A "Warning" may be corrected or by-passed.
6. Double-check all entries through the links displayed on the Validation page.
7. You may save your work for submission at a later time by clicking on the Download Portable Data button at the bottom of the Validation page.
8. When ready to file, use the Pay/Submit button at the bottom of the Validation page. This will allow you to choose from three (3) different payment methods: credit card, automated deposit account, or electronic funds transfer.
9. After accessing the proper screen for payment, and making the appropriate entries, you will receive a confirmation screen if your transmission is successful. This screen will say SUCCESS! and will provide your assigned serial number.
10. You will receive an e-mail acknowledging receipt of your submission, which will include the assigned serial number and provide a summary of your submission.

Once you submit this application, we will not cancel the filing or refund your fee. The fee is a processing fee, which we do not refund even if we cannot issue a registration after our substantive review.

Important: ONCE YOU SUBMIT AN APPLICATION ELECTRONICALLY, THE USPTO WILL IMMEDIATELY ISSUE AN ELECTRONIC ACKNOWLEDGMENT OF RECEIPT. Please contact TEAS@uspto.gov if you do not receive this acknowledgment within 24 hours of transmission.

Contact Points:

- **General trademark information:** Please review the information posted at Where Do I Start. If you have remaining questions, e-mail TrademarkAssistanceCenter@uspto.gov, or telephone 1-800-786-9199.
- **Help:** For instructions on how to ***use*** the electronic forms, or help in resolving ***technical*** glitches, please e-mail TEAS@uspto.gov. Please include your telephone number in your e-mail, so we can talk to you directly, if necessary. Also, include the relevant serial number or registration number, if existing.
  NOTE: The TEAS Support Team focuses on problems related to the process of completing the electronic forms, **not** on what information would be correct for entry within a form, or other broader trademark issues. Please route those types of inquiries to the Trademark Assistance Center. However, please be aware that neither group can provide any sort of information in the nature of "legal advice." For legal advice, please consider contacting an attorney who specializes in intellectual property.
- **Bug Report:** If you think there is a "bug" within one of the electronic forms, please click Bug Report.
- **Status Information:** For an application with an assigned serial number, check the Trademark Status & Document Retrieval (TSDR) system to view current status information, as well as the complete prosecution history. Do **not** attempt to check the status of a filing until at least 7-10 days after submission of the filing, to allow sufficient time for all USPTO databases to be updated. You can view **all** items listed in the prosecution history section online via the TSDR system, including all Office actions sent by the USPTO.

WARNING: This form has a session time limit of 60 minutes. Your "session" began as soon as you accessed this initial Form Wizard page. If you exceed the 60-minute time limit, the form will not validate and you must begin the entire process again; you can, however, extend the time limit. You should always try to have all information required to complete the form prior to starting any session.

1. Is an attorney filing this application?

Yes No

2. [*OPTIONAL*] To access previously-saved data, use the "Browse/Choose File" button below to access the file from your local drive. NOTE: For specific instructions, please click here. FAILURE TO FOLLOW THESE NEW INSTRUCTIONS WILL RESULT IN THE DISPLAY OF YOUR DATA IN AN XML FORMAT THAT CANNOT BE EDITED. **NOTE: Do NOT attempt to use the button below to upload an image file (for example, a specimen). You must use the button that will be presented for that purpose *within the proper section of the actual form.***

Choose File no file selected

Figure 3

Carefully read the information at the top of the screen. The first block explains the help system (which you can access by clicking any underlined word) and lets you turn off the help text that automatically appears at the bottom of the page. It also explains that only the blanks marked with an asterisk are mandatory. We recommend that you leave the help on and read the help for each step. We also recommend that you be as complete as possible in your responses; even if the information isn't mandatory, supplying it may save you time and trouble down the line.

Some of the nonmandatory information could be useful to the examiner when evaluating your application and expeditiously communicating with you if a problem arises. For example, your phone number isn't mandatory, but suppose the examiner has a question, whose answer could support the granting of your application? How can the examiner call you if you don't include your number?

Near the bottom of the page is the first question in the process—whether an attorney is filing the application. If the answer is "No," click that button.

Beneath that question, the USPTO gives you the option to import any previously saved data, if you have any. (First-time filers won't need this option.) Click "Continue." This will take you to the page where you enter "Applicant Information."

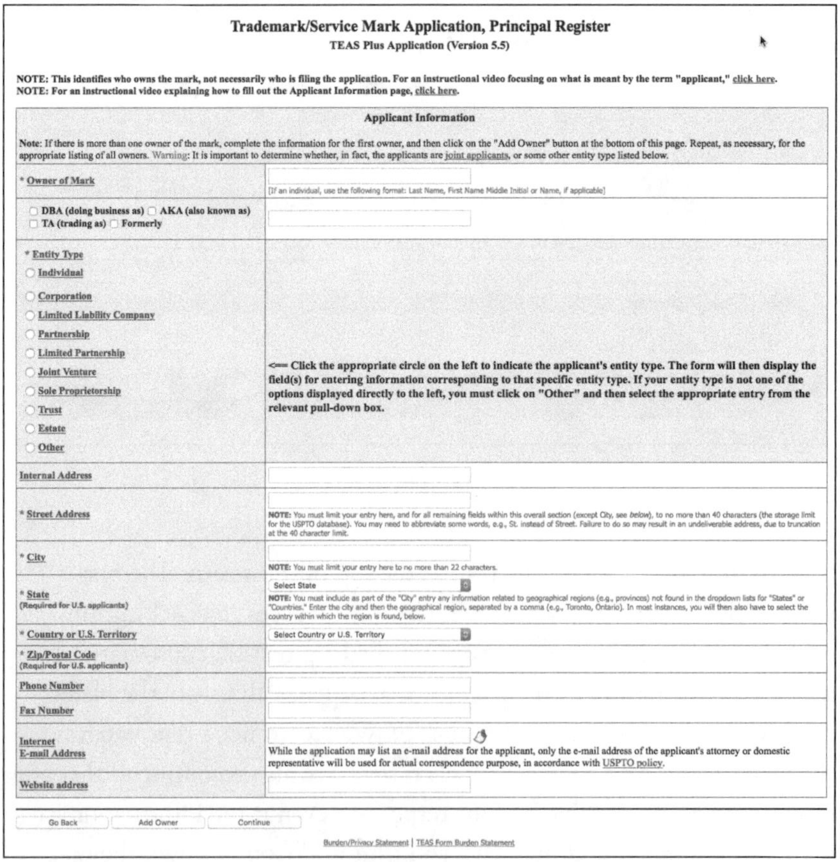

Figure 4

Applicant Information. Provide the name of the owner (your business or you), choose your Entity Type, and complete the relevant associated drop-down information—country of citizenship, and so on. Provide your street address, city, state, country, zip code, phone number, fax number, and email address. All of these information blanks come with excellent help should you need it.

When finished, click "Continue." This will take you to a page where you will enter information about your mark (see Figure 5).

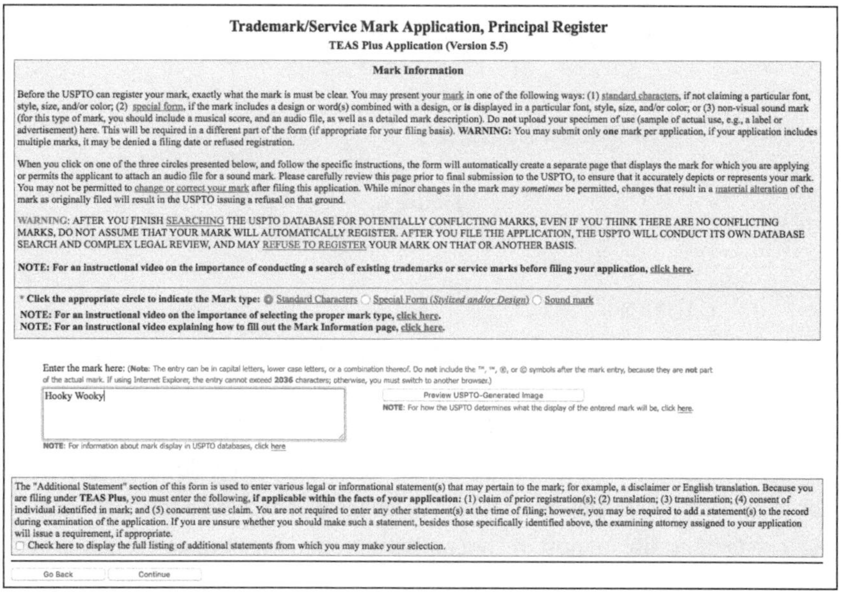

Trademark/Service Mark Application, Principal Register

TEAS Plus Application (Version 5.5)

Mark Information

Before the USPTO can register your mark, exactly what the mark is must be clear. You may present your mark in one of the following ways: (1) standard characters, if not claiming a particular font, style, size, and/or color; (2) special form, if the mark includes a design or word(s) combined with a design, or **is** displayed in a particular font, style, size, and/or color; or (3) non-visual sound mark (for this type of mark, you should include a musical score, and an audio file, as well as a detailed mark description). Do **not** upload your specimen of use (sample of actual use, e.g., a label or advertisement) here. This will be required in a different part of the form (if appropriate for your filing basis). **WARNING:** You may submit only **one** mark per application, if your application includes multiple marks, it may be denied a filing date or refused registration.

When you click on one of the three circles presented below, and follow the specific instructions, the form will automatically create a separate page that displays the mark for which you are applying or permits the applicant to attach an audio file for a sound mark. Please carefully review this page prior to final submission to the USPTO, to ensure that it accurately depicts or represents your mark. You may not be permitted to change or correct your mark after filing this application. While minor changes in the mark may *sometimes* be permitted, changes that result in a material alteration of the mark as originally filed will result in the USPTO issuing a refusal on that ground.

WARNING: AFTER YOU FINISH SEARCHING THE USPTO DATABASE FOR POTENTIALLY CONFLICTING MARKS, EVEN IF YOU THINK THERE ARE NO CONFLICTING MARKS, DO NOT ASSUME THAT YOUR MARK WILL AUTOMATICALLY REGISTER. AFTER YOU FILE THE APPLICATION, THE USPTO WILL CONDUCT ITS OWN DATABASE SEARCH AND COMPLEX LEGAL REVIEW, AND MAY REFUSE TO REGISTER YOUR MARK ON THAT OR ANOTHER BASIS.

NOTE: For an instructional video on the importance of conducting a search of existing trademarks or service marks before filing your application, click here.

*** Click the appropriate circle to indicate the Mark type:** Standard Characters Special Form (*Stylized and/or Design*) Sound mark

NOTE: For an instructional video on the importance of selecting the proper mark type, click here.
NOTE: For an instructional video explaining how to fill out the Mark Information page, click here.

Enter the mark here: (**Note**: The entry can be in capital letters, lower case letters, or a combination thereof. Do **not** include the ™, ℠, ®, or © symbols after the mark entry, because they are **not** part of the actual mark. If using Internet Explorer, the entry cannot exceed **2036** characters; otherwise, you must switch to another browser.)

Hooky Wooky

NOTE: For information about mark display in USPTO databases, click here

Preview USPTO-Generated Image

NOTE: For how the USPTO determines what the display of the entered mark will be, click here.

The "Additional Statement" section of this form is used to enter various legal or informational statement(s) that may pertain to the mark; for example, a disclaimer or English translation. Because you are filing under **TEAS Plus**, you must enter the following, **if applicable within the facts of your application:** (1) claim of prior registration(s); (2) translation; (3) transliteration; (4) consent of individual identified in mark; and (5) concurrent use claim. You are not required to enter any other statement(s) at the time of filing; however, you may be required to add a statement(s) to the record during examination of the application. If you are unsure whether you should make such a statement, besides those specifically identified above, the examining attorney assigned to your application will issue a requirement, if appropriate.

Check here to display the full listing of additional statements from which you may make your selection.

Go Back Continue

Figure 5

Mark Information. Here you have a choice. If your mark consists of unstylized words or numbers (or both), click the button next to the words "Standard Characters." In the box just below the words "Enter the mark here," enter your mark. If your mark is a domain name, you can enter the complete domain name, including the .com, or just the unique part of your name. For instance, Nolo might choose to register its domain name as Nolo.com or just Nolo. Because domain names are such a new species of trademark, there are no firm rules. If your mark is stylized or in design format (such as a logo or trade dress), read the help and attach a JPEG file showing the mark. Keep in mind that the USPTO has a two-megabyte limitation on each graphic file. By clicking the button "Preview USPTO-Generated Image" you can see how your mark will appear in the USPTO system (see Figure 6). When done, click "Continue" on the bottom of the page.

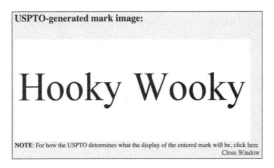

Figure 6

⚠ CAUTION

If you are filing for a stylized mark (you want the word to appear in a specific graphic manner) or design mark, you must submit two types of image files. One is the graphic file showing the mark, as described above. The other is the specimen—the mark as used in commerce (see below). Be careful not to confuse the images by attaching an image meant to be a specimen as the mark image, because in most instances this is often difficult to correct.

⚠ CAUTION

If you're scanning a black-and-white image, set the scanner for black and white, not color. If you use an improper setting, the produced image might appear to be black and white, but it will actually consist of thousands of colors. This mélange will result in an image of unacceptable quality when received by the USPTO. In addition, images with thousands of colors might exceed the two-megabyte limitation.

Next you will see the page where you enter "Goods/Services Information" (see Figure 7, below).

Trademark/Service Mark Application, Principal Register
TEAS Plus Application (Version 5.5)

Goods/Services Information

Instructions:

Step 1: Click on the "Add Goods/Services by Searching IDManual" button below to select goods/services from the *Manual of Trademark Acceptable Identifications of Goods & Services* (IDManual).

Step 2: After creating the complete list of goods/services for this application, you will then be able in the next section of the form to designate the filing basis (or bases) appropriate for each listed item.

NOTE:

1. Your selection of goods/services must be precise and accurate. Do NOT simply select a listing that is "close" to your goods/services. If you do not find a listing that accurately identifies your goods/services, you may e-mail TMIDSUGGEST@uspto.gov to request that your identification be added to the IDManual, and then wait for the addition before filing using TEAS Plus. For more information on this process, click here. If your request is not approved or you wish to file immediately, you must use either the TEAS Regular or TEAS RF form.

2. The TEAS Plus version of the IDManual intentionally does not include the following: (1) items classified in Classes A, B, or 200, because those marks are not eligible for filing under TEAS Plus; (2) any listings that appear in the "regular" manual under "000," because correct classification is required under TEAS Plus, and classification for these listings varies according to the additional information provided within the listing; and (3) the Class 25 listing of "Clothing, namely, ...", because this entry is too open-ended, and could result in items being listed that do not truly fall within this class. Since specific clothing items must be listed anyway, the TEAS Plus version of the form requires the *initial* selection of those specific items.

3. Some entries include instructional language beneath the actual entry, within < > symbols. This language is only to assist in the proper selection of an entry, and will NOT be included as part of the actual identification after the checked entry is inserted into the form.

4. If you cannot access the IDManual through the "Add Goods/Services by Searching IDManual" button, try switching to another browser. If after changing browsers you still cannot access the IDManual through the "Add Goods/Services by Searching IDManual" button, please contact TEAS@uspto.gov.

WARNING: This form has a session time limit of 60 minutes. Your "session" began as soon as you accessed the initial Form Wizard page. If you exceed the 60-minute time limit, the form will not validate and you must begin the entire process again; you can, however, extend the time limit. You should always try to have all information required to complete the form prior to starting any session.

NOTE: For an instructional video on goods and services and the importance of making the proper selection, click here.
NOTE: For an instructional video explaining how to fill out the Goods and Services page, click here.

| Add Goods/Services | Remove Checked Goods/Services |

NOTE: Clicking "Go Back" will take you directly back to the MARK section of the form.
Go Back

Figure 7

Because you are using TEAS Plus, you will need to search the *ID Manual* to describe your goods or services. Click the "Add Goods/ Services" button, which will take you to a search page where you can type in your goods to get the proper International Classification (see Figure 8). We typed in "hats" and then checked Class 25. Then we clicked "Insert Checked Entries."

Next you will be taken to the page seeking your "Basis for Filing" (see Figure 9).

Filing Basis. If you are already using the mark on goods or services, select the button for "Section 1(a)" to file an actual use application. If you are not yet up and running with your mark, select "Section 1(b)" to file an intent-to-use application.

The procedures for each filing basis are somewhat different, and the intent-to-use basis will cost an additional $100 once you do put the trademark into actual use.

⊙ CAUTION

Previous foreign registration. If you are filing in the United States on the basis of a previous foreign registration, see a lawyer before continuing. This book doesn't cover U.S. registrations based on foreign registrations.

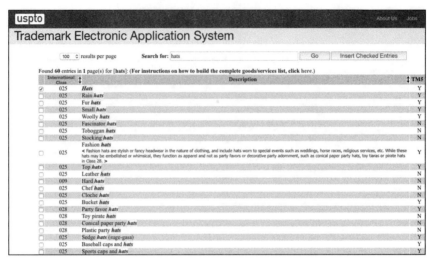

Figure 8

Figure 9

After you click the button for your basis for filing, you will need to enter additional information and attach a specimen (see Figure 10).

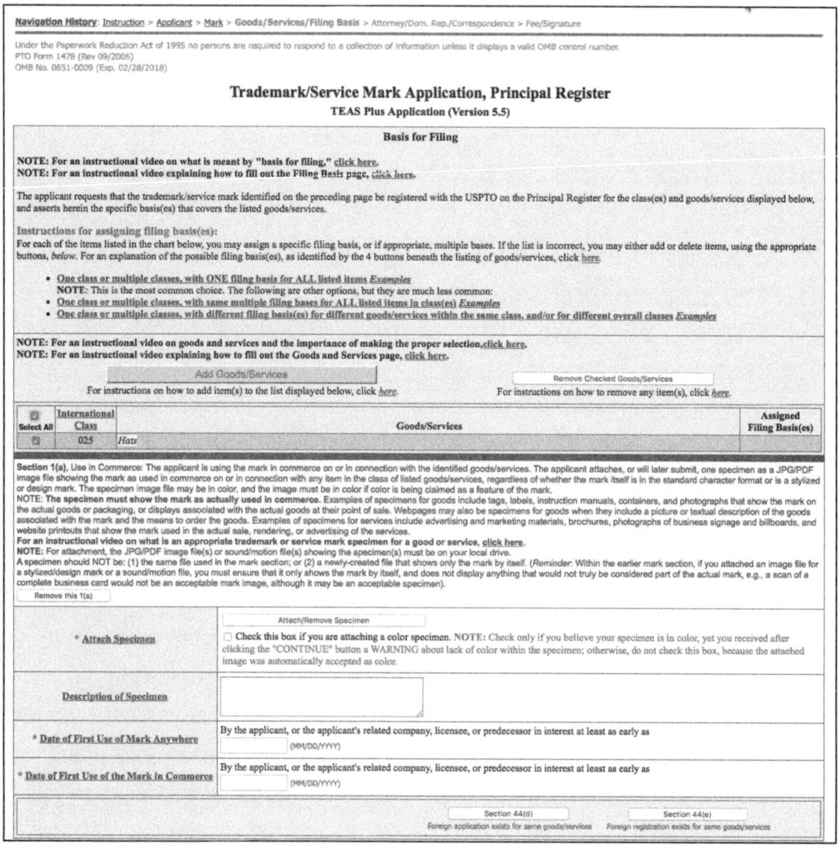

Navigation History: Instruction > Applicant > Mark > Goods/Services/Filing Basis > Attorney/Dom. Rep./Correspondence > Fee/Signature

Under the Paperwork Reduction Act of 1995 no persons are required to respond to a collection of information unless it displays a valid OMB control number.
PTO Form 1478 (Rev 09/2006)
OMB No. 0651-0009 (Exp. 02/28/2018)

Trademark/Service Mark Application, Principal Register

TEAS Plus Application (Version 5.5)

Basis for Filing

NOTE: For an instructional video on what is meant by "basis for filing," click here.
NOTE: For an instructional video explaining how to fill out the Filing Basis page, click here.

The applicant requests that the trademark/service mark identified on the preceding page be registered with the USPTO on the Principal Register for the class(es) and goods/services displayed below, and asserts herein the specific basis(es) that covers the listed goods/services.

Instructions for assigning filing basis(es):
For each of the items listed in the chart below, you may assign a specific filing basis, or if appropriate, multiple bases. If the list is incorrect, you may either add or delete items, using the appropriate buttons, *below*. For an explanation of the possible filing basis(es), as identified by the 4 buttons beneath the listing of goods/services, click here.

- One class or multiple classes, with ONE filing basis for ALL listed items *Examples*
  NOTE: This is the most common choice. The following are other options, but they are much less common:
- One class or multiple classes, with same multiple filing bases for ALL listed items in class(es) *Examples*
- One class or multiple classes, with different filing basis(es) for different goods/services within the same class, and/or for different overall classes *Examples*

NOTE: For an instructional video on goods and services and the importance of making the proper selection, click here.
NOTE: For an instructional video explaining how to fill out the Goods and Services page, click here.

Add Goods/Services — For instructions on how to add item(s) to the list displayed below, click *here*.
Remove Checked Goods/Services — For instructions on how to remove any item(s), click *here*.

Select All	International Class	Goods/Services	Assigned Filing Basis(es)
☑	025	*Hats*	

Section 1(a), Use in Commerce: The applicant is using the mark in commerce on or in connection with the identified goods/services. The applicant attaches, or will later submit, one specimen as a JPG/PDF image file showing the mark as used in commerce on or in connection with any item in the class of listed goods/services, regardless of whether the mark itself is in the standard character format or is a stylized or design mark. The specimen image file may be in color, and the image must be in color if color is being claimed as a feature of the mark.
NOTE: **The specimen must show the mark as actually used in commerce.** Examples of specimens for goods include tags, labels, instruction manuals, containers, and photographs that show the mark on the actual goods or packaging, or displays associated with the actual goods at their point of sale. Webpages may also be specimens for goods when they include a picture or textual description of the goods associated with the mark and the means to order the goods. Examples of specimens for services include advertising and marketing materials, brochures, photographs of business signage and billboards, and website printouts that show the mark used in the actual sale, rendering, or advertising of the services.
For an instructional video on what is an appropriate trademark or service mark specimen for a good or service, click here.
NOTE: For attachment, the JPG/PDF image file(s) or sound/motion file(s) showing the specimen(s) must be on your local drive.
A specimen should NOT be: (1) the same file used in the mark section; or (2) a newly-created file that shows only the mark by itself. (*Reminder*: Within the earlier mark section, if you attached an image file for a stylized/design mark or a sound/motion file, you must ensure that it only shows the mark by itself, and does not display anything that would not truly be considered part of the actual mark, e.g., a scan of a complete business card would not be an acceptable mark image, although it may be an acceptable specimen).
Remove this 1(a)

* Attach Specimen	Attach/Remove Specimen ☐ **Check this box if you are attaching a color specimen.** NOTE: Check only if you believe your specimen is in color, yet you received after clicking the "CONTINUE" button a WARNING about lack of color within the specimen; otherwise, do not check this box, because the attached image was automatically accepted as color.
Description of Specimen	
* Date of First Use of Mark Anywhere	By the applicant, or the applicant's related company, licensee, or predecessor in interest at least as early as (MM/DD/YYYY)
* Date of First Use of the Mark in Commerce	By the applicant, or the applicant's related company, licensee, or predecessor in interest at least as early as (MM/DD/YYYY)

Section 44(d) — Foreign application exists for same goods/services
Section 44(e) — Foreign registration exists for same goods/services

Figure 10

Attach Specimen. If you're filing under Section 1(a), you'll need to provide a specimen image file in JPEG format, as well as a description of the specimen in the next box. Scan the file and be sure it's less than five megabytes. When you click to attach the specimen you will be shown a typical upload screen (see Figure 11) that you can use to find the file and upload it from your computer.

When you are done, click "Return to Application." If you're an intent-to-use applicant, you will not have a specimen information section on your application and should go to the next step.

Description of Specimen. The next part of the specimen box asks you to describe the specimen. For example, if you are submitting a label, write "scanned label applied to goods." See the help topic for more details.

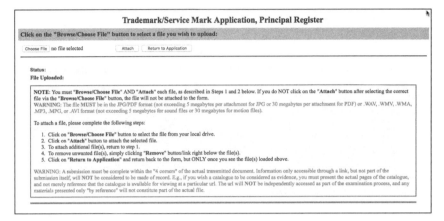

Figure 11

CAUTION

As you fill in the form, make sure that your specimen, mark information, and description of goods and services are all consistent with each other. If your specimen shows a different mark than what you enter on the Mark Information page (or submit in a JPEG file), you'll have some explaining to do. Similarly, if your specimen shows a different product or service than you describe in the application, you'll have to submit another specimen or change your product/service description. If you are filing an intent-to-use application, you won't have to submit a specimen at this stage, but you will ultimately have to submit a specimen (once you begin using the mark) to complete your registration.

Date of First Use of Mark Anywhere. Here you provide the date you first started using the mark in the marketplace in connection with your product or service.

Date of First Use of the Mark in Commerce. Enter the date when you first used the mark in commerce across state, territorial, or international borders. If you have an existing business, this date might be different than the date of first use that you just entered. For example, you might have first used the name to market your local business and later gone national or international. The first date would be your use anywhere, and the second date would be the date the scope of your business expanded.

Fraudulent Statements Can Result in Loss of Your Trademark Registration

The Trademark Trial Appeal Board cancelled three trademark registrations after receiving evidence from a competitor that the trademark owner had made fraudulent statements regarding its dates of use. (*Standard Knitting, Ltd. v. Toyota Jidosha Kabushiki Kaisha*, 77 U.S.P.Q.2d 1917 (TTAB 2006).) Note that not every false statement made on a trademark application amounts to fraud. In one case, a misstatement regarding whether commerce was intrastate or interstate did not amount to a fraudulent statement. (*Maids to Order of Ohio, Inc. v. Maid-to-Order, Inc.*, 78 U.S.P.Q.2d 1899 (TTAB 2006).)

If you've been using a mark for years and don't remember the exact date of its first use anywhere or across state lines, make your best estimate. Use dated documents that you have gathered over the years, such as old advertisements or business licenses, to help jog your memory. Use the earliest possible date that you can reasonably assert as correct.

Correspondence Information. Next you will be taken to a page where you will provide your contact information for the USPTO to communicate with you regarding the application (see Figure 12). This information becomes part of the public record. You can also use this page of the form to indicate whether you want the USPTO to communicate with you via email. Then you will be taken to a page where you will verify fee information and provide an electronic signature. (See Figure 13.)

What signature approach do you want to use? Here you have several choices: sign electronically directly on this application (the easiest choice), email the text form to a second party for electronic signature, provide a handwritten pen-and-ink signature, or submit your application unsigned (a signature must be supplied later).

Amount. If you are registering in just one class and using regular TEAS, the fee will be $400. If you are using TEAS RF, your fee will be $275. If you are using TEAS Plus, your fee will be $225.

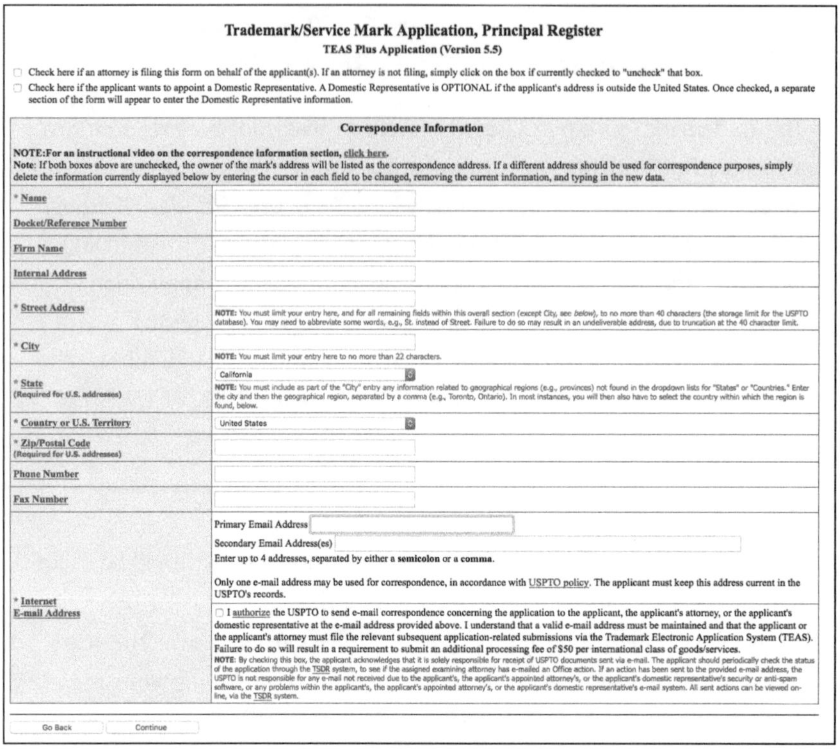

Figure 12

Declaration. The declaration is a statement that the facts in the trademark application are true. Read it carefully. If statements in the declaration raise serious doubts or questions in your mind, do not file the application until you see a trademark lawyer. (For information on finding a lawyer, see Chapter 14, "Help Beyond This Book.")

Signature. The information box right above the signature section provides the surprising information that your electronic "signature" can be any combination of letters, numbers, or other characters. Each signature must begin and end with a forward slash (/). For example, /pat smith/; /ps/; and /268-3421/ are all acceptable signatures. There's no trick here. Unless you've developed some special internal system for tracking electronic signatures in your office, entering your own name is the simplest option. Click the signature link just below the information box for the USPTO's own words on this subject.

Figure 13

Validate. Once you click the "Validate" button, you will be taken to a "Validation Page" (see Figure 14, below). This page alerts you if you forgot to include any information that is mandatory. You will have a chance to go back and fill in the missing information. A warning message will also appear for nonmandatory missing information, but you are not required to go back and include that information.

Once you have finished the validation, click "Pay/Submit" at the bottom of the validation screen. Because you are using a credit card for payment, you will be asked to enter payment information (see Figure 15, below). If your transaction is successful, you will receive a confirmation screen.

Later, you will receive an email acknowledging the submission of your application. Hold on to that email, because it is the only proof you'll have that the USPTO has your application. It is also proof of your filing date and contains the serial number assigned to your application.

Trademark/Service Mark Application, Principal Register

TEAS Plus Application (Version 5.5) - Validation Page

On Thu Dec 17 21:25:57 EST 2015 **You completed all mandatory fields and successfully validated the form. It has NOT been filed to the USPTO at this point. Please complete all steps below to submit the application.**

NOTE:For an instructional video on the Validation Page, click here.
■ **STEP 1:** Review the application data in various formats, by clicking on the phrases under Application Data. Use the print function within your browser to print these pages for your own records. If the Mark and Specimens appear huge, click here.

Note: It is important that you review this information for accuracy and completeness now. Corrections after submission may not be permissible, thereby possibly affecting your legal rights.
Note: If you are using the e-signature approach or the handwritten pen-and-ink signature approach, you must click on the final link to access the specific "text form" for that purpose.

Application Data				
■ Input	■ Mark	■ Specimen	■ XML File	■ Text Form

■ **STEP 2:** If there are no errors and you are ready to file this application electronically, confirm the e-mail address for acknowledgment. Once you submit the form electronically, we will send an electronic acknowledgment of receipt to the e-mail address entered below. If no e-mail address appears, you must enter one. If we should send the acknowledgment to a different e-mail address, or to an additional address(es), please enter the proper address or additional address(es). For **multiple addresses/receipts**, please separate e-mail addresses by either a **semicolon or a comma.**
NOTE: This e-mail address is only for the purpose of receiving the acknowledgment that the transmission reached the USPTO, and is not related to the e-mail that will be used for correspondence purposes (although it could be the same address. The official e-mail address that the USPTO will use for any future communication is whatever appears in the specific correspondence section of the form.)

     * **E-mail for acknowledgment** [_____]

     To ensure we can deliver your e-mail confirmation successfully, please re-enter your **e-mail address(es)** here:

     * **E-mail for acknowledgment** [_____]

■ **STEP 3:** To download and save the form data, click on the **Download Portable Data** button at the bottom of this page. The information will be saved to your local drive. To begin the submission process with saved data, you must open a new form, and click on the "Browse/Choose File" button displayed on the initial form wizard page, at "**[OPTIONAL] To access previously-saved data, use the "Browse/Choose File" button below to access the file from your local drive."** REMINDER: Do NOT try to open the saved .obj/.xml form directly. You must return to the very first page of the form, as if starting a brand new form, and then use the specific "Browse/Choose File" button on that page to import the saved file. Clicking on the "Continue" button at the bottom of that first page will then properly open the saved version of your form.

■ **STEP 4:** Read and check the following:

Important Notice:
(1) Once you submit this application, we will not cancel the filing or refund your fee. The fee is a processing fee, which we do not refund even if we cannot issue a registration after our substantive review. This is true regardless of how soon after submission you might attempt to request cancellation of the filing. Therefore, please review ALL information carefully prior to transmission.
(2) All information you submit to the USPTO at any point in the application and/or registration process will become public record, including your name, phone number, e-mail address, and street address. By filing this application, you acknowledge that YOU HAVE NO RIGHT TO CONFIDENTIALITY in the information disclosed. The public will be able to view this information in the USPTO's on-line databases and through internet search engines and other on-line databases. This information will remain public even if the application is later abandoned or any resulting registration is surrendered, cancelled, or expired. To maintain confidentiality of banking or credit card information, only enter payment information in the secure portion of the site after validating your form. For any information that may be subject to copyright protection, by submitting it to the USPTO, the filer is representing that he or she has the authority to grant, and is granting, the USPTO permission to make the information available in its on-line database and in copies of the application or registration record.
(3) Be aware that private companies not associated with the USPTO often use trademark application and registration information from the USPTO's databases to mail or e-mail trademark-related solicitations (samples of non-USPTO solicitations included).
☐ If you have read and understand the above notice, please check the box before you click on the **Pay/Submit** button.

■ **STEP 5:** If you are ready to file electronically:
Click on the **Pay/Submit** button *below,* to access the site where you will select one of three possible payment methods. After successful entry of payment information, you can complete the submission to the USPTO. A valid transaction will result in a screen that says **SUCCESS!** Also, we will send an e-mail acknowledgment within 24 hours.
WARNING: Click on the Pay/Submit button ONLY if you are now entirely prepared to complete the Pay/Submit process. After clicking the button, you can NOT return to the form, since you will have left the TEAS site entirely. Once in the separate payment site, you **must** complete the Pay/Submit process within **30 minutes.** If you are not prepared to complete the process now, you should select the "Download Portable Data" option to save your form, and then complete the Pay/Submit process later. Or, if you have discovered any error, use the "Go Back to Modify" button to make a correction.
WARNING: Fee payments by credit card may **not** be made from 2 a.m. to 6 a.m. Sunday, Eastern Standard Time. If you are attempting to file during that specific period, you must use either (1) the deposit account or electronic funds transfer payment method; or (2) the "Download Portable Data" option to save your form, and then complete the Pay/Submit process later for a credit card payment.

Go Back to Modify	Download Portable Data	Pay/Submit

Figure 14

Figure 15

Disclaimers—Do It Now or Later?

If part of your mark includes a word or phrase that cannot be protected under trademark law, the USPTO will want you to disclaim (give up) trademark rights in those specific words, even though you have a trademark in the name as a whole. For example, suppose you manufacture a highly successful line of perfume called Candor, and you wish to register the trademark Candor Perfume. The USPTO will likely ask you to disclaim the word "perfume" because it is generic. Similarly, if you had a gossip website called candor.com, the USPTO would require that you disclaim the ".com." That's okay, because these generic terms "perfume" and ".com" can't be registered or protected anyway. Disclaiming a term doesn't mean that you lose part of your trademark, it only means that you cannot stop competitors from using a similar generic term as part of their marks. For example, in the case of Candor Perfume, you have the exclusive right to use "perfume" with the mark "Candor," but you cannot stop others from using "perfume" with their marks as well.

If you are positive that you will have to disclaim part of your mark—for example, you know that all of your competitors have had to disclaim the word "sauce" or "shuttle"—then you might as well make the disclaimer now. Check the "Additional Statement" box (see Figure 5) and enter the term you are disclaiming. If you are not absolutely positive, we recommend that you not disclaim anything until required to do so during the examination process. If this becomes necessary, the trademark examiner will tell you what you should disclaim.

If You Are Filing by Mail

If filing your application by mail, you must pay a filing fee of $600 per class. You can request a hard copy of the application form by calling the USPTO at 800-786-9199. Make a copy of your completed application for your records, and mail your application to Commissioner of Trademarks, P.O. Box 1451, Alexandria, VA 22313-1451. The USPTO keeps track of all applications by assigning them serial numbers. Once your application is filed, all your communication with the USPTO must include this serial number. The fastest way to be sure your application has reached the USPTO and to get your serial number is to include with your application a self-addressed, postage-paid postcard with your mark printed clearly on it. The USPTO will stamp the card with your serial number and the date your application was received and mail it to you. You should receive it within two weeks after you mailed the application. Keep the card in a safe place, as you may need to refer to your serial number frequently during the process.

We recommend using the mailing method that will get your application to the USPTO in the shortest amount of time, so that you may obtain the earliest possible filing date. Express Mail sent "Post Office to Post Office" is your best option.

About six to eight weeks after mailing your application, you should receive the USPTO's filing receipt. The current form is an 8½" x 11" white form titled "Filing Receipt for Trademark Application." The filing receipt includes the application serial number, the date of filing, the mark, the applicant's name and address, and other information. Check the information on the receipt carefully. If there is a mistake, send a correcting letter to the USPTO immediately.

The USPTO filing receipt will explain that you should not expect to hear anything about your application for approximately three months. If you have not heard anything in three and a half months, it is wise to inquire as to the status of your application. There are three ways to do this:

- **Check TSDR.** The online Trademark Status and Document Retrieval system page (http://tsdr.uspto.gov) allows you to access information about pending trademarks obtained from the USPTO's internal database by entering a valid trademark serial number.

- **TRAM automated system.** TRAM stands for trademark reporting and monitoring. From any touch-tone phone, Monday through Friday, from 6:30 a.m. to midnight, Eastern time, dial 703-305-8747. After the welcome message and tone, enter your mark's eight-digit serial number and the pound symbol. You should immediately hear the computer give you the current status of your mark along with the effective date of the status.

- **If you want additional information or would prefer talking with a person,** call the Trademark Assistance Center at 800-786-9199 and request a status check.

What Happens Next?

You will likely receive some communication from the USPTO within three to six months. If there is a problem with your application, you will receive what's called an "action letter." This is a letter from your examiner explaining what the problems are. Most problems can be resolved with a phone call to the examiner.

When the examiner approves your application for publication, you will receive a Notice of Publication in the mail. Your mark will then be published in the *Official Gazette.* For 30 days following publication, anyone may oppose your registration. Only 3% of all published marks are opposed, so it is very unlikely you will run into trouble.

Once your mark has made it through the 30-day publication period, you will receive a Certificate of Registration, if you filed on an actual use basis. The USPTO sometimes has a difficult time moving applications through this long process. As a result, it might take a year or more to process your application.

Citizens Can Challenge Trademark Registrations

A law professor filed an opposition for a trademark registration for RAPUNZEL toys and dolls. The applicant sought to dismiss the opposition because the professor was not a competitor. The TTAB disagreed and established that the professor, a consumer of dolls, had standing to oppose because as a consumer, "she has purchased and continues to purchase said goods and that registration of the applied-for mark by applicant would constrain the marketplace of such goods sold under the name 'Rapunzel,' and raise prices of 'Rapunzel' dolls offered by other manufacturers." The TTAB held "Consumers, like competitors, may have a real interest in keeping merely descriptive or generic words in the public domain." (*Rebecca Curtin v. United Trademark Holdings, Inc.,* Opposition No. 91241083 (December 28, 2018).)

> CAUTION
> **Once your registration is complete, you'll still have some paperwork to do five years down the line.** See Chapter 8 for more on what awaits you.

If you filed on an intent-to-use basis, your mark will not be placed on the trademark register until you file an additional document with the USPTO once you put it into actual use. This form is called the Statement of Use/Amendment to Allege Use for Intent-to-Use Application. It tells the USPTO the date you started using the mark and completes the registration process. You must also provide a specimen at that time, showing how you are using the mark.

Communicating With the USPTO

The chances are great that you will be communicating with the USPTO after you have filed your application. Few applications sail through completely unscathed.

You should be diligent when pursuing your application. If you are expecting some action from the USPTO (the ball is in their court) and more than six months have passed without your hearing from them, check the TSDR system (http://tsdr.uspto.gov). Type your serial number and review the application's status as well any documents that have been filed. If you discover a problem, bring it to the USPTO's attention. If you fail to respond in a timely manner to a USPTO request, your application will be considered abandoned. If that happens, you must petition the commissioner for trademarks within 60 days to reactivate your application.

If the examiner wants you to change your application, such as offering a different description of services or goods, there is usually some room for negotiation.

> EXAMPLE: Frieda claimed her mark was used in connection with "buying services for nonprofit institutions and organizations" and submitted a specimen showing an advertisement of food products aimed at schools. That description was found to be too indefinite, and the examiner suggested "buying services for nonprofit organizations and institutions in the field of food products." If Frieda's services extended beyond food

products to include items such as medical and automotive supplies, she probably wouldn't want to agree to the examiner's suggestion. However, after talking with the examiner, she should be able to arrive at a description inclusive enough for her, yet definite enough for the examiner. For instance, this might be "buying services for nonprofit institutions and organizations in the fields of food products, medical supplies, and automotive parts."

An examiner with a brief question might call you and then mail or email you an Examiner's Amendment. This is a form on which the examiner records in handwriting a phone conversation or meeting with an applicant. Read the amendment carefully to make sure it matches your understanding of the conversation. If you disagree, or don't understand the amendment, first call the examiner. Then, if necessary, write the examiner a letter or an email with your concerns, explaining your point of view on the communication.

A common Examiner's Amendment comes up when you use words as part of your mark that, by themselves, don't qualify for registration. The examiner will ask you to formally disclaim those words (see "Disclaimers—Do It Now or Later?" above). After making the disclaimer, your mark will be registered in its entirety, but you cannot prevent your competitors from using the disclaimed terms as parts of their trademarks.

EXAMPLE: The Exotic Perfume Company manufactures a line of fragrances fancifully named after various wildflowers that themselves don't carry any particular fragrance. One of these is called Violet Snapdragon Parfum. If Exotic wants to register this mark, it will have to disclaim "parfum"— a foreign-language term for perfume—because it is a generic term and thus not registrable. If Exotic refuses to disclaim "parfum," the USPTO will probably refuse registration. If the filer makes a disclaimer, however, the USPTO can register the entire mark and the company will be able to stop others from using the combination of terms "violet," "snapdragon," and "parfum." However, the company will not be able to stop someone who is using only "parfum." For example, if a competing fragrance company comes out with Wild Rose Parfum, there will be no infringement. On the other hand, if a competitor produces Purple Snapdragon Fragrance or Dragon Snap Parfum, a court would likely find infringement.

If the Examiner Issues a Rejection Letter

An examiner may write three kinds of action letters that constitute trademark application rejections:

- **Technical rejections.** These usually involve minor or procedural matters that can be corrected by amendment as described earlier.
- **Substantive rejections.** These usually involve issues such as potential confusion with another mark. Responding to these rejections takes more effort and may well require the help of a trademark lawyer.
- **Final rejections.** These usually are written only after you have been given at least one chance to respond to a technical or substantive rejection.

The examining attorney may notify the applicant of the basis for the rejection by telephone or mail. Often, smaller issues are resolved over the phone while more substantive issues require mail notification. USPTO correspondence usually includes an adhesive-label caption with a mailing date. This caption can be peeled off and placed on an applicant's reply.

Rejections always specify how much time you have to respond (usually six months). If the USPTO doesn't receive your response within the time specified, you risk having your application deemed abandoned (which means you have to start over if you wish to pursue registration of the mark), so always send the response as early as possible.

If you receive a rejection, you have three choices:

- respond to it yourself,
- hire a trademark attorney to prepare the response, or
- abandon your application.

Responding to an Objection Yourself

Whether you should respond to a rejection yourself depends on the nature of the problem and your comfort level in dealing with a trademark examiner. You'll have to weigh both issues and make your decision.

In the event of an objection by the examining attorney, it might be necessary to amend the application or provide a response to a rejection. An amendment is a correction usually made in response to a request by the USPTO. A response is a legal argument advanced by the applicant to overcome an objection. The response should include the caption (an adhesive label peeled off the examining attorney's letter). A response *must* be provided to the USPTO within six months of the date of mailing of the office action. If not, the application will be deemed abandoned.

Common Rejections That Are Easy to Address

Below are some common correctable errors that most applicants can rectify easily:

- **Incorrect name of applicant.** The application lists the wrong trademark owner. For example, the founder of a company might mistakenly believe that he owns the mark, not the company.
- **Ambiguous authority for applicant.** The authority and position of the person signing the application is ambiguous. Officers of a corporation, for example, should be specifically identified by their titles.
- **Using the class heading as listing of goods.** Instead of identifying and describing the specific goods or services in the application, an applicant describes the goods by the International Class heading.
- **Scattered listing of goods.** The applicant filed for registration in several classes but did not clearly group the goods in appropriate classes. The USPTO prefers that goods be grouped according to class in the description of goods and in the drawing.
- **Incorrect or inadequate description of goods.** The application does not accurately describe or reflect the goods or services. For example, the applicant describes the goods as "computer programs" instead of "computer programs and accompanying manuals intended for use in instructional applications."

Substantive Rejections Are More Challenging to Correct

The errors in the previous section were fairly easily to correct. However, certain objections by a trademark examining attorney require substantial effort to overcome. These objections are usually based on the statutory bars to registration established in Section 2 of the Lanham Act. These bars include:

- **Likelihood of confusion.** The trademark examining attorney determines that the mark—when used on the identified goods—is likely to be confused with a registered mark. For example, a shoe manufacturer attempts to register Knike for shoes.
- **Generic or other disclaimed material.** The trademark examining attorney determines that a portion of the mark is generic and must be disclaimed. For example, the owner of the trademark Nebraska Opry may have to disclaim the word Opry, as it is a generic term for country and western music entertainment.

  If the examining attorney determines that the entire mark is generic, then overcoming the objection is much more difficult. For example, in 2006, registration was refused for the term Fresh Organics on the basis that the term was a generic reference to a "variety of fresh, unprocessed, and/or raw food items that have been grown organically." (*In re Nutraceutical Corp.*, Serial No. 78975072 (March 13, 2006).)

- **Descriptive mark.** The trademark examining attorney determines that the mark—when used on the identified goods—is merely descriptive of the goods. For example, the mark Nasal No-Hair for a nose-hair clipper.

Sometimes you'll need to provide extensive legal and factual arguments to overcome objections. Because these arguments are often similar to the arguments made in infringement lawsuits (for example, likelihood of confusion or descriptiveness), the bases for such responses are discussed in various chapters throughout this book. (For example, Chapter 6 discusses likelihood of confusion.) The procedure for preparing responses is also documented in treatises such as *Trademark Registration Practice 2d*, by James E. Hawes (Thomson Reuters), and *McCarthy on Trademarks* (Thomson Reuters).

Hire a Trademark Attorney to Prepare a Response

It is almost never necessary to use an attorney to successfully respond to a technical rejection. Because this type of rejection usually is based on a clerical deficiency in your application, it does not take a legal education to figure out the correct response. Substantive rejections are another matter. This type of rejection is based on an examiner's assessment that the mark itself doesn't qualify for registration. Changing the examiner's mind on this point requires advocacy skills and a good working knowledge of trademark law—both attributes of competent trademark attorneys. (See Chapter 14, "Help Beyond This Book," for information on how to find a good trademark attorney.)

As desirable as it may be to use an attorney to help push your application through the USPTO, this is almost always an expensive option. If you have a significant amount of money or business goodwill already tied up in your mark, then the expense may be justified. However, if you don't have a lot invested in your mark, it may be the wiser course to handle the matter yourself, even though an attorney might get better results. Why? Pure economics. Keep in mind that you are only out $225 to $400 if you don't succeed in your first application and need to file a new one.

This amount is roughly the same as the normal hourly fee charged by trademark attorneys—and fighting with the USPTO can easily end up costing you $4,000 to $5,000 worth of an attorney's time. Though you may not be able to register your chosen mark, there are plenty of other potential marks in the world.

Abandon Your Application

If your application is based on actual use of your mark, your ownership of the mark will depend on the first date of that use. Registration itself does not confer ownership except when the application is based on an intent to use (in which case the filing date becomes the date of first use).

If you already own your trademark, registration only gives notice to the world of your mark, and it gives you a leg up (in terms of what you have to prove) if you end up in court in an ownership or infringement dispute.

Rather than pay an attorney or spend dozens of hours of your own time haggling with the USPTO, you might be better off dropping your application and continuing to use your mark as you have before. This is especially true in the case of a descriptiveness rejection. If your mark is, in truth, descriptive, getting it registered will not offer much in the way of additional protection. If, however, the rejection is based on "likelihood of confusion" grounds, take a close look at the reasons for the rejection and decide whether you might be sued for infringement if you continue to use your chosen mark.

TIP

You can expressly abandon your application by filing a Request for Express Abandonment (Withdrawal) of Application using TEAS. Click "Apply Online" under "Trademarks" on the USPTO home page (www.uspto.gov). Scroll down to "All TEAS Forms" and select "Miscellaneous Forms."

CAUTION

All abandonments are not equal. Here we are talking about abandoning an application, which will result only in the loss of whatever rights you would have obtained by completing the application. If, however, you stop using a mark over a period of time, or fail to maintain quality control over how the mark is used, you could be considered to have abandoned the mark itself, and therefore lose the exclusive right to use it. (See Chapter 8, "How to Use and Care for Your Trademark," for more on how to avoid abandoning the mark itself.)

Also, if you filed an intent-to-use application, abandonment of the application might affect your ownership of the mark. For example, assume a business starts using the same or a similar mark after you file your intent-to-use application but before you put your mark into actual use. If you follow through with your registration, you can claim the original filing date as the date of first use and be considered the owner of the mark. If, on the other hand, you abandon the application, the other user will be considered the owner—because you will no longer be entitled to the filing date as your date of first use.

Final Rejection: An Objection That Cannot Be Overcome

If the examiners at the USPTO determine that a mark is not registrable, they will mail a final rejection to the applicant. In the event of a final rejection, the applicant can:

- **Appeal to the Trademark Trial and Appeal Board (TTAB).** An appeal to the TTAB is possible when the basis for the final rejection is substantive, for example, your application has been rejected for descriptiveness or likelihood of confusion.
- **File a Petition to the Director.** Applicants use a Petition to the Director when the basis for the rejection is that the applicant or the USPTO failed to adhere to procedural rules. For example, a final rejection that is based upon an improper time limit for response would be a procedural basis for a Petition to the Director.
- **Request further reconsideration.** The applicant can request that the examining attorney perform another examination of the mark.
- **Abandon or suspend the application.** Abandoning the application terminates the application process. Suspending the application permits more time to prepare a response.
- **Amend the application to seek registration on the Supplemental Register** (37 C.F.R. § 2.75). If the basis for rejection is that the mark is descriptive, the mark might still qualify for registration on the Supplemental Register.

Follow-Up Activity Required for Intent-to-Use Applications

SKIP AHEAD

If you are filing an actual-use application, skip this section. An intent-to-use application involves more steps than an actual-use application. This is because to complete your registration and own the mark, you must actually get it into use in commerce, tell the USPTO about it, and pay an additional fee.

The Allegation of Use for Intent-to-Use Application

To actually get your mark registered, you will use a form called a Statement of Use/Amendment to Allege Use for Intent-to-Use Application. This form may be filed at any time prior to the date the USPTO authorizes the publication of your proposed mark and any time after the USPTO issues a Notice of Allowance. It may not be filed between those two dates, which has come to be known as the "blackout" period.

Intent-to-Use Applicant Must Have Actual Intent to Use

Don't file an ITU application if you just want to put a trademark on hold until you decide whether to go ahead with it. You must have a bona fide intent to use the mark at the time you file. For example, an applicant who was unable to provide any documents or other evidence of an actual intent to use a mark (ENYCE on custom auto accessories) was denied trademark rights by the Trademark Trial and Appeals Board (TTAB). (*L.C. Licensing, Inc. v. Berman*, 86 U.S.P.Q.2d 1883 (TTAB 2008).) In a similar case involving a foreign registrant, the TTAB held that an applicant who "has not had activities in the United States and has not made or employed a business plan, strategy, arrangements or methods there," and "has not identified channels of trade that will be used in the United States," does not have a bona fide intent to use the mark. (*Honda Motor Co., Ltd. v. Friedrich Winkelmann*, 90 U.S.P.Q.2d 1660 (TTAB 2009).)

You can prepare and file the Statement of Use online using TEAS. You do not need to supply specimens with an intent-to-use application, but you'll have to include one with your Statement of Use. In addition to the information in this chapter, the USPTO's help system should easily get you through this form.

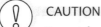

CAUTION

Remember that your specimen, mark drawing, and description of goods and services must all be consistent. That is, if your specimen shows a different mark than what you put in your original application, you'll have some explaining to do. Similarly, if your specimen shows a different product or service than that described in your application, you'll have to submit another specimen or change your product/service description.

When to Divide Your Application

When using TEAS, you will be asked whether you wish to divide your application. You would want to divide your application only if all of the following are true:

- Your original application designated your mark to apply to more than one product or service.
- You have used the mark in connection with one or some, but not all, of those goods or services.
- You still intend to use the mark in connection with one or more additional good(s) and service(s).

The benefit of dividing an application, rather than waiting until the mark is in use for all goods or services originally contemplated, is that the mark in use can be placed on the Federal Register more quickly.

If your situation meets the three criteria described above, you should consider dividing your application so that one application now claims actual use for one or more of the goods or services, while the other application remains on an intent-to-use status with respect to the remaining goods or services.

> EXAMPLE: Suppose Etta's intent-to-use application claimed she was going to use Quick-Bytes in connection with computer consulting services and computer programs. If she began offering consulting services two months after her application was filed, she might want to amend her application to claim use of Quick-Bytes in connection with the services. When she divides the application, she will then have two applications: one in which she alleges actual use of the mark for her services, and one in which she plans to use the mark for computer programs in the future.

The downside of dividing the application is that additional paperwork is involved (another Statement of Use), and you will have to pay an additional filing fee each time you claim usage under an additional classification. If money is scarce, or you soon expect to have the mark in use with all the goods or services you claimed, it's probably better not to divide your application. Just wait until you are using the mark in all the ways you intend and then file one Statement of Use.

If you decide to divide your application, use the form that TEAS offers for this purpose (called a Request to Divide Application). However, we recommend that you not file it with the USPTO until a trademark attorney has reviewed your work.

 CAUTION
Even if you are filing a Request to Divide, you must respond to any USPTO communications on time, or risk abandoning your application.

Getting a Six-Month Extension to File Your Statement of Use

As long as you still intend to use your mark on at least one of the goods or services mentioned in your application and are willing to pay $150 per class as a filing fee, you can request an extension and get an extra six months before you have to file your Statement of Use. As stated earlier, you must file the request before your six months run out.

You can request six-month extensions up to five times, as long as you file each one before the last extension runs out. For the first request, you need not give the reason why you need it. But after that, you must convince the USPTO that there is a good reason why your mark hasn't been used yet, as explained below. The USPTO won't give an extension of time beyond 36 months after issuing the Notice of Allowance. If you're asking for your second, third, fourth, or fifth request, you will need to explain what you have done to get ready to use the mark in commerce. Your explanation need not be lengthy; a sentence or two will do. Some possible explanations include the following:

- the need for more research or development of your product or service
- the need for more research about your market, including where and how to sell the product or service
- a delay in efforts to arrange for product manufacturing
- the need for more time to develop advertising or promotional activities
- attempts to get government approval are still in progress
- attempts to set up marketing networks are still in progress, and
- any other reasonable explanation (for instance, a prolonged illness or destruction of vital records at your factory due to fire or another disaster).

You might be tempted not to seek these extensions but to abandon the application and file a new application when the mark is finally put into use in commerce. Although this could save you money, you will lose the date of first use (your original filing date) that you would be able to claim if you get your mark into actual use within the 36-month period.

If you are mailing these forms, see the section "If You Are Filing by Mail," above, regarding mailing information to the USPTO. Mail your Statement of Use and fees to this address:

Commissioner for Trademarks
BOX AAU/SOU
P.O. Box 1451
Alexandria, VA 22313-1451

Follow-Up Activity Required After Registration

While you are entitled to hearty congratulations upon receiving your Certificate of Registration, your efforts will be for naught if you fail to take the next important step. You'll need to file with the USPTO some additional paperwork known as the Section 8 and Section 15 Declarations (which tell the USPTO that you are still using the mark). (We cover this in Chapter 8.) Because these declarations must be filed between the fifth and sixth year after your original registration date (unless you purchase a six-month grace period), it's easy to let the deadline slip.

You will also have to renew your registration prior to ten years after your registration date, and submit both a renewal form and a Section 8 Declaration (which proves that your mark is still in use). The combined filing is called a Section 8/9 Declaration and Renewal and is explained in Chapter 8.

How to Use and Care for Your Trademark

In this chapter, we assume that you are a trademark owner who wants to take all the right steps to keep your mark legally healthy. Trademark ownership can be lost if you don't use the mark correctly. And if you have registered the mark with the USPTO, your registration may lapse if you fail to take certain required follow-up steps. This chapter identifies the major pitfalls that owners of marks—registered or unregistered—can encounter and suggests some easy steps for keeping your mark strong against all potential copiers.

Use of the Trademark Registration ® Symbol

If your mark is federally registered—on either the Principal or Supplemental Register—you have the right to use the symbol ® with your mark and should begin doing so immediately. If your mark is not on either of the federal trademark registers, you may not use the ® symbol.

The ® symbol, which lets others know that the mark is federally registered, is usually printed in a very small type—next to the mark. By placing the ® next to your mark, you place potential infringers on notice as to your federal registration, which improves your chances of collecting damages if you need to take an infringer to court. However, you won't lose ownership of the mark by omitting this notice.

> **EXAMPLE:** While searching for a name for his new word-processing program, Phil Programmer sees an advertisement in a trade magazine for a new program called Sorcerer's Apprentice, which allows the user to construct databases for hobby collections. No notice of registration is displayed in the advertisement, so Phil foolishly decides the mark is probably not registered and proceeds to use it as a trademark for his program. The mark is in fact registered. The owners of the mark Sorcerer's Apprentice could sue Phil for infringement because the goods are so closely related (they're both software); and they can probably force him to stop using the mark. But they might have trouble collecting the damages allowed for willful infringement (triple damages, the defendant's profits, and possibly attorneys' fees) because they didn't use the ®.

You'll get the desired protection afforded by the symbol if it appears at least once on each label, tag, or advertisement. You don't need to use the symbol on every occurrence of your mark. Incidentally, instead of using the ® symbol, you may state that "[*your mark*] is a registered trademark of [*your name*]." This has the same legal effect as the ® symbol, but it takes up much more space.

Be sure to specify how you want the symbol used when hiring advertising services or printers or when you allow others to use your mark—for example, on a website or in conjunction with another product or service. It is your responsibility to make sure the world knows your mark is registered. However, it isn't necessary to include the symbol when your mark is being referred to for reasons that have nothing to do with the underlying goods and services. For instance, this book refers to many marks, including McDonald's, without an accompanying registration symbol, because the reason we are referring to the marks is to discuss their characteristics as marks and not to sell the goods or services associated with them.

Use of ® If Your Federal Registration Is Canceled

The USPTO will cancel your federal trademark registration if you fail to file certain required follow-up documents after your initial registration. However, you won't receive notice of this fact from the USPTO. It is easy, therefore, to inadvertently continue using the ® on a mark that is no longer technically registered. Obviously, the easiest way to prevent this from happening is to meet the follow-up requirements. But if you slip up—and many do—use your best efforts to stop using the ® unless and until you reregister the mark.

Using the TM or SM Symbol for Unregistered Trademarks

You may use TM (for trademark) or SM (for service mark) alongside an unregistered mark to show that you claim ownership of the mark and intend to assert your rights against imitators. These symbols are usually placed in smaller type to the right of the mark, as in The Purple World™. Use of the TM or SM symbol provides no legal benefits—that is, their presence is disregarded by the courts—but it warns would-be copiers that the name or other device has been claimed as a mark, and in many instances this will keep others away from using the mark. As with the ® symbol, you don't need to place the TM or SM symbol next to every appearance of your trademark. Nothing can be more distracting than seeing the same word appear over and over again on a page with a little TM mark appearing next to it. The reason to use these symbols is to make sure you get your "Back off—this is a trademark!" message across once, or if there are many pages, at most once on every page. Neither courts nor the USPTO have a rule for how often you should use the symbol; let common sense be your guide.

The USPTO Can Help You Maintain Your Registration

The owner of a federally registered trademark must timely file several documents over the course of the trademark's lifespan. Failure to file some of these documents often results in the loss of the registration. Until recently, the USPTO offered little help to trademark owners in determining when these documents had to be filed. This changed in 2015 when the USPTO's Trademark Status and Document Retrieval (TSDR) system introduced a "Maintenance" tab, showing owners the follow-up documents they must file and by when (see image below). To locate this information, find your registration in the USPTO TESS database and click on the TSDR button.

In 2015, the USPTO also began sending courtesy email reminders of registration renewals to trademark owners who:

- had "live" registrations
- provided a valid email address to the USPTO, and
- authorized the USPTO to communicate by email.

The USPTO does not send reminders by regular postal mail, and when an email comes back as undeliverable, the agency won't attempt to reach you again. The USPTO's failure to provide a courtesy email reminder does not excuse an owner who fails to file required documents on time.

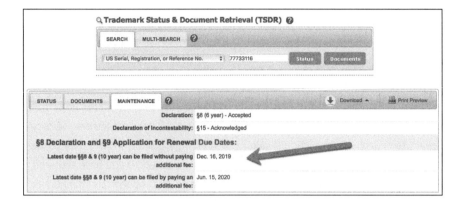

File Your Section 8 and Section 15 Declarations

Between the fifth and sixth year after federally registering your mark, you must complete and file two important forms with the USPTO: the Section 8 Declaration and the Section 15 Declaration. You can file each declaration separately, or you can use one form that combines both the Section 8 and 15 Declarations. You can complete and file these forms online, using the TEAS program.

By filing these declarations, you'll protect your mark in two extremely important ways. The Section 8 Declaration officially advises the USPTO that your mark is still in use and that your registration should continue in force. The Section 15 Declaration advises the USPTO that your mark has been in continuous use from the date of registration and therefore deserves extra protection against potential challengers. In USPTO jargon, you're requesting "incontestability status" for your mark. You'll need to briefly evaluate the use of your mark to make sure you're eligible to file these declarations. Here's how.

Is Your Mark Still in Use?

To file the Section 8 and Section 15 Declarations, you must still be using your mark in the manner described in your registration certificate. This means that you must still be using it, at a minimum, on the same products or services and in the same way (on packaging or pamphlets, and so on) as you originally stated. And, you must be able to come up with samples that demonstrate your continued use.

> **CAUTION**
>
> **File in the name of the current owner.** The Section 8 and Section 15 Declarations must be filed by the current owner of the federal trademark registrations. (The current owner should calculate the filing period from the date of registration, not the date the mark was transferred or acquired.) If you have acquired the trademark registration by an assignment, or if your company has changed its business name or form (for example, from a sole proprietorship to a corporation), you will also need to file a record of the transfer of ownership with the USPTO.

Has Your Mark Been in Continuous Use for Five Years?

You will qualify for incontestable status (the Section 15 Declaration) if your mark is in continuous use for five years after being placed on the Principal Register. More specifically, your mark can become incontestable if all of the following apply:

- Your mark was placed on the Principal Register at least five years ago and you have used the mark continuously—without a lapse—since that registration date in the same manner and on the same goods or services for which it was originally registered. (If you are using the mark for some of those original goods or services but not for others, it can become incontestable for the goods and services you are still using it for.)
- No court has rendered a final decision that affects your ownership claim since the date of registration.
- There is no pending court or USPTO challenge to your right to use the trademark.
- You file the Sections 8 and 15 Declarations on time.
- The mark is not and has not become generic (that is, synonymous with the underlying product or service).

Incontestability status makes it more difficult—but not impossible— for anyone to challenge the validity of your mark. The result is that it will be easier for you to protect your mark from infringement. Even though an incontestable mark can still be challenged on a number of grounds in an infringement lawsuit (see "'Incontestable' Really Means 'Harder to Contest,'" below), it is safe from attack on the basis that it lacks distinctiveness. This is a key benefit—once a mark is considered distinctive beyond argument, it gets very strong protection.

> **EXAMPLE:** Park 'N Fly, Inc., sued Dollar Park and Fly, Inc., for trademark infringement. Dollar Park and Fly defended on the ground that the Park 'N Fly mark was too weak to deserve protection. But the U.S. Supreme Court ruled that the Park 'N Fly mark had obtained incontestability status and couldn't be challenged on that ground. (*Park 'N Fly, Inc. v. Dollar Park and Fly, Inc.*, 469 U.S. 189 (1985).)

Of course, even after a mark attains incontestability status, the mark can be deemed abandoned and dropped from the Federal Register if you stop using it for a sufficiently long time.

"Incontestable" Really Means "Harder to Contest"

Paradoxically, you can contest an incontestable trademark in quite a few ways. The upshot is that "incontestable" really means "harder to contest."

If accused of infringing a particular mark that has achieved incontestability status, you can defend on any of the following grounds:

- The registrant obtained the registration or its incontestability fraudulently.
- The registrant has abandoned the mark .
- The registrant is using the mark to misrepresent the source of the goods or services with which it is being used (for instance, a mark is used to deceive consumers into believing they are buying another company's products or services).
- Your mark is your own name being used in your own business or is descriptive of your goods or services or geographic locale.
- Your mark was used in interstate commerce before the incontestable mark was used and registered.
- Your mark was registered before the incontestable mark was registered.
- The incontestable mark is being used to violate the antitrust laws of the United States. (37 U.S.C. § 1115(b).)

Can You File on Time?

Both the Section 8 and Section 15 Declarations must be signed and filed with the USPTO between the fifth and sixth years of registration. The fee for the combined filing is currently $325 per class ($125 for the Section 8 Declaration, and $200 for the Section 15 Declaration). Timing is critical: If you miss the deadline, you'll have only a six-month grace period to file the declarations, and you'll have to pay an extra $100 fee per class. To avoid missed or late filings, use the "Maintenance" tab in the TSDR database to double-check your required filing dates (see "The USPTO Can Help You Maintain Your Registration," above). It's also wise to file these declarations well before the six-year deadline, so that you'll have time to clear up questions or provide the USPTO with more information, if needed.

> EXAMPLE: If your mark was registered on July 27, 2014, you must sign and file your Sections 8 and 15 Declarations by July 27, 2020 to avoid paying an additional fee. The latest you can file the declarations is six months later on January 27, 2021, in which case you'll have to pay the additional fee.

Failure to file the Section 8 Declaration on time will result in your federal registration being canceled (unless you pay the $100 fee and file within the six-month grace period). If the USPTO cancels your mark, you will have to reregister if you still want the benefit of federal registration. But although you'll be registered again, you'll be behind in one important respect: You won't be able to obtain incontestable status for the mark until an additional five years has passed from your reregistration date. To avoid waiting extra time for the protection of incontestable status, it is in your interest to make sure you file this document on time.

Filing Sections 8 and 15 Declarations Online

The Sections 8 and 15 Declarations (whether filed separately or as one application) are available for filing online through the TEAS program.

On the USPTO home page (www.uspto.gov), under "Trademarks," click "Apply Online." Scroll down and then click "Registration maintenance/ renewal/correction forms." Then choose either the combined 8 and 15 form or the Section 8 form, depending on your needs. After that, you must answer a series of questions similar to those asked of applicants under the TEAS new trademark application (see Chapter 7). Like other TEAS forms, you can pay by credit card at the end of the procedure.

File Your Section 8 Declaration and Section 9 Application for Renewal

If your mark was registered on or after November 16, 1989, you must renew it within ten years from the date of registration. If your mark was registered before November 16, 1989, it must be renewed 20 years from the date of registration. In addition to filing a renewal application (Section 9), you also must file another Section 8 Declaration at the same time. These two documents have been combined into one document and can be filled out online using the TEAS program. You can access the form online, in the same place where the Section 8 and Section 15 Declarations can be found.

File the renewal application within the six-month period directly before the ten-year anniversary of your mark's registration. The fee for the combined filing is currently $425 per mark per class ($125 for the Section 8 Declaration, $300 for the Section 9 renewal application). For an additional $100-per-class fee, the renewal may be filed within a six-month grace period after the anniversary date. The USPTO will not accept a renewal application after that date. For instance, if your registration expires on May 15, 2020, your renewal application (1) must be dated after November 15, 2019, and (2) may be filed between November 16, 2019, and May 15, 2020 (or between May 16 and December 15, 2020, with the $100 grace period fee). We strongly recommend that you file your renewal application as soon as you are able, to allow the maximum time possible for curing glitches.

Use It or Risk Losing It

The adage "use it or lose it" applies to trademark protection. A mark must be in continuous use for the owner to keep others from using it. If the mark falls out of use for a long enough period of time, it may be considered abandoned. A mark that has been registered with the USPTO, if not used for three years or more, will be presumed abandoned. A "presumption" is a legal standard that means it is more likely than not that something has happened. Every presumption can be rebutted by credible evidence to the contrary. For example, suppose a company challenges the validity of a trademark arguing that it has not been used for three years. If the trademark owner can present a good explanation of why the nonuse does not constitute an "intent to abandon," the USPTO will not consider the mark to be abandoned. Despite the "use it or lose it" rule, the law often permits nonuse for a considerable amount of time. Such contingencies as temporary financial difficulty, bankruptcy proceedings, and the need for a product revision may qualify as satisfactory explanations for nonuse of a mark. The USPTO has no particular time period that the mark must be out of use to be considered abandoned (other than the three-year presumption mentioned above). Rather, abandonment will be decided on a case-by-case basis.

Maintain Tight Control of Your Mark

As we explain in other parts of the book, trademarks serve the primary function of identifying a particular product or service in the marketplace. If an owner allows others to use its trademark without restriction, the mark will no longer serve as a meaningful indicator of a particular product's or service's origin. When this occurs, the mark can be considered abandoned. For instance, if a fast food hamburger chain allows its franchise operators to have complete discretion as to the food, decor, and type of service they offer under the company logo, the logo quickly loses its ability to indicate a particular type of food service. In this situation, the logo can be abandoned—it no longer serves its original function of product or service identification—and anyone will be free to use it.

Beware Naked Licenses

If you grant others the right to use your trademark (known as a trademark license), you must always supervise the nature and quality of the goods or services being produced using that trademark. For example, if you are the owner of a trademark for clothing and you license its use to a shoe company, you must supervise the quality of the shoe company's products using your trademark. Your failure to supervise is referred to as a "naked license," and the results can be disastrous. For example, in a 2002 case, a court cancelled the trademark rights of an owner of a wine trademark because the company failed to supervise a company to which it had licensed the trademark. (*Barcamerica International USA Trust v. Tyfield Importers Inc.*, 289 F.3d 589 (9th Cir. 2002).) In *Eva's Bridal Ltd. v. Halanick Enterprises*, 639 F.3d 788 (7th Cir. 2011), the Seventh Circuit held that a family-owned bridal shop failed to supervise its licensees, and as a result the bridal shop abandoned its right to the mark. A similar result was reached when an organization (The Freecycle Network) did not exercise contractual or actual control over a licensee. The court considered the arrangement a "naked license," resulting in trademark abandonment and the owner's loss of all trademark rights. (*Freecycle Sunnyvale v. Freecycle Network*, 626 F.3d 509 (9th Cir. 2010).) Most trademark licenses are drafted to avoid a finding of abandonment by requiring that samples of all licensed trademark goods be periodically submitted by the licensee to the trademark owner for approval and quality control.

The way that McDonald's controls its marks exemplifies the type of vigilance over the product or service that is necessary to avoid the possibility of abandonment. McDonald's uses its service mark not only to distinguish its service from its competitors generally but also to call to a consumer's mind such characteristics as a specific level of service, a specific type of meal at a specific price, and a specific level of cleanliness. It does this by requiring every owner of a McDonald's franchise to operate the franchise under tight rules and restrictions, designed to ensure that the characteristics associated with the McDonald's mark are always present. Without such restrictions, the McDonald's mark soon would stand for nothing; a McDonald's franchise operation would cease to provide the consumer with meaningful information about its products based on its usage of the McDonald's mark.

Another aspect of controlling your mark is to police its use by others with whom you do not have a license agreement. Even if you don't particularly care whether others use your mark, your failure to assert your exclusive ownership rights means that the mark might be considered abandoned. Policing your mark might mean annual checks of the trade literature applicable to your business, weekly scrutiny of the *Official Gazette* for new trademark applications, or even periodic full trademark searches.

You can also hire a third party to police your trademark. Most trademark search companies (see Chapter 4) offer trademark-watching services for a monthly or annual fee.

Authorized Uses of Your Trademark

Not all uses of your trademark by others place it in jeopardy. For example, it is common for stores to use marks belonging to other companies to tell their customers that the goods or services identified by the marks can be purchased at that store. When using marks in this way, however, the stores must make it clear that the marks belong to their owners, not to the store. Usually this fact is clear from the context ("Levi's sold here" or "An authorized distributor of Apple Computer products"). Often, you will see—on labels of goods that incorporate others' products, like a sofa—a message like "Wear-Dated ® is a trademark of the Monsanto Company," indicating that the name of the sofa's fabric is a trademark of another company. Such uses become a problem only when it is not clear that the trademark belongs to the rightful trademark owner.

Generally, textual use of a trademark—simply typed—is not a problem. However, if used in a comparative advertisement, the mark must have the same typeface and logo as used by the original mark owner. If the trademark does not look like it normally does, the use of the mark may be confusing or diluting.

If you do discover other businesses using your mark, you can respond in the ways we suggest in Chapter 11, "When Someone Infringes Your Mark." Or you could hire a lawyer to sue if necessary. To maintain your rights, you don't have to take an unauthorized user to court, but you should send a letter protesting the use of the mark and asserting your claim of ownership. If the infringer's use goes on for a long time—for example, several years— any delay on your part might provide the infringer with a defense against your legal action. Or, once you finally file a lawsuit, you could lose your right to obtain an injunction (to order them to stop using the mark).

"I Googled It!"

In a 2017 federal lawsuit, an individual who had forfeited various Google-related domain names asked the court to cancel the GOOGLE trademark on the grounds that it had become generic. The appellate court held that the plaintiff mistakenly assumed that using the mark as a verb ("I Googled that") by a majority of the public would automatically convert the mark to generic status. In ruling to preserve the Google trademark, the court stated that what matters is whether the primary significance of the word "google" to the relevant public was as a mark identifying the Google search engine in particular. (*Elliott v. Google, Inc*, 860 F.3d 1151 (9th Cir. 2017).)

Use the Mark Properly—Avoid Genericide

A few businesses—mostly large ones—have the apparent good fortune of owning a mark that has become a household word. But, paradoxically, once the mark becomes so much of a household word that it becomes synonymous with any product or service of the sort it originally represented, it ceases to be a mark—it becomes generic. For example, some people refer to all paper facial tissues as Kleenex, and all personal watercrafts as Jet-Skis. These marks would be in danger of becoming lost through "genericide" if the companies did not make an effort to prevent such improper uses of the marks.

The problem is this: The more well-known a particular mark becomes, the more the public is prone to equate the mark with the underlying product rather than view it as one brand name among many. This is just another way of saying that the mark loses its ability to identify a particular brand and becomes generic. Only a tiny number of companies will face this problem—it tends to arise with revolutionary new products that the public comes to associate with the name their first manufacturer gives them, like Rollerblades for in-line skates. But because genericide is avoidable, you ought to know how to prevent your mark from going generic if that seems to be even a remote possibility.

The best ways to keep a mark from becoming generic are:

- Accompany every use of the mark with the generic name for the product or service (for example, Kleenex tissues).
- Avoid using the mark as a verb (for instance, you never go "roller blading," you skate on Rollerblade skates).
- Always capitalize your mark (Tylenol).
- Never use the mark as a general noun (for instance, don't call a photocopy a "Xerox").

Transferring Ownership of a Trademark

You should consider your registered mark as property with a title, the same as a house or car. The title document is your Certificate of Registration. If you sell your business or the rights in products you manufacture or distribute, you will also need to sell the marks used to identify the business and products in the marketplace. The complete transfer of ownership in a mark to another person or entity is called an "assignment." An assignment of a registered mark must be in writing to be valid. It can—and should—be filed with the USPTO. The new owner can obtain a new Certificate of Registration in his or her name. If you anticipate a sale (assignment) of your mark, see a trademark attorney. A sample assignment form is set forth below.

You can file an assignment of trademark ownership with the USPTO online. On the home page (www.uspto.gov), click "Trademarks" and then click "Filing Online." Scroll down and then click "Assignment Forms."

Assignment

_____ [*Name of registrant*] _____ (Assignor),

of _____ [*mailing address*] _____ ,

has adopted, used, and is using a mark that is registered in the United States Patent and Trademark Office, Registration No. [*get number from registration certificate*] ,

dated _____ [*get date from registration certificate*] _____ .

[*Name of person (and citizenship) or company that will be the owner of the mark**]

(Assignee) of _____ [*mailing address*] _____ ,

wants to acquire the mark and the registration thereof.

For good and valuable consideration, receipt of which is hereby acknowledged, Assignor hereby assigns to Assignee all right, title, and interest in and to the mark, together with the goodwill of the business symbolized by the mark, and the above-identified registration.

_____

Signature of Assignor

[*If assignor is a business, list official title of person signing*]
Title

State of _____)

)

County of _____)

On this _____ day of _____ [*month*] _____ , [*year*] , before me

appeared _____ [*assignor's name*] _____ , the person

who signed this instrument, who acknowledged that he/she signed it as a free act on his/her own behalf (or on behalf of the identified entity with authority to do so).

_____

Signature of notary public

NOTE: This form is valid only when the assignee is a United States resident or company.

* If the assignee is a domestic general partnership or domestic joint venture, you must also provide the names, legal entity type, and national citizenship (or the state or country of organization) of all general partners or active members that compose the partnership or joint venture.

This takes you to ETAS (Electronic Trademark Assignment System) where you can proceed through the process of preparing a Trademark Assignment Recordation Coversheet and attaching your assignment.

Because the USPTO does not examine trademark assignments, the simple act of recording the assignment is not determinative of the assignment's validity. In other words, filing the assignment doesn't guarantee its enforceability. (*Richards v. Burgett, Inc.*, 2011 WL 6156838 (N.D. Ill., December 12, 2011).)

If you are selling a business, chances are you are also selling any trademarks associated with it. If so, it makes sense to assign your ownership of the marks in a document that is separate from the contract of sale. This enables the new mark owner to record only the transfer of mark ownership with the USPTO, while keeping private the many details of the deal that do not affect the transfer of trademark rights.

SEE AN EXPERT

Seek an attorney's assistance if you plan on bequeathing a trademark as part of your estate plan. If you want to give a trademark as an inheritance gift, you'll need professional advice to ensure that the business and associated goodwill are also transferred (and that you have the right to bequeath the mark).

CAUTION

Note that in the sample assignment form, above, the trademark owner transfers ownership of the business's "goodwill" as well as the mark itself. Goodwill is an intangible asset measured in large part by customer recognition of—and loyalty to—the mark in question. Any transfer of ownership in the mark must include a transfer of the goodwill associated with the mark.

FREQUENTLY ASKED QUESTION

Transferring TMs to new corporation

"I have two trademarks registered to a corporation and will be transferring the rights to use these trademarks to a new corporation. Do I have to notify the Patent and Trademark Office and how would I do that? Also, I notice that someone asked about renewing a patent. Is that also necessary for trademarks?"

You need to do two things: (1) Assign the marks to your new corporation; and (2) file the assignment, along with a Trademark Assignment Recordation Coversheet, at the USPTO website.

What about renewal? You must file a renewal and declaration of continued use between the ninth and tenth anniversaries of registration and you should file a declaration of continued use and (optionally but recommended) a statement of incontestability between the fifth and sixth years of registration. The failure to file the declaration of continued use will result in the loss of the registration.

Evaluating Trademark Strength

This chapter helps you evaluate a particular mark's legal strength—that is, the degree to which the courts will protect it or something similar against use or misuse by others. You will want to read this chapter if you feel the need for a deeper understanding of the material in Chapter 3, or if you have:

- been accused of violating someone else's mark, or
- think that someone else is treading on your mark.

Assuming you are involved in a conflict situation, once you digest this material you should read Chapter 10, which discusses who has priority in case two marks—or a mark and an Internet domain name—come into conflict. Then you should go to Chapter 11 (if your mark is being infringed) or Chapter 12 (if you are accused of infringement) for suggestions on how to deal with the dispute.

In Chapter 3, we explained the basics of what makes a mark legally strong—inherent distinctiveness or distinctiveness acquired through secondary meaning. This chapter teaches you how to classify your mark by type (for instance, geographic names and personal names) and explains how far the courts are willing to go to protect that type of mark in case of a dispute.

A Brief Review of What Makes a Strong Mark

A legally strong trademark successfully identifies your goods or services in the consumer's mind. It achieves its strength either (1) by being inherently distinctive, or (2) by acquiring distinctiveness through long-term use and customer recognition. The following sections will help you determine your mark's strength.

CAUTION

The tools we give you to evaluate a trademark's strength are guide-lines, not guarantees. These rules represent the best guesses that most lawyers would likely make based on the relevant court decisions. But we don't promise specific results for a specific mark because that depends on many factors, including use, timing, and how the facts strike the judge who decides the particular dispute.

For Marks Consisting of Words, Identify the Distinctive Part of the Mark

To evaluate the strength of your product or service mark, first separate its distinctive component from the part of the mark that identifies the type of product or service it identifies. For example, the mark Apple Computers contains a distinctive element—Apple—and a product/service identifier, computers. Another example: The distinctive aspect of the name Guess? jeans is the word "Guess" followed by a "?"

Sometimes all or most of the individual words of a mark are equally distinctive (or nondistinctive), and it is the combination of the words that is distinctive. Examples: include Trader Joe's (food market) and Music Now and Then (a disc jockey service). Even when a word mark lacks a specific distinctive part, the mark will still have a tail that identifies the underlying product or service. So, it's still important to understand where the words that give the mark at least some distinctiveness drop off and common identifiers of goods or services kick in. Because the nondistinctive aspect of a word mark can never be protected, we simply disregard it in evaluating the legal strength of the name as a mark.

After you have isolated the word or phrase that forms the distinctive aspect of your mark, match it with one or more of the categories listed below to understand why your mark does or doesn't have legal strength.

Assess the Legal Strength of the Trademark Aspect of Your Word Mark

The distinctive part of your word mark is, in fact, the trademark aspect of your mark. Here, we place the different categories of trademarks on a spectrum. We start with the most distinctive marks—the ones with the greatest legal strength. We then move to more ordinary marks, which might be easier to promote but harder to protect legally, and finally conclude with generic marks, which can't be protected at all because they utterly lack distinctiveness. Along the way, we provide lists of examples of each category and discuss why various names are classified as they are.

Remember to consider the whole effect of your mark—its sound, its look, and all the meanings of the individual elements of the mark—before drawing conclusions about its legal strength. This includes the style of the typeface, as well as its color, shape, size, and any other aspect of the overall impression the mark makes. In addition, how the mark is used and the timing of its first use are all relevant in determining relative trademark strengths.

Some of the distinctions that place a mark in one category or another might appear arbitrary and even, at times, hairsplitting. At first, you might feel that it is impossible to tell the difference. Bear with it: The more time you spend with this material, the more it will make sense.

> CAUTION
> **Reasonable minds can differ when it comes to deciding on a mark's strength.** Do keep in mind that live human beings—with their individual strengths and weaknesses—are the ultimate deciders of whether a particular mark is strong or weak. Whether the person is a trademark examiner (an employee of the U.S. Patent and Trademark Office), a judge, a juror, or one of the authors of this book, his or her analysis of a particular mark is based on a subjective response to mostly visual stimuli, which makes for fuzzy decision making. So, if you find yourself disagreeing with the category a particular mark has been consigned to by the USPTO, courts, or even the authors of this book (in the many made-up examples provided), try to understand the rationale rather than reject the conclusion in the name of some absolute truth.

Varieties of Distinctive Marks

Distinctive marks fall into three basic categories—coined, arbitrary, and suggestive. All are strong, but coined and arbitrary marks are considered stronger than suggestive marks and therefore receive more protection.

Coined Marks

These are words that you won't find in any dictionary; they have been made up just to serve as trademarks, so they have no other meaning. Words such as Blistex, Häagen Dazs, Exxon, Tylenol, and Actifed are the marks lawyers like best. They are inarguably distinctive and therefore legally strong. Whether a coined mark is registered or not, chances are that it will automatically entitle you to the strongest protection against copying that courts can provide.

In practice, coined marks can't be used by others in any commercial context. By contrast, most other types of marks can be used by more than one owner as long as both of the following are true:

- The goods and services they are used on are not related and don't compete with each other.
- It is unlikely that customers will be confused by the multiple use of the mark.

The reason for the special treatment afforded a coined mark is its uniqueness. Because a coined mark's exclusive role is to identify a specific product or service (or product line) in the marketplace, most consumers would expect a connection among all businesses that use the mark, and would therefore be confused as to the origins of the products or services carrying it. So it is highly unwise to borrow a famous coined trademark even for a vastly different product or service.

Not all made-up marks fall into this strongest-of-all category. Marks that are coined wholly new, like Maalox, are treated differently and are given more protection than marks that are composites of recognizable elements of words, like Accuride. Maalox is automatically strong because it is not like anything we have heard before. But Accuride is too close to "accurate ride" to be considered a purely coined term. Such a mark is therefore usually considered suggestive rather than coined. (We discuss composite marks at the end of this chapter.)

Fanciful or Arbitrary Marks

Fanciful or arbitrary names, such as Penguin books, Arrow shirts, and Camel cigarettes also make distinctive and legally strong marks. These marks use common words in an unexpected or arbitrary way, so that their normal meanings have nothing to do with the nature of the product or service they identify. That's how a skating rink came up with the appealing name Jellibeans. Another example of a fanciful name is We Be Bop for women's clothing, and it's difficult to think of a more arbitrary name than Diesel, for a bookstore.

These arbitrary or fanciful marks have almost as broad a scope of exclusive use as do coined marks. Most of the time, using an arbitrary or fanciful mark for one type of product or service will prevent the use of the same mark on similar or related services or products. However, unlike a coined mark, arbitrary or fanciful marks may be used if the context of use is entirely different and the original mark is not too well known. If, on the other hand, the arbitrary or fanciful mark has become famous, then—under a principle known as trademark dilution—the mark may be protected against use by others, no matter what the context of use. (See Chapter 1, "A Trademark Primer.")

Suggestive Marks

A close relative of the arbitrary mark is the suggestive mark. This type of mark uses ordinary words in a clever manner to create a desirable idea or feeling about a product or service, but stays away from literally describing any aspect of the product or service. Examples of suggestive marks are Dropbox (for data storage services), Banana Republic (for a style of clothing), Greyhound (for bus service), Thistle Dew Inn (for a bed and breakfast service), and Panache (for a beauty salon).

Suggestive marks are considered distinctive and therefore legally strong because they indirectly associate favorable qualities with specific goods and services in a creative way. For example, a Jaguar car conveys the idea of aggressiveness, beauty, and speed—desirable attributes for a car; Dove soap conveys softness and gentleness; Greyhound implies speed and sleekness—not adjectives normally associated with bus lines but desirable ones nonetheless.

Sunkist is an interesting example of a suggestive mark. Although it is just a novel spelling of the adjective "sun-kissed," its creative use on fruit and juices evokes a wonderfully fresh and healthy image. The originality of the mark makes it legally strong.

Categories of Distinctive Trademarks		
Suggestive	Fanciful/Arbitrary	Coined
Accuride tires	Ajax cleanser	Actifed
Chicken of the Sea tuna	Apple computers	Amtrak
Coppertone tanning lotion	Arrow shirts	Barbasol
Esprit clothes	Banana Republic clothes	Blistex
Glacier ice	Beefeater gin	Curel
Greyhound bus	Camel cigarettes	Exxon
Liquid Paper	Domino sugar	Kodak
Maternally Yours clothes	Double Rainbow ice cream	Maalox
Q-tips	GoDaddy Internet services	Nyquil
Roach Motel insect trap	Hang Ten clothes	Reebok
7-Eleven stores	Hard Rock Cafe	Tylenol
Suave shampoo	Ivory soap	
Wearever cookware	Nova TV series	
	Penguin books	

Another excellent example of a suggestive mark is Thistle Dew Inn, used by a quaint bed and breakfast establishment just off the town square in Sonoma, California. The composite term Thistle Dew evokes both a ubiquitous local purple-flowered plant and a feeling of freshness and renewal that people in Northern California seek when they visit Sonoma, the heart of wine country. (It also—perhaps unintentionally— echoes the sentiment, "This'll do.")

And finally, Panache, a French word that means spirited self-confidence, style, flamboyance, and daring elegance of manner, suggests the qualities that customers might hope to obtain from an upscale beauty shop located in Lakeport, California.

More Examples of Distinctive Marks by Category

The line between arbitrary or fanciful and suggestive marks is often a fine one. A mark that might appear to be fanciful or arbitrary might in fact be derived from a little-known source and might, therefore, be suggestive to those in the know. For example, some marks employ mythical or fantasy allusions to suggest desirable connotations, like the Janus investment fund (Janus = Roman god of beginnings) or Midas Muffler (King Midas = the golden touch). A clever mark of this sort is Prints Valiant for a copy shop, which combines the name of a cartoon hero with a pun on the kind of shop it is and implies heroic effort.

Above is a chart showing examples of the different categories of distinctive trademarks. Examine it carefully to see if these distinctions make sense to you.

Perplexed? Don't be. Many of these examples can go either way. For example, while some trademark authorities consider Ivory soap to be an arbitrary trademark, others argue that it describes the color of the soap, or that it suggests the desirable qualities of ivory—smooth, clean, white, valuable. Nyquil, a cold remedy, can be seen either as a coined term, or a composite suggestive mark, combining "night" and "tranquil" to evoke peaceful sleep. Banana Republic could be either arbitrary, because it has nothing to do with clothes, or it could be suggestive of adventure and travel.

As long as your mark is distinctive in the sense of it being unique, clever, or just plain memorable, the practical importance of what category it fits in is nil—until you find yourself in a conflict with another mark. Then, to the extent that your mark qualifies as a coined term, it will get the widest scope of protection.

Varieties of Nondistinctive (Ordinary) Marks

In Chapter 3, we lumped all the marks that aren't inherently distinctive into a category called ordinary marks. An ordinary mark is one that communicates in a descriptive or otherwise mundane way something about the product or service to which it is attached. It includes five sorts of terms:

- **descriptive**, describing the nature of the service or product (Self-Help Divorce Center for a consulting service helping people file their own divorce forms)
- **laudatory**, praising the business or the customer (Pretty Nails, for a manicurist; Fast Feet, for athletic shoes)
- **geographic**, describing the geographic area the service is in (Downtown Auto Service, if it's really downtown)
- **personal names**, consisting primarily of first names, surnames, personal initials, or nicknames (Maury's Deli, Gooden Chevrolet), and
- **business name initials**.

While these types of word marks are considered to be legally weak initially, they can each become distinctive through long use and customer recognition, via the secondary meaning rule (discussed in Chapter 3). For example, IBM, the acronym for International Business Machines, originally was a legally weak mark until it became well known over time, thereby acquiring legal strength under the secondary meaning rule.

In the following subsections we detail the pros and cons of each kind of ordinary mark and give you rules about when a term will be considered strong enough to qualify for protection in the courts.

Descriptive and Laudatory Marks

We lump marks using these kinds of words together because there is little practical difference between them. As long as you know your mark is one or the other, you'd be wasting your time trying to decide between the two.

Descriptive marks are those that literally describe a feature or attribute of a product or service, such as 10-Minute Lube (auto care), Hi-Tech Computers, Char-broiler hamburgers, FindUHome (real estate broker), or Nuts and Bolts (hardware store).

Laudatory marks (words of praise) hype a product or service's quality or quantity, using common words like Original Blend (cat food), America's Freshest Ice Cream, Maple Rich (syrup), or Blue Ribbon (bakeries); or they describe the qualities of the product or service a business hopes to deliver, like Joy detergent or Pride furniture polish.

These marks make very weak trademarks for two reasons:

- Consumers are so used to commercial hype that a descriptive or laudatory term doesn't make the kind of impact on them that would help them to effectively distinguish one product or service from another. For example, the name Canine Clipping Centers doesn't by itself clearly differentiate that pet care shop from any other.

- Descriptive and laudatory terms need to remain freely available for everyone's commercial or everyday use. Trademark law will protect only terms that are unique to a particular product or service brand and that aren't, therefore, necessary for another business to use if it wishes to describe or hype its business in advertising or marketing copy.

You might think that changing the spelling or language—from English to French, for example—makes an otherwise weak mark strong. It usually doesn't work that way. So La Bread Shoppe or Tastee Kookie remain weak marks despite the spelling/language variations. But a relatively obscure foreign term, or one that most consumers wouldn't recognize as a foreign language equivalent of a descriptive term, can create a strong mark. So, although "xerox" is the ancient Greek word for dry, and dry describes the photocopying process Xerox invented, Xerox was a strong mark from the beginning—because only a few Greek scholars knew its meaning. In addition, La Posada Inns, directed at English speakers, is considered a distinctive mark even though the Spanish translation (The Inn) is descriptive.

How Xerox Almost Became a Generic Mark

Over a number of years, Xerox became more and more synonymous with photocopy machines and the photocopying process ("I need a xerox" or, "I'm going to xerox that"). This common usage put the Xerox mark in danger of becoming generic and therefore not protectable at all. To prevent this, Xerox undertook an aggressive and expensive advertising campaign to encourage people to use Xerox properly, as a proper adjective, and not as a generic term (a verb or a noun). Generic marks are discussed further below.

As we have emphasized in earlier chapters, even descriptive names can become legally strong enough to get full trademark protection, through the secondary meaning rule. That's when a trademark becomes so closely identified with a specific product or service that the public no longer thinks first of the original ordinary meaning of the words. The mark is said to have taken on a new secondary—and distinctive—meaning, and rivals can no longer use it to identify their products or services.

But even after descriptive marks have acquired distinctiveness through the secondary meaning rule, others still can use the ordinary words that make up such marks in nontrademark ways—that is, to legitimately describe their products or services in advertising. This is known as "fair use" of a trademark, and it is a valid defense in court if a mark owner challenges the use of certain words in your mark.

Deceptive and Misleading Marks Get No Protection

Marks that describe a product or service in a misleading way get no protection at all. So neither Neo-Hide nor Softhide can be protected as marks for imitation leather. Most state and federal trademark laws specifically bar these types of marks from registration both to protect consumers from being ripped off and to protect businesses that accurately describe their products from unfair competition by those who don't.

A second category of marks that are only slightly misleading—called "deceptively misdescriptive"—is viewed as less deceptive. American Beauty as a mark for a Japanese sewing machine is one example of this type of mark. When first used, this type of mark does not receive legal protection either. But once it acquires secondary meaning, then it becomes distinctive, and protectable as a mark, on the theory that it is no longer considered misleading. That's because the public no longer thinks of the literal meaning of the words and instead only associates the words in the mark with the product or service.

For example, once Standard Brands acquired secondary meaning and became protectable as a trademark, others could not use those words as a trademark on goods, but a store could advertise that it carries "all standard brands" of paint, tools, or whatever they sell, without fear of infringing.

> **TIP**
> **Continuous use for five years.** If the owner of a weak mark can prove that the mark has been in continuous use for a five-year period, the USPTO will presume that it has acquired secondary meaning and is eligible for placement on the federal Principal Register. (See Chapter 7.)

One final point: Even without secondary meaning, ordinary marks can get limited protection—under unfair competition laws—from a rival with a confusingly similar name in the same geographic area and in the same line of business. (See Chapter 10, "Sorting Out Trademark Disputes.")

Geographic Marks

Geographic marks have a geographic term in them, such as Eastern, Miami, Indiana, English, or any other place names, from streets to continents, or regions to rivers. There are several subspecies of marks containing geographic terms:

- **Literal geographic descriptors.** Like other ordinary marks, the general rule is that if you use a geographic term descriptively (for example, if the product or service is really connected to the place name), it can't be protected as a mark, absent a showing of secondary meaning. That's because everyone has a right to use accurate geographic words to describe the origin of their services or products. So marks like Manhasset Drugs, Central Realty, North Moline Hardware, or Chestnut Street Pub (if it's on Chestnut Street) are weak and can't be protected, unless, of course, they gain secondary meaning in connection with the particular product or service for which they're used. Examples of geographic marks that got protection by acquiring secondary meaning are American Airlines, Continental Can Corp., and *The New Yorker* magazine.

CAUTION
Even if they're not protectable as marks, these extremely common geographic types of business names might be entitled to some relief in court under unfair competition laws. For example, Manhasset Drugs could stop a competitor from using that exact name in Manhasset. (See Chapter 1, for more information.)

- **Indirect geographic descriptors.** Even if your service or product is not factually associated with the place named in your mark, the mark might still be weak if the public is likely to assume that such a link exists. For example, Chicago is famous for a kind of pizza, so it's descriptive, not distinctive, to call a Dallas pizzeria Chicago Pizza. Likewise, Thai Videos is weak if it sells videos from Thailand, even though it does so in Los Angeles. So, too, Phnom Penh is weak for a Cambodian restaurant located in Trenton, New Jersey.
- **General geographic descriptors.** Some words like "world," "globe," and places in outer space might be far too broad to suggest any specific place of origin, but they are still weak because they operate like laudatory or descriptive marks. Thus, *American Engineer* on an engineering trade magazine is descriptive and weak because it's aimed at a readership made up of American engineers.
- **Ambiguous geographic descriptors.** Some geographic terms are ambiguous in meaning when used in a trademark. For instance, the term "continental" can be interpreted as referring to a literal continental land mass or, more quaintly, to the European continent; or to suggest a refined foreign experience (such as "a continental breakfast"). "National" could indicate nationwide scope or patriotism, again depending on how it is used. Whether it's a weak or a strong mark would depend on which meaning applies.

As with all marks consisting of ordinary terms, there are times when geographic marks are protectable, even before they acquire secondary meaning. The best way to make a geographic term distinctive as a mark is to use it in an arbitrary or fanciful way. For example, American Express (for travel and credit services) and California Girl (for clothes) don't really describe either the service or the product or imply their origins. Instead, these words project an image that is fanciful and distinctive for the items on which they are used. So, they are protectable as marks.

Likewise, English Leather is a distinctive (suggestive) mark, as long as it does not describe a leather product. If it did, it would be either descriptive, if it comes from Britain, or deceptive, if it does not. And a fabric store called Taos Fabrics has a weak mark if it's in New Mexico but a strong one if it is in Chattanooga, Tennessee.

Giving strong status to marks that don't obviously describe the product, and allocating weak status to marks that simply identify the item makes sense. The sellers of products or services have a right to truthfully tell where an item came from without infringing another's mark. It would be unfair to all other New York businesses to give any one company in that city a monopoly on the name. But if an entrepreneur elsewhere wants to evoke the Big Apple in Fargo, North Dakota, for example, that's fair. (If the owner of the Fargo-based Big Apple decided later to market its products in New York City, it's possible that its rights would be greater than if the business had started there from the beginning. This would depend on how well-known the Big Apple mark had become in the meantime, whether the mark had been placed on the Federal Register, and what competing uses of the mark already existed in New York City at the time of the desired expansion.)

Personal Names

Words in this category refer to persons, whether their first names, last names, whole names, nicknames, or initials. Examples are Juan's, Houlihan's, Larry Blake's, C.J.'s, and H&R Block. As a general rule, anyone can use a personal name as a mark for a service or product, unless the same name is already in use on directly competing products or services.

This means that personal names (at least common ones) make weak marks. But as we discovered in an informal study of the yellow pages, more small businesses use a surname or first name as their marks than any other kind of name. Marks using personal initials are also popular. It's understandable why businesspeople are drawn to these types of names; they demonstrate pride of ownership. But using a personal name or initials has potentially serious drawbacks from a trademark point of view.

First, most personal names are legally weak because they are not particularly memorable, especially if they are used in one or more competing businesses. We saw this problem with Ray's Pizza in New York. When someone there says "Ray's Pizza," no one can tell which of the 24 Ray's in the city is the right one. Merely adding an initial does not make a personal name inherently distinctive enough to become a legally strong trademark. On the other hand, the more unique your name, the less likely others will use it on a similar business and the more memorable it will be. Will the real Orville Redenbacher please stand up?

Second, as with other ordinary marks, a personal name trademark must usually acquire secondary meaning to be protected as a strong trademark. However, many personal names have garnered such a large degree of public recognition that the courts permit only very limited other uses of them. McDonald's and Levi's are two good examples.

Despite these general principles, a few personal name marks do manage to get strong trademark protection without secondary meaning. The general rule is that if the public would not view the mark primarily as a personal name, then it can be protected outright. Put another way, a personal name works as a trademark if it is so unusual that no one recognizes it as a personal name, like Garan. Other personal names that can be distinctive trademarks are ones that have additional meanings, like Bird, Kent, or Fairbanks, which also have common descriptive or geographic significance. The distinctiveness of such marks would depend on how they are used.

Well-known historical names, like Da Vinci, Lincoln, Rameses, and Robin Hood, are another exception to the general rule that personal names make weak trademarks because they're considered fanciful and distinctive. Using such marks obviously does not imply that the person named is commercially connected to the product or service—so their trademark use is not primarily as a personal name. On the other hand, some historical names, like Webster and Longfellow, have been treated as weak marks. What's the difference? Perhaps because the latter names are less mythic—Daniel Webster and Henry Wadsworth Longfellow are less famous by far than Leonardo Da Vinci or Abraham Lincoln—they carry more of a personal name meaning than do the former. We're in another of those gray areas of the law, where the differences are slim.

The Right of Publicity

A related but separate right protects people's names and personas from commercial use by others. It's called the right of publicity, and it allows celebrities to prevent others from making money by the unauthorized use of their names. Although the right of publicity is commonly associated with celebrities, every person, regardless of how famous, has a right to prevent unauthorized use of his or her name or image to sell products. The right of publicity extends beyond the commercial use of a person's name or image and includes the use of any personal element that implies an individual's endorsement of a product, provided that the public can identify the individual based upon the use. In many states, the right of publicity survives death and can be exercised by the person's heirs.

Even using a famous name on unrelated services or products can be a problem. John Walker probably can't operate a motel under the name Johnny Walker Inn, but he might be able to use a name that sounds sufficiently different, like John M. Walker Inn. Often, in order to resolve such potentially confusing uses, a disclaimer such as "not associated with …" is required. For example, Hyatt Corp. sued Hyatt Legal Services over the use of that surname. The suit was eventually resolved when the defendant agreed to use the statement: "Hyatt Legal Services is named after its founder, Joel Z. Hyatt."

Some names are so famous and applied to such a variety of products that any additional use of them would be confusing to the public, even on a completely unrelated product or service. DuPont or Yves St. Laurent are examples.

Using the Name of a Living Person

In one famous case detailed by Calvin Trillin in the *The New Yorker* magazine, a small bar opened up in Milwaukee under the name of Mike Houlihan's (the first name of one of the owners and the last name of the other owner). W.R. Grace, a conglomerate, already owned a chain of family restaurants called Houlihan's Old Place, one of which was in Milwaukee.

The two establishments coexisted peaceably in the same city for a couple of years. It was only when Mike Houlihan's opened a second pub in St. Louis, where there was another Houlihan's Old Place, that the conglomerate protested the bar's use of a similar mark and threatened to sue. The pub owners were furious and refused to back down: "What do you mean I can't use my surname?" fumed John Houlihan to his lawyer.

The lawyer knew that W.R. Grace appeared to have the law on its side— the Houlihan name was first used and first federally registered in connection with Houlihan's Old Place. But then luck intervened. It turned out that there really was a Mr. Houlihan, after which Houlihan's Old Place was named, and that his written consent for the use of his name had never been obtained—a prerequisite to registering a mark using the name of a living person. Because of this omission, the court canceled W.R. Grace's trademark registration of Houlihan's Old Place. And yet the restaurant eventually succeeded in barring the bar's use of the mark in Missouri based on unfair competition, common law trademark rights, and state dilution laws. Moral of the story: Using personal names in a mark can be tricky, so always get permission when using the name of a living person.

Other names might be equally famous but are associated so exclusively with specific products or services that even though the public would recognize any use of a similar name, no actual confusion is likely to result where the mark is used on a totally different type of product or service. If such is the case, then you can use your name even if it's also a famous mark. That's why Bob Fanta successfully defended against a lawsuit brought by Coca-Cola over his use of "Keep Tab with Fanta" to advertise his tax return service: His business is so logically remote from soft drinks that actual confusion is unlikely.

Generic Labels and Terms

In Chapter 3, we introduced you to the concept of generic labels—words that are synonymous with the underlying product or service and that therefore can't be distinguished from others. Examples of generic terms are "aspirin," "linoleum," and "lite beer." Here we follow up on that discussion to help you distinguish generic labels from marks that are merely weak. It's an important distinction, because while weak marks can gain protection once they acquire secondary meaning, generic labels will never receive any protection at all.

You will see problems with generic words in three different trademark contexts:

- when you try to protect your weak mark against an infringer, and they defend by saying your mark is generic and therefore freely copyable
- when you adopt a mark and seek to have it registered under the secondary meaning rule, but it is rejected because the term is generic rather than merely weak, and
- when a mark that was once distinctive (and perhaps even registered) loses all legal protection because it has become synonymous with the product and not just one brand of it. An example of a distinctive mark that is in danger of becoming generic is Rollerblades, which many people use for the product itself (more accurately called in-line skates).

We are more concerned with the first circumstance than with the second or third, but most of our examples are drawn from court cases in which a mark was denied protection because it always was or had become synonymous with the product. For example, Thermos was once a trademark, but is now seen as a generic term for a kind of insulated bottle. Although they emerge from a different context, such examples are useful because they illustrate the thinking of a judge or trademark examiner in determining if a mark is protectable at all or simply generic.

Distinguishing generic labels from weak marks is not always easy to do. Courts ask what buyers are likely to think of when they hear the term—the product itself or a specific source for that product? Another approach is to try to come up with a generic label for the underlying type of product or service that is different from the mark itself. As long as a generic label for a product or service can be articulated, a name that is different from the label could qualify for treatment as a mark, no matter how weak it is. Only if the name and the generic label merge over time will the mark suffer genericide.

It usually takes some market research to discover a term's generally accepted meaning, and some legal advocacy to convince a court of this point of view.

Below is a list of generic labels.

Generic Labels		
aspirin	escalator	pilates
baby oil	hoagie sandwich	shredded wheat
bath oil beads	jujubes candy	softsoap
brassiere	lite beer	superglue
cellophane	matchbox toys	thermos
cola	monopoly game	the scooter store
copperclad	montessori method	yo-yo
dry ice		

Why, you might ask, is matchbox on this list but not Tinkertoy? Perhaps the public associates Tinkertoy more specifically with one company, whereas matchbox indicates a variety of small toy. Why is copperclad generic but not *Teflon*? Again, *Teflon* is a material that the public associates with a company, whereas copperclad is more of a process.

Let's take one example a little further. Montessori has been ruled a generic term for child care centers that share a general philosophy of early childhood education based on the teachings of Maria Montessori. Even though the American Montessori Society certifies certain Montessori schools but not others, any school is free to use the Montessori name to describe the kind of education it provides.

But what makes the name Montessori generic instead of being descriptive of the philosophy of the school? The bottom line is, what does the public think when it hears such a term? It thinks, "Montessori —that's an educational method." Put simply, because the name describes the kind of service involved, it's generic. By contrast, if the name tells you which service is involved—even if it does so very descriptively— it has the potential for being a trademark.

Does this mean that no Montessori school can ever have a protectable trademark? Not at all. Many protectable marks have generic terms in them. As long as the trademark contains a nongeneric part that distinguishes the service or product from others, in addition to the generic part, then the whole is not generic and may be protected. So to have a protectable name, any Montessori school can simply add a distinguishing modifier to its name, such as Big Trees Montessori School. The modifier, Big Trees, is the nongeneric part of the mark.

Is "Zero" Generic for Soft Drinks and Sports Drinks?

For ten years, Royal Crown opposed Coca-Cola's ZERO trademark. The Trademark Trial and Appeals Board (TTAB) held that the ZERO mark was descriptive, not generic but the Federal Circuit ruled that the TTAB failed to consider if the term is generic when applied to a specific genus of "soft drinks, sports drinks, and energy drinks." If the term, ZERO, is understood "to refer to a key aspect of that genus" then it is generic. (*Royal Crown Dr. Pepper, and Seven Up v. Coca Cola*, 2016-2375 (Fed. Cir. 2018).)

Composite Terms and Slogans

In this section, we discuss composite terms, slogans, designs, shapes, and containers. These types of marks also can be inherently distinctive or ordinary, so we discuss them at some length to help you evaluate what makes them weak or strong.

Composite Terms

These marks can also be called cross-category marks. They are made up of one or more of the different sorts of marks discussed above. Examples are: Shorty's Mean Motorcycles, Gino's New York Pizza, Stormy Weather Home Rehab Services, and Kmart.

Composite marks are not easy to analyze. They usually consist of weak components but still may be considered strong marks. As a general rule, if all the components of a mark are descriptive, the trademark as a whole is also descriptive, and therefore weak. But this is by no means always true. In some circumstances, the kind of service or product a mark is attached to, the context of the mark's use, and even the public's reaction to the mark can result in weak words combining to form a strong mark.

Composites of Whole Words

This type of composite mark consists of individual words with different trademark strengths, like *Gino's Chicago style pizza*, which contains a personal name and a geographic term. The first rule about these types of marks is that the whole name is stronger than the sum of its parts. So, for example, *Risky Business* is a strong mark for an extreme sports supply store. It consists of ordinary words, but they are not used descriptively: that is, "Risky Business" tells you nothing about what the business is or what it hopes to purvey. It's the combination of the phrase and the nature of the service that makes it funny, surprising, unique, and memorable. The same could be said of *pea in a pod* for a maternity store.

Another recent example is a line of books that uses "Don't Know Much About" as a prefix to the subject matter of the book, as in *Don't Know Much About the Civil War*. This prefix is a well-known line from an old Sam Cooke song. The line is sure to grab the attention of most prospective readers over the age of 50 and therefore serves admirably as a trademark, even though it consists entirely of ordinary words. Incidentally, book titles are not, by themselves, entitled to trademark status, but a name that indicates a series of books (*Hardy Boys, Nancy Drew, Dummies*) is entitled to protection.

Other composites of weak elements can also make a stronger whole. For example, Houlihan's Old Place is an effective trademark for a restaurant. This composite of two sorts of names is much more suggestive than simply Houlihan's (which as a personal name can get no trademark protection without secondary meaning), or The Old Place (which, although not necessarily descriptive, is vague and not particularly memorable). Again, taken together, the elements of this mark are more distinctive than either is alone.

On the other hand, Bette's Oceanview Diner, in the Oceanview section of Berkeley, California, is a moderately weak composite mark. That's because it combines two ordinary terms—a personal name and a geographic term—and uses them descriptively. As we have learned, this is not a recipe for a strong mark. Unless such a mark has acquired secondary meaning, the only protection Bette is likely to get is under state unfair competition laws, and then only if a rival restaurant uses a similar mark in the same local area and if customers are likely to be confused by it.

Now consider the composite mark, I Can't Believe It's Not Butter! For the uninitiated, this is a brand of margarine, not just a promotional slogan. It is descriptive because it conveys the information that the product is a close imitation of butter. Furthermore, it's exactly the kind of phrase that a rival margarine producer might want to use in advertising. But the fact that the brand name is a complete sentence with an exclamation point at the end makes it unusual, and even memorable, which means it's distinctive, which gives it legal strength.

Take another example. Colin Moriarity runs a chimney cleaning service called The Irish Sweep. The mark is a composite of descriptive terms, because he is in fact an Irish chimney sweeper. But we bet you'd remember the name. Why? Because it plays on a famous horse race, the Irish Sweepstakes. Also, one word, "sweep," is an archaic term for a chimney sweeper and gives the whole trademark a more evocative feel. To some extent, the strength of this trademark depends on whether many people recognize "sweep" as equivalent to chimney cleaner. If they do, it's descriptive. And yet, people can know what it means and still recognize it as archaic. On the other hand, if the mark's key feature, "sweep," is just a term in common use, then the trademark using it is just descriptive and too ordinary to be a protectable mark, without secondary meaning.

Composites of Elements of Words

These are one-word marks, such as Ultraswim, Bushhawk, and Microsoft, made up of recognizable separate words. These marks are different from those consisting of coined words. Coined terms are wholly new words that mean nothing. But because composite marks contain elements of words, they carry meaning, even if it is only to evoke an image. That makes them more akin to suggestive or descriptive marks than to coined terms. What makes this kind of composite mark strong or weak is not what its elements are, but how it is used. For example, Ultraswim as a trademark for a piece of swimming equipment would be descriptive, and therefore weak. But as used on a shampoo designed for swimmers, it is suggestive, and thus stronger. On the other hand, Bufferin is considered a descriptive mark, even though it's a composite that's not in the dictionary. That's because it's simply a contraction of "buffered aspirin," and the result is too close to the descriptive word "buffered" and the generic term "aspirin" to be distinctive.

Many businesses have latched on to the idea of creating a mark out of word fragments. Unfortunately, they often select terms, at least in computer and technological fields, that are so overused that they have become hackneyed and therefore descriptive. The result is that trademarks using elements like web-, laser-, super-, macro-, -tech, -soft, data-, and compu-, even though they are made up, are not unusual and therefore not very distinctive or memorable. This is really an instance where the early bird got the worm. Only the first companies to pick such marks, like Microsoft, that got in before the genre became so common, had a strong mark even before they built up extensive public recognition.

Slogans

Slogans such as "What Happens Here, Stays Here" (Las Vegas Visitor's Bureau), "What's In Your Wallet?" (Capital One), and "Can you hear me now?" (Verizon) are valuable trademarks because they create indelible consumer impressions. Distinctive slogans can be registered as trademarks with the USPTO. Some slogans are inherently distinctive— that is, by their very nature they create a memorable association with a particular product or service. For example, "Reach out and touch someone" is inherently distinctive because it does not describe phone services; rather, it cleverly suggests or promotes a quality of life enhanced by phone communication. The same is true of "Just Do It," a slogan that connotes the active life without describing any aspect of Nike or its products. An inherently distinctive slogan is usually a pithy, short phrase that does more than inform or describe—it promotes.

By contrast, a slogan such as "Extra Strength Pain Reliever" is merely informative and does not, by itself, distinguish Excedrin from other analgesics. However, even though this particular slogan is not inherently distinctive, it has become distinctive by acquiring a secondary meaning through sales and advertising. This was also the case with "Hair Color So Natural Only Your Hairdresser Knows For Sure" for Clairol hair products.

Some slogans, like some generic terms, can never function as marks. For example, the phrases "Why Pay More!" and "Proudly Made in the U.S.A." were both rejected for registration because they were common commercial phrases and failed to distinguish the goods or services to which they were attached.

If your mark is a combination of a business or product name and a slogan, such as Happy Clown—America's Favorite Ice Cream, the slogan part must meet the same standards for distinctiveness as if the slogan stood alone. For example, if you attempted to federally register Happy Clown—America's Favorite Ice Cream as a mark, the trademark examiner would break the mark into two parts—"Happy Clown" and "America's Favorite Ice Cream." Although "Happy Clown" would by itself probably qualify as a distinctive mark, "America's Favorite Ice Cream" would not be considered distinctive, primarily because it uses a common phrase to describe rather than promote the product. For that reason, the trademark examiner would require you to disclaim the slogan as a condition of having "Happy Clown" placed on the Principal Register. (See Chapter 7 for more on what it means to disclaim a word or phrase.)

Tips for Selecting a Slogan

- Avoid using common commercial phrases, especially if the phrase is part of the trade language ("Think Green" for recycled paper).
- Avoid describing the product or service ("Finest Salsa That Money Can Buy").
- Keep it short and pithy ("Just Do It").
- Use the slogan vigorously on the product, in conjunction with the service and with all advertising.

Sorting Out Trademark Disputes

Most commonly, a business first becomes aware of trademark principles in one of the following situations:

- The business learns—usually from a customer or trade journal—that a competitor is using a copycat name for a similar product or service in a situation where money might be lost as a result of customer confusion.
- The business receives a stiff letter (called a "cease and desist letter") from another company's lawyer alleging that the business is improperly using a trademark that belongs to the lawyer's client and demanding that the business stop using the mark or suffer the legal consequences.
- The USPTO denies the business's application to register a trademark or use its business name as its Internet domain name because the name is already being used.

Few things disturb a business owner quite as much as a dispute over the exclusive right to use the business's chosen name to identify its goods or services. A business's mark is normally intimately linked with the recognition and goodwill the business enjoys in the marketplace. So, a dispute over that mark sets off alarm bells. In this chapter, we provide information on sorting out these types of squabbles.

The world of trademark disputes can be boiled down to three main types of disagreements:

- infringement
- dilution, and
- cybersquatting.

Infringement disputes arise when the simultaneous use of the same or similar marks by two different businesses is likely to confuse customers. Two main issues underlie an infringement dispute:

- Who first used the mark?
- Are customers of the first trademark user likely to be confused by the second user's use of a similar trademark on similar goods or services?

Dilution involves the wrongful use of a famous mark, either by weakening the famous mark or tarnishing its reputation. The primary inquiry in a dilution dispute is whether the mark is famous. If the mark is found to be famous, the owner of the mark has the power to stop certain uses of the mark that dilute the strength of the mark or that harm the mark's reputation for quality.

Traditionally, infringement and dilution were the only two types of trademark disputes. With the rise of the Internet, however, a third main type of dispute arose—cybersquatting.

Cybersquatting involves holding domain names hostage. It happens when someone registers and owns a domain name that mirrors a valuable trademark, for the sole purpose of selling the domain name to the owner of the mark. Cybersquatting was made illegal in the United States in 1999 by the passage of the Anticybersquatting Consumer Protection Act by Congress. Cybersquatting also has been found to violate the rules of the Internet Corporation for Assigned Names and Numbers, the international committee that regulates the Internet. Cybersquatting disputes peaked in the early days of Internet business (1998-2010) and as businesses became more cyber-savvy, they declined.

Your particular trademark dispute could involve one or more of these main types of conflicts. For example, suppose you find that someone has registered your trademark as a domain name and, at the address, has set up a website selling goods that are similar to yours under the same name. You contact the scoundrel, and he says that if you want him to stop, you can just buy the domain name from him. This person is infringing your trademark by using the mark in a manner likely to confuse your customers. He might also be cybersquatting, because he is holding the domain name of your trademark hostage. Thus, it is important to keep in mind that your dispute could involve a number of types of wrongful activity. The first two sections of this chapter deal with infringement, including the main issues underlying infringement and the common types of disputes. The third section covers dilution, and the last section describes cybersquatting and arbitration of cybersquatting disputes.

RELATED TOPIC

If you are not familiar with basic trademark principles, we recommend that you review Chapter 1, "A Trademark Primer," in which we explain trademark basics and the sources of trademark law.

CAUTION

The rules in this chapter are based on the premise that the business complaining of infringement, dilution, or cybersquatting has a valid trademark. If a trademark is not distinctive, has been abandoned, or has become generic, the owner has no rights to enforce and will not prevail in a trademark dispute.

Trademark Infringement

As a general rule, the first user of a trademark in a marketing territory (known as the "senior user") will be able to stop a subsequent user (called the "junior user") from using the same or a similar mark on similar goods and services. Below, we discuss the most important elements a court uses when sorting out an infringement dispute between a senior and junior user.

Customer Confusion

When courts attempt to sort out trademark disputes, the most important issue is often whether customers are likely to be confused. Will the purchaser of goods or services likely be confused as to the source of the goods or services? Or will the purchaser of goods or services likely be confused as to which product or service is being purchased?

EXAMPLE 1: Sally Lee Humbold sells frozen pizzas under the name Sally Lee's Italian. Because customers might think that the pizzas are a Sara Lee product, chances are excellent a judge would prevent her from using the name, even though pizzas and baked goods don't directly compete with each other. In addition, because Sara Lee is used on such a wide variety of frozen foods that it's reasonable to foresee a Sara Lee frozen pizza in the future, Sally Lee's use will likely cause confusion.

EXAMPLE 2: Oliver LaRocque of Sedona, Arizona, markets a brand of garlic-stuffed olives to several Sedona markets under the name Ollie's Stinking Olives. Pollie Jones, an unfriendly neighbor, decides to compete with Oliver and names her product Pollie's Garlic Olives. Because Ollie and Pollie have competing products under marks that could easily be confused by customers (they might mistakenly buy Pollie's olives thinking they are Ollie's olives), the marks legally conflict.

It's fair to say that customer confusion will be a factor in either of these situations:

- You believe that customers might currently confuse your goods or services with a competitor's because of a physical or perceptive similarity between the two marks and an overlapping of marketing territories or channels
- You purposely selected your mark because of its similarity to another mark, and the owner of the other mark is now calling you on it.

The purpose of the customer confusion rule is to ensure that a business that invests in a mark benefits from the resulting goodwill that attaches to the mark and to protect consumers from marketplace confusion that would result from overlapping marks.

Here we briefly discuss three of the main factors in a customer confusion inquiry. These include the similarity of the goods or services, the marketing territories, and the intent of the junior user of the mark. (For a list of all of the factors used to evaluate customer confusion, see Chapter 6.)

Answers Are Hard to Come By

No book can give you the definitive answer as to when customer confusion is likely in a given case. Even an attorney can give you only an educated guess. Many trademark cases involve attorneys on opposite sides who are seriously convinced that customers either would or would not be confused by a simultaneous use of the disputed marks. The bottom line is, it is very difficult to tell who is right in any trademark dispute.

No Proof of Confusion Required for Counterfeit Goods

A district court ruled in 2008 that the likelihood of confusion standard is simplified for counterfeit goods. When goods are classified as counterfeit— that is, unauthorized look-alike goods using another's trademark—there is no need to conduct a factor-by-factor analysis of likelihood of confusion. In a case involving two merchandising companies, the district court ruled that by their very nature, counterfeit goods cause confusion. (*Bravado International Group Merchandising Services v. Ninna, Inc.*, U.S. Dist. LEXIS 78040 (E.D. N.Y., October 6, 2008).)

Similar Goods and Services

As a general rule, a junior user can use a similar mark on dissimilar goods. That's because customers are less likely to be confused when similar marks are used on different goods and services. Therefore, when courts consider the likelihood of confusion in a given case, they ask whether the products or services are similar to each other. If the goods or services in question are not similar or even related, confusion is not likely to result, so no infringement will be found. For example, many similar names coexist legally as marks on different goods, like Cascade, which separately identifies a whiskey, a baking mix, and a dishwashing detergent—all of which are names owned by different companies. Dunhill cigarettes and Dunhill shoes, and Sunkist fruits and Sunkist baked goods, are other examples of identical names used to identify goods in product categories that are sufficiently different to avoid the likelihood that customers will be confused as to the products or their sources. One exception to the principle of similarity of goods is if the senior user is likely to expand into the junior user's product area (see "Bridging the Gap," below).

Similarity of goods is not a factor in dilution cases. (See "Dilution," below.)

Bridging the Gap

Even where the two parties in an infringement dispute have dissimilar products, a court may consider whether consumers would reasonably expect the senior user to expand its product line into that of the junior user. This potential expansion of the product base is referred to as "bridging the gap." For example, a federal court determined that consumers would be likely to confuse the McDonald's trademark for food establishments with McSleep for motel services because the "Mc" prefix has been used so extensively by the McDonald's Corporation that its expansion into non-food categories is expected by consumers. "Bridging the gap" is usually an issue only in disputes involving the mark of a well-known company, such as Microsoft, McDonald's, or Nike, because their customers are more likely to expect an expansion of the company's product base.

Marketing Territories

Two marks come into legal conflict only if they are used in the same market or marketing territory. Trademark law as it exists today developed at a time when geography played an important role in resolving trademark conflicts. If the same trademark was used by different businesses in different parts of the country, there was no likelihood of customer confusion and, therefore, no need for intervention by a court unless and until one of the users expanded into the other user's territory.

In the age of the Internet, the definition of what constitutes a marketing territory is rapidly changing. Because of services such as YouTube, Ebay, Twitter, and other online businesses, more and more goods and services are able to claim a national marketing territory.

Still, many businesses in the United States are local in nature, and unless they are doing business on the Internet and reaching out to a wider customer base, they may reasonably claim only a relatively small portion of a city or county as their marketing territory. For instance, two movie rental businesses using the same name are likely to have completely different marketing territories if one of them is in Pasadena and the other is in Manhattan Beach, cities that are 30 miles apart yet still within the greater Los Angeles area. And even if both businesses have sites on the Internet, their customer bases will almost certainly remain local.

But what if you are operating a business online and offline that can deliver goods or services on a mail-order basis? As the use of the Internet increases, the chances are greater that you and any other user of the same mark in the country or the world will be offering goods and services that will compete in that new territory we call cyberspace. This competition will put your marks in conflict, a state of affairs that can only lead to trademark infringement issues.

Though a marketing territory is impossible to define with precision, it is relatively easy to recognize. It is the rough geographic area from which a business of your type can reasonably expect to attract its customers. If anyone anywhere can order products or services from you through your website, or your mail-order business is advertised in national periodicals, or your products are regularly reviewed in national trade magazines, your marketing territory is the entire country.

Intent of the Junior User: Good Faith/Bad Faith

The outcome of a likelihood-of-confusion analysis is often influenced by the junior user's intent. In an infringement dispute, courts will inquire as to whether the junior user initiated use of its mark in good faith. Good faith involves two issues:

- Did the junior user know of the existing mark at the time it began using the mark in commerce?
- Was the existing mark known in the junior user's marketing territory at that time?

If either question can be answered "yes," then good faith is not present, and the junior user must stop use of the mark upon a challenge by the senior user. Let's take a closer look at these questions.

CAUTION

A fine legal point. Technically, the issue of good faith extends only to whether the junior user knew of the existing mark. The issue of whether the existing mark was known in the junior user's marketing territory is usually discussed in terms of remoteness—that is, the junior user must qualify as a distant user, separated in distance from the marketing territory of the senior user, in order to preserve some rights. We have combined the good faith and remoteness factors under the good faith label for greater simplicity of presentation. It should cause no problem in understanding your rights as we discuss them in this chapter.

How Most Disputes Are Resolved

If you can't tell for sure who is in the right, how should you proceed if you are locked in a trademark dispute? The only way to force a resolution is to go to court and find out what a judge has to say. But lawsuits are expensive. It might be possible—if both parties agree—to resolve the dispute through mediation or by submitting the issue to arbitration. However, most trademark disputes are resolved through negotiation and typically end up with the economically weaker party agreeing to back down, regardless of who was first to use the mark. If, however, the economically weaker party has a strong legal claim to ownership of the mark, the larger company usually will be willing to pay something in exchange for the weaker party's acquiescence. While this might appear to be a cynical view of how trademark disputes get resolved, it's unfortunately just the way things are.

If the junior user knew of the first use before adopting the mark, the dispute will be resolved entirely in favor of the senior user. However, if the junior user didn't know of the first use, that user might have some rights—although limited—in case of a dispute, unless the mark was known to the customers in the junior user's marketing territory. If it was, it won't make any difference that the junior user didn't actually know of the mark. The senior user will be given priority on the ground that its marketing territory was already established when the junior use was initiated. If, on the other hand, neither the junior user's customer base nor the junior user had knowledge of the existing mark, the junior user may continue to use the mark in its current marketing territory, but nowhere else.

The Concept of Reverse Confusion

In traditional trademark infringement cases, the junior user of a trademark confuses consumers into believing that they are buying goods from the senior user. In the 1970s, a federal court created a variation on this principle, known as "reverse confusion." In a reverse confusion case, a senior user can sue a junior user for infringement, even if the public has come to associate the mark with the junior user.

In early 1974, Big O Tires, a midsized regional tire distributor, began marketing a bias, belted tire under the unregistered mark BigFoot. The tire giant Goodyear coincidentally decided to market a radial tire under the BigFoot mark in late 1974. The larger company pumped millions of dollars into its advertising effort, which overlapped Big O's advertising effort to some extent. As a result, the public began coming to Big O asking for Goodyear's tire. Angry and disappointed, consumers suspected Big O of stealing the idea from Goodyear.

But, in fact, Goodyear had become aware of Big O's prior use of the same mark midway into its marketing plans and had tried unsuccessfully to buy the mark from them. Nevertheless, Goodyear continued to use the mark. In this case, Goodyear spent so much money on advertising in such a short period of time (including expensive Super Bowl advertisements), that the public associated Goodyear with the trademark "Big Foot" and believed that Big O was the junior user (and thus an infringer). This resulted in a judgment for Big O of $4.7 million and the debut of a new type of infringement based on reverse confusion.

As we'll see in the rest of this chapter, the junior user will be presumed to know about any mark that is on the Principal Register. This, of course, means that searching the federal trademark register is always wise before adopting and using a new business name or other device as a service mark or trademark. Although courts will not presume that a junior user ought to know of an unregistered mark just because it is well known, we are fast becoming a global village, and more and more marks can be said to have nationwide exposure. And, as we explained above, if the senior user can establish this fact, the senior user will prevail over the junior user.

Priority of Use: Who Used the Mark First?

As a general rule, if a legal conflict erupts between two businesses using the same or a similar mark, a judge will consider the business that first used the mark as the owner of the mark, who will prevail against the junior user. Therefore, it should not be surprising that most of the rules that we use in this chapter for resolving trademark disputes turn on the question of who used the mark first. "Use" is either:

- actual use in commerce, or
- constructive use through an application to the USPTO to register the mark on an intent-to-use basis.

Actual Use in Commerce

A mark is in actual use when it is attached to a product that is being sold in the marketplace or is used in a business's marketing materials for the purpose of selling the business's service. Actual use must be a commercial use, not simply a token use to obtain trademark priority. (See Chapter 7 for more on what constitutes actual use.)

Constructive Use (Intent to Use)

A person can apply to have a mark placed on the federal Principal Register on the basis of intended use—even though the mark is not yet in actual use. The date an intent-to-use application is filed with the

USPTO is considered the date the mark was first used, assuming the applicant goes on to actually use the mark at a later time and files the necessary documents to place the mark on the Principal Register. This type of use is termed a constructive use because it is created by the law rather than by real events.

> **EXAMPLE:** In March 2019, Paul begins distributing a line of distinctive jewelry (bracelets and earrings) called Cleopatra Designs. Unbeknownst to him, Oscar had previously applied to register Cleopatra Designs on the Principal Register in connection with his intended use for a line of women's clothing. Even though Paul actually began using the mark first, Oscar will have priority based on his intent-to-use application, as long as he puts the mark into actual use and completes the registration process.

Priority of use is a crucial question in infringement disputes and often turns on the status of the mark (federally registered or unregistered) and the territory. We discuss various priority scenarios below.

Domain Names and Trademark Infringement

If a domain name is used as a trademark—that is, it's being used to identify goods or services in the marketplace—it is subject to the same rules regarding infringement as any other trademark. If the domain name is not being used for a commercial purpose, then it would not be subject to a claim of infringement.

> **EXAMPLE 1:** Jonah Ishmael creates a personal website with the domain name Ahab.com. Jonah uses the site to post pictures of his family, some poems he writes from time to time, and a statement of his political philosophy. Because Jonah is not using the term "Ahab" as a means to identify goods or services or an entity doing business on the Web, the domain name isn't being used as a trademark. If Ahab Tours, a business that offers whale-sighting tours and a collection of historically famous whale art, decided to accuse Jonah of trademark infringement, Jonah would respond that because he isn't using the name as a trademark, there is no likelihood of customer confusion and therefore no infringement.

EXAMPLE 2: Jonah becomes interested in whale art and decides to open a cyberart gallery featuring contributions by various contemporary artists who feature whales as part of their art. At this point, there is little question that Jonah is using ahab.com as a trademark, and Ahab Tours would have a basis to sue for trademark infringement.

As with any trademark owner, a domain name registrant uses its new domain name at its peril if it doesn't first conduct its own thorough trademark search. If someone else is already using the proposed domain name as a mark, and the context of the two uses would likely lead to customer confusion, the business seeking to register the domain name should pick a different name.

 FREQUENTLY ASKED QUESTION

Can we copy logos to save money on company shirts?

"I work for a corporation that requires us to wear uniform shirts with the company logo. The boss supplies the shirt at what we believe to be an elevated cost, and we were wondering about creating the shirts on our own. Would it be legal for an embroiderer to use the company's trademark to produce the shirts for us, or would we need to obtain permission to use the trademark?"

The short answer to that question might be in your company's employee handbook (assuming your company has one), in the "uniforms" section. In other words this would be a case of your employment rules taking precedence over trademark rules.

Even if your employee handbook has rules on where to buy your shirt, you should still check your state's labor laws. Many states regulate costs of company uniforms or other dictated dress codes. For example, in California, your employer must pay for your uniforms or other required on-the-job dress.

If your employee handbook doesn't address the issue and your state laws don't help, then the question is: "Does it violate your company's trademark rights to create unauthorized T-shirts with the company logo?" We're pretty sure you will run into a problem. We think your unauthorized use of the corporate logo would likely cause confusion (and if done badly, it might dilute the company mark, assuming the mark is famous). And of course, unlike other types of infringement, the company is very likely to learn about the infringement.

Defensive Maneuvers

In addition to disproving priority and likelihood of confusion, a junior user accused of infringement has other potential defenses, most of which have been introduced in previous chapters. Below, we provide a brief summary of the available defenses, most of which will apply to infringement, dilution, and cybersquatting. For more information on these legal defenses, review the related chapters or, in the case of more obscure defenses, such as laches, estoppel, unclean hands, trademark misuse, and fair use, consult an attorney versed in trademark law. The possible defenses include:

- **The mark is descriptive.** A junior user can defend its use if a senior user's mark is weak and lacks secondary meaning (see Chapter 1).
- **Abandonment.** A junior user can defend its use if the senior user has abandoned its mark (see Chapter 8).
- **Genericness.** A junior user can defend its use if the senior user's mark has become the generic term for the goods or services (see Chapter 8).
- **Trademark misuse.** A senior user may be prohibited from recovering damages for infringement if it has violated antitrust laws or fraudulently obtained registration.
- **Fair use.** Can you run an ad for your company selling dishwashing machines that refers to the "joy of dishwashing" without infringing the trademark "Joy" as used for dishwashing soap? Yes. A company may defend its use of a trademarked term (owned by someone else) when the term is used to describe products or services. In 2005, the U.S. Supreme Court ruled that the fair use defense can be asserted even when the use results in consumer confusion.
- **Free speech and parody.** In certain cases, a junior user can defend its use under First Amendment principles. For example, the makers of the video game, "Grand Theft Auto: San Andreas" were permitted to parody an East Los Angeles strip club, "The Play Pen," (referred to as "The Pig Pen" in the game). The court permitted the parody under First Amendment principles noting that artistic use of a mark is permitted when: (1) the use has artistic relevance to the work at issue (the video game), and (2) it doesn't explicitly mislead consumers as to the source of the mark or the work. (*E.S.S. Entertainment 2000, Inc. v. Rock Star Videos, Inc.*, 547 F.3d 1095 (9th Cir. 2008).)

Defensive Maneuvers (continued)

- **Unclean hands.** A junior user can defend its use by claiming that the senior user acted in bad faith.
- **Estoppel.** A junior user can defend its use if the junior user has justifiably relied on the senior user's behavior.
- **Laches.** A junior user can defend its use if the senior user waited too long to file the lawsuit.
- **Trade dress and product configuration defenses.** In cases of trade dress infringement, two defenses are particularly important: functionality and distinctiveness. If a senior user's trade dress or product shape is functional or lacks distinctiveness, it is not protectable and cannot be infringed (see Chapter 1).

Determining Priority in an Infringement Dispute

Now that you have some general information about trademark disputes under your belt, it's time to get specific. The rest of this guide will give you a pretty good idea of who has legal priority over the use of a mark in case a legal conflict develops between you and another business. But to apply the discussion to your particular situation, you will need to answer the following questions:

- Is the other mark registered on the Principal Register?
- If the other mark is federally registered, what is the date of registration?
- Was the federal registration based on actual use or intended use?
- When was the other mark first used, if the federal registration is based on actual use?

If you don't know the answers to these questions, you can get them through a trademark search. (See Chapters 4 and 5 for more on trademark searching.) Below are some of the common scenarios involving a determination of priority.

Your Unregistered Mark Conflicts With a Federally Registered Mark

Here we discuss who has priority in case your mark is *not* registered on the Principal Register and the other mark is.

Assume you receive a letter from a lawyer informing you that your unregistered mark conflicts with another mark that is on the federal Principal Register and demanding that you cease and desist from any further use of your mark. The fact that the other mark is on the federal Principal Register while yours is not might be pretty scary. And in truth, the other mark's owner holds some high cards. But as you will see from the discussion and examples below, you might still have some rights, depending on the timing of events.

If You Are the Senior User

If you used your mark before the other party used its mark and can prove it, you have a right to continue using your mark based on the rules discussed below.

In your existing marketing territory

You may use your mark in the same part of the country where you were using it when the junior user applied for federal registration.

> **EXAMPLE:** You opened the Date Palm Restaurant in Kansas City in 2015. In 2017, a chain, Date Palm Inn, opens hotels in four Southeastern states. The Date Palm Inn mark was registered with the USPTO that same year. In 2020, the Date Palm Inn chain discovers your Date Palm Restaurant, and a lawyer sends you a cease and desist letter, citing the Date Palm Inn's registration of the Date Palm Inn mark on the Principal Register and demanding that you immediately change the name of your restaurant. You may continue operating in Kansas City on an exclusive basis under your existing name because you were the senior user of the Date Palm mark in that territory.

In all other areas

You may claim the exclusive right to use your mark in all other parts of the country if you can prove that the owner of the registered mark actually knew of your mark's use at the time of the registration application and failed to disclose this fact to the USPTO. The deliberate failure of a junior user to disclose the existence of a conflicting mark can lead the USPTO to cancel the trademark registration.

If the owner of the registered mark didn't know of your unregistered mark's use, however, the registered owner will be given priority (that is, the right to exclusive use) in all other parts of the country where a later simultaneous use of the two marks would create the likelihood of customer confusion.

EXAMPLE 1: Continuing the above example, assume you can prove that the Date Palm Inn owners actually knew of your use of the Date Palm mark prior to 2017, the year it registered the mark with the USPTO. This fact would allow you to continue using the Date Palm mark in Kansas City on an exclusive basis and to expand your right of exclusive use to the rest of the country, even to the four states in which the Date Palm Inn currently operates. That's right. If the owner of the Date Palm Inn trademark knew of your mark's prior use on a restaurant when it registered its mark and failed to disclose the fact to the USPTO, you would most likely be able to have the federal registration canceled, and the company would have to change its name if you decided to enter its marketing territory.

EXAMPLE 2: Now assume that you can't show that the Date Palm Inn knew of your mark prior to the time it registered its mark. In this situation, you can remain in your current marketing territory, but the Date Palm Inn will have the exclusive right in the future to use the mark in any other part of the country it chooses to expand into, even if later you have expanded into that area ahead of the Date Palm Inn. This is because the Date Palm Inn's registration was in good faith (neither it nor the USPTO knew of your mark, and your mark wasn't known in the Date Palm Inn's original marketing territory).

If the Registered Owner Is the Senior User

If the owner of the federally registered mark is the senior user (either by actual use or constructive use through the filing of an intent-to-use application), the following rules apply.

In your marketing territory—without knowledge of the senior user's mark

If neither you nor the customers in your marketing territory had knowledge of the senior user's mark when you first used your mark, and your first use was before the senior user's mark was placed on the federal trademark register, you can continue using the mark in your marketing territory on an exclusive basis.

> EXAMPLE: Modifying our Date Palm example, after the Date Palm Inn chain starts operating in 2013 and, without knowledge of that earlier use, you open the Date Palm Restaurant in Shreveport, Louisiana, in 2014, an area in which the Date Palm Inn is unknown. The Date Palm Inn then places its mark on the Principal Register in 2015. You may continue using the Date Palm mark on an exclusive basis in your marketing territory. This territory is probably only Shreveport, but could be argued to include nearby areas of Louisiana.

In your marketing territory—with knowledge of the senior user's mark

If you knew that the senior user's mark was in use prior to yours, or if the senior user's mark was known in your marketing territory even though you didn't know of it, the senior user may expand into your marketing area and force you to stop using your mark. If you first used your mark after the senior user's mark was registered, knowledge of the senior user's first use will be presumed. In either situation—actual or presumed knowledge—you may continue using the mark only in your area until the senior user decides to expand its market into your area. Then you will have to stop using the mark altogether. Otherwise, you might be liable for large damages as a willful infringer.

EXAMPLE: Assume that you know of the Date Palm Inn's registered mark when you open your restaurant in 2019, and the Date Palm Inn can prove it. (In this situation, all the Date Palm Inn would have to do to prove your knowledge is to show that their federal registration occurred prior to your first use of the mark.) If and when the Date Palm Inn decides to expand into Shreveport, you can be forced to change your restaurant's name. Your name could also be at risk if the Date Palm Inn expands into any area that draws its customers from Shreveport, because Shreveport would then be part of its marketing territory, and it would have a right to exclude your use of the name. If the Date Palm Inn launches an advertising campaign designed to draw customers from all over the country—or creates and maintains a site on the Internet—its marketing territory will be national, even if it doesn't move into Shreveport.

What If You Are Asked to Change Your Mark?

Many marks used by small and medium-sized businesses can be modified without significant damage, especially when there is time to plan the change. While some customers might be lost when the business introduces a new mark, most will continue patronizing a business or using a product that has served them well. And a name change can even provide a convenient opportunity for a business to draw attention to its goods or services by announcing the change in the media and direct mail pieces. Also, if a big company is challenging a small company's mark, the small company can often get a lot of mileage in the media if it emphasizes how it has been bullied into making the change.

In other marketing areas

If the other company is the senior user but did not federally register the mark until after you started using your mark, the other company will have priority wherever the two marks come into conflict.

EXAMPLE: You start using the Date Palm mark before Date Palm Inn's registration of the mark. You can use the mark as long as it doesn't come into conflict with the Date Palm Inn's registered mark. In territories where conflicts do develop, you will have to withdraw, and Date Palm Inn will be able to use the mark.

If the registered mark is being used nationwide and you started using your mark after the date of registration, you could be subject to heavy damages as a willful infringer.

EXAMPLE: A San Francisco Bay Area comedy group puts together Lawdaudible, a series of podcasts about lawyers and their bizarre professional speech patterns. The comedy group places Lawdaudible on the Principal Register and seeks national bookings. A year later, without actual knowledge of the California group, you start a similar act in Vermont. Because the California Lawdaudible group first used and federally registered the mark prior to your use, you have infringed the California group's service mark. And, because that group's registration gave you "presumed knowledge" of its prior ownership of the mark, you will be considered a deliberate infringer if the matter gets to court, even though you actually were unaware of the prior use.

Your Unregistered Mark Conflicts With Another Unregistered Mark

Conflicts between unregistered marks are the most common types of business name disputes that small businesses are likely to face. These types of disputes are usually between business names that are also being used as service marks. They are usually governed by state trademark and unfair competition principles, which are designed to combat customer confusion in the marketplace and protect the first user of a mark because of fairness considerations. However, you may also invoke the federal unfair competition provision of the Lanham Act if one of the unregistered marks is used in interstate, interterritorial, or international commerce.

As a general rule, the more distinctive the mark in issue, the more willing the courts are to find the likelihood of customer confusion and protect the senior user's right of exclusive use.

> EXAMPLE 1: You open a day care center for the elderly in St. Paul, Minnesota, named The Seniors Club. Several years later, in the same part of town, another day care center called The Senior Citizen's Club opens its doors. You will be able to get the second business to change its name if you can convince a court that customer confusion between the two names is likely—that is, the other center is likely to draw from your customer base—and that your name is distinctive enough to protect. In this example, however, the court might find that your name is ordinary and weak rather than distinctive, and rule that The Senior Citizen's Club is different enough to not risk customer confusion (because customers attach little significance to weak marks). It is also possible that a court could invoke the state's unfair competition laws (see Chapter 1) to order the second user to alter its name in some respect to protect your business.

> EXAMPLE 2: Since 2015, you have sold your ready-to-eat barbecued ribs to a number of Missoula, Montana, supermarkets under the mark Clarence's Rockin' Ribs. They are very popular throughout the Missoula area. In 2021, Steve starts selling Steve's Rockin' Ribs to markets in a three-state area, including Missoula. You can force Steve to adopt another mark for his ribs, since "Rockin'" as applied to ribs has become a distinctive mark over time and belongs exclusively to you, at least in the Missoula area.

If your mark and another unregistered mark have been used in different geographical areas without coming into conflict, but then simultaneously (more or less) come into conflict in a new marketplace, unfair competition principles may resolve the conflict in several ways. Dual use may be authorized with certain conditions attached:

- One of you might prevail on the grounds that the area in question was a natural part of your original marketing territory.
- One of you might be ordered to change your mark somewhat to distinguish it from the other.

> **EXAMPLE:** You start a sign business in Newport, New Hampshire, that specializes in magnetic signs for trucks (they stick to the truck panel). You call your business Sign Up but don't register the name, even though you do a little business across state lines with Massachusetts and Vermont customers. Within the next several years, other entrepreneurs start similar sign businesses in San Francisco, Dallas, Chicago, and Miami, using the same name. They also don't register the name. Because the name is used in different marketing areas, there is no legal conflict.

What happens, however, if you and one of the other businesses simultaneously decide to operate a national online mail-order sign business under Sign Up? Because both businesses would be in conflict everywhere in the country, and because both businesses would be in conflict with the other regional users of the name, even if those regional businesses weren't on the Web, clearly something would have to give.

Theoretically, of the two companies that were marketing the sign service online, the senior user would have priority and could stop the other Web-based company (the junior user) from using it. As for the other regional companies, it's possible that they also could be prevented from further use of the mark on the ground that when they adopted their names, they did so at the risk of being forced to stop using them if and when one of the senior users decided to go national.

Traditionally, these regional companies might have been able to continue using the mark in their regions on an exclusive basis, but because of the way the Internet works, regional markets are becoming less feasible.

The solution ultimately favored by the courts in this type of scenario is to order an adjustment of one of the marks so that both businesses can continue their operations with minimum disruption and without creating customer confusion. But if it appears that the junior user is deliberately trying to piggyback on the senior user's goodwill, the junior user may be forced to choose a completely different name and even pay some damages as punishment.

Your Federally Registered Mark Conflicts With Another Federally Registered Mark

Here we explain your rights when your mark and the other mark are both registered on the federal trademark register. On occasion, two marks that have each been placed on the federal trademark register come into conflict with each other in the marketplace. The USPTO might approve two identical or very similar marks for registration because:

- The registration applications state that the marks will be used on goods and services in different classes, and it appears that the goods or services won't compete in the marketplace and aren't related enough to create a likelihood of customer confusion.
- An examiner honestly, but mistakenly, believes the two marks are sufficiently different to eliminate the likelihood of customer confusion.

As stated earlier, once a trademark is placed on the Principal Register, its owner is presumed to be the rightful nationwide owner of the mark. When you have two presumed rightful nationwide owners claiming title to the same (or a very similar) mark, the conflict can be difficult to unravel. Sometimes, this can be accomplished in proceedings brought in the USPTO itself, while other times, court action may be necessary. The result will depend on why and when the conflict developed.

EXAMPLE 1: You use the mark TeeTotaler on a brand of fruit juice, while Julie uses this same mark on her chain of vegetable juice bars. Although unlikely, it is possible that you and Julie will both get your respective marks onto the federal trademark register because one is a trademark being used on a juice product sold in supermarkets while the other is a service mark used on a health drink service business. Though there is no direct competition between you and Julie, it's easy to see that consumers might think that your product is really being marketed by Julie's business or vice versa. In short, customer confusion is likely if the mark is used in a context where consumers might be exposed to both uses. In this instance, you and Julie might be restricted by a court in the use of your marks to your respective and distinct marketing territories, and whoever can prove first use might be given priority when expanding to areas where the mark is not yet in use.

EXAMPLE 2: Assume now that you originally applied to register the mark TeeTotaler for use on a brand of biodegradable golf tee but later changed your mind and used the mark on your fruit juice line. Because your use of the mark was vastly different than described on your registration application, your registration would not count when resolving the conflict with Julie's mark. In other words, Julie would be treated as the registered owner of the mark, and you would be an unregistered owner for purposes of resolving the dispute.

Your Federally Registered Mark Conflicts With an Unregistered Mark

You're in a strong position if your mark is registered and the other mark is not. You are presumed to be the nationwide exclusive owner, and the other owner is definitely on the defensive. However, the fact of registration doesn't mean you'll win a trademark dispute. It depends, as with other disputes over your mark, on the principles discussed below.

If You Were First to Use the Mark Anywhere and Registered the Mark Before the Second Use Began

If you used your mark and federally registered it before the other business used its mark, you have the exclusive nationwide right to use the mark and can stop the other owner from using the mark in any geographic market in which you decide to market your goods or services. If you maintain a website or otherwise nationally market your goods or services, you can require the other business to stop using the mark immediately. However, if your use is local or regional and the other user's local or regional market is completely separate from yours, you will have to wait until you are on the verge of entering the other market to require your competition to adopt another mark.

EXAMPLE: You are a Rhode Island publisher of travel guides that specialize in the Northeastern states under the mark Yankee Visions. You successfully obtain a federal registration for the mark. Two years later, you learn that a travel guide publisher for the Northwestern states began using the same mark for its publications after the date of your registration, but has not registered the mark itself. Because of your registration, the USPTO and the courts will deem a competitor to have had knowledge of your mark's previous use, which means you can force the competitor to stop using the mark if and when you decide to market your guides in the Northwest. But if your marketing efforts remain restricted to one portion of the country—say the Northeast and Eastern Seaboard—and the competitor stays in the Northwest, you won't win a trademark infringement case unless you can show that you want to enter the Northwestern market and are prepared to do so.

As we emphasize throughout this material, the Internet and other national marketing techniques make a collision between marketing territories more and more likely.

If You Were First to Use the Mark Anywhere But Registered the Mark After the Second Use Began

Here is yet another scenario: The other user started to use the mark after your first use but before you registered your mark. In this situation, the rights of the second (junior) user will turn on the answers to these two questions:

- Did the junior user have actual knowledge of your mark's use?
- Was your mark known in the junior user's marketing territory?

If the junior user had actual knowledge of your mark's previous use (and you can prove it), the junior user has no rights and must give way if and when your mark expands into its marketing territory.

And regardless of the junior user's knowledge, if your mark was known within the marketing territory from which the junior user's customer base was being drawn, the junior user will have to give way if you decide to use your mark in that territory.

> EXAMPLE: Continuing our Yankee Visions example, assume you can show that the Northwest competitor knew of your mark before it started using its mark. If you later decide to market your guides in that area, you can force the competitor to drop the name. Similarly, if your guides were being distributed in the Northwest prior to the junior use, you can force the competitor to stop using the mark if you now decide to market the guides in the Northwest.

If, however, neither your competitor nor its customer base knew of your Yankee Visions mark when the competitor's use of the mark began, the competitor can continue using the mark in the Northwest and freeze you out of that market. This result stems from the fact that the competitor would be deemed to be a good-faith junior user in a remote marketing territory.

If the Other Owner Used the Mark Both Before You Used It and Before You Registered It

If the owner of the unregistered mark was the senior user, you may continue to use your registered mark in the marketing territory where you are currently using it if the following two statements are true:

- You didn't know of the senior use when your use began.
- The senior use was largely unknown in your marketing territory when your second use began.

EXAMPLE: You invent a digital device that attaches to a tennis racquet handle and keeps track of the score during the game. You attach the trademark Total Recall to your invention and register it with the USPTO. You begin test marketing in California and Arizona. Unknown to you, Felix was already using this same mark on a product designed to keep track of the score of ping pong games he is test marketing in Miami, Florida. Because you had no knowledge of Felix's earlier use when you registered the mark, and because knowledge of Felix's device had not penetrated into your test markets, you may continue using it in your test markets. However, Felix has the exclusive right to use the Total Recall mark in Miami, and you would be excluded from marketing your invention in that area.

If you didn't know of the other mark's previous use when you registered your mark, you will have priority over the senior user in all areas of the country that the senior has not yet entered. In other words, you will be rewarded for promptly registering your mark, and the senior user will stay frozen in his or her territory.

EXAMPLE: Assuming that you didn't know of Felix's use of the Total Recall mark when you registered, Felix's use will be limited to the Miami area, and you can market your product nationwide.

Dilution

Famous trademarks acquire additional rights compared to their not-so-famous cousins. Owners of the famous marks can halt another company's use of a similar mark if it would weaken or degrade the famous mark, regardless of whether there would be customer confusion. This rule, known as dilution, permits the owner of a famous trademark to sue because the famous trademark will lose its distinctive character and legal strength if degrading or diluting uses of the mark are permitted. Also, according to some courts, the public would necessarily be confused by such use in that they would expect the business owning the famous mark to be associated in some way with the second user.

In 1996, Congress added the Federal Trademark Dilution Act (FTDA) to the Lanham Act, prohibiting activity that leads to the dilution of famous marks. (42 U.S.C. § 1125(a)(c).) Ten years later, Congress enacted the Trademark Dilution Revision Act of 2006, which provided additional remedies and clarified and reinforced provisions of the 1996 act. About half the states also have antidilution laws.

Federal Dilution Laws

The Federal Trademark Dilution Act provides that the owner of a famous mark will be entitled to protection against a junior user's commercial use of a mark if the use begins after the mark has become famous and causes dilution of the distinctive quality of the mark. The act defines dilution as "the lessening of the capacity of a famous mark to identify and distinguish goods or services" regardless of whether the dual use would likely confuse customers. So, to prevail under the FTDA, a senior user must prove all of the following:

- The senior mark is famous.
- The senior mark is distinctive.
- The junior use is commercial in nature.
- The junior use began after the senior mark became famous.
- The junior use lessens the senior mark's capacity to identify and distinguish goods and services.

The Trademark Dilution Revision Act of 2006 establishes that the owner of a famous mark does not need to demonstrate actual or likely confusion, competition, or actual economic injury when the owner seeks to stop dilution.

What Makes a Mark Famous?

The Trademark Dilution Revision Act of 2006 defines a mark as "famous" if it is widely recognized by the general consuming public as a designation of the source of the goods or services of the mark's owner. The revision generally does away with a concept known as "niche fame" in which a mark owner argued that its mark was not well known by the public but was famous within its niche industry. The law instructs courts to consider "all relevant factors" when determining whether a mark is famous, including:

- the duration, extent, and geographic reach of advertising and publicity of the mark
- the amount, volume, and geographic extent of sales of goods or services offered under the mark
- the extent of actual recognition of the mark, and
- whether the mark was registered on the Principal Register.

None of these factors is more important than the others, and the list is not exclusive. As a practical matter, this means that courts have discretion in deciding whether a particular mark is famous for purposes of protection under federal law. Federal law, by associating fame with the factors listed above, has created analogies between fame and distinctiveness. (We covered distinctiveness in Chapters 3 and 9.)

Blurring and Tarnishment

In 1996, Hasbro, the owner of the trademark Candyland (used on children's games) stopped a company providing adult sex services and products from using the name "Candyland" for its website. (*Hasbro Inc. v. Internet Entertainment Group, Ltd.,* 40 U.S.P.Q.2d 1479 (W.D. Wash., 1996).) In 1999, the National Basketball Association stopped a rap music company from using an altered version of its logo featuring a silhouette of a basketball player holding a gun. (*NBA Properties v. Untertainment Records LLC*, 1999 U.S. Dist. LEXIS 7780 (S.D. N.Y., 1999).)

In both cases, it was unlikely that consumers would confuse the junior and senior users' goods, yet both Hasbro and the NBA prevailed because the junior use tarnished and blurred their famous marks. The Trademark Dilution Revision Act of 2006 clarified the importance and meaning of these two types of dilution. In general, blurring occurs when someone chips away at a mark's distinctiveness. Tarnishment occurs when someone chips away at a mark's reputation for quality.

Blurring a Mark's Distinctiveness

Part of what makes a famous mark actually famous is that it stands out in the minds of consumers for one product or service. So when a similar mark appears that makes the mark *less* distinctive because of an unrelated association, blurring has occurred. Bacardi, for example, stands out in the minds of consumers as a source of rum. The use of the same mark for a jewelry store blurred its power and distinctiveness for consumers. In the same way, a Boston restaurant's use of Tiffany's blurred the consumer connotation with the famous jewelry store. In each of these cases the goods/services did not compete, and no likelihood of confusion existed. Rather, the question was whether the distinctive and famous mark in each of those cases was made less distinctive by the second use of the mark—a question decided in favor of the famous mark owners.

When legislators enacted the Trademark Dilution Revision Act of 2006, they defined "dilution by blurring" as an association arising from the similarity between a mark or trade name and a famous mark that impairs the distinctiveness of the famous mark. When determining whether blurring has occurred, a court can consider factors such as:

- the degree of similarity between the marks
- the degree of inherent or acquired distinctiveness of the famous mark
- the extent to which the owner of the famous mark is engaging in substantially exclusive use of the mark

- the degree of recognition of the famous mark
- whether the second user of the mark or trade name intended to create an association with the famous mark, and
- any actual association between the mark or trade name and the famous mark.

Parody and Satire Are Not Dilution

Satirical uses or parodies of marks might appear as obvious examples of tarnishment. Nevertheless, our Constitution's First Amendment (as well as the Trademark Dilution Revision Act of 2006) protects satires and parodies that clearly aren't using a mark to market goods or services commercially. In addition, federal law excludes from its definition of dilution the use of a famous mark for noncommercial purposes, such as parodies, comparative advertising, consumer product reviews, and news coverage. For example, in one case dealing with a website titled "Bally sucks," a U.S. District Court ruled that because the website was operated for a noncommercial purpose—to criticize Bally's (a health club)—the use of the Bally mark did not offend the Lanham Act's antidilution provisions. (*Bally Total Fitness Holding Corp. v. Faber*, 29 F. Supp.2d 1161 (C.D. Cal., 1998).)

In another case, the Louis Vuitton Company's dilution claim was undone by a parody defense. The defendant sold tote bags that read "My other bag is a Louis Vuitton" (as well as other high-end fashion designers). Louis Vuitton sued, claiming the tote bags diluted the Vuitton mark. In an unpublished opinion, the Second Circuit upheld the summary judgment against Louis Vuitton because the tote bags, though they mimicked LV, were clearly "a joke on LV's luxury image." (*Louis Vuitton Malletier, S.A v. My Other Bag, Inc.* 674 Fed. Appx. 16 (2016).)

Tarnishment, or Injury to Reputation for Quality

The Trademark Dilution Revision Act of 2006 defines "dilution by tarnishment" as an association that harms the reputation of a famous mark. Tarnishment is usually some unsavory association. For example, the phrase "Where there's life there's Bud" could be tarnished by an insecticide maker's use of the phrase, "Where there's life, there's bugs." In other words, an association with bugs can tarnish a beer maker's image.

Courts are especially likely to find tarnishment—and trademark owners are more likely to sue—when the offending marks are attached to products that are "unwholesome or unsavory." Examples of marks that have been stopped under this prong of the dilution theory are the fake American Express card shown with a condom that said, "Never Leave Home Without It," the use of Dallas Cowboy cheerleader uniforms in a pornographic film, and the "Enjoy Cocaine" poster that used a script and coloring identical to Coca-Cola's.

Federal Dilution Defenses

The Federal Dilution Act and Trademark Dilution Revision Act of 2006 provide that certain actions won't give rise to dilution under federal law including:

- **Comparative advertising.** It is not dilution to use a famous mark in comparative advertising. However, the mark should not be altered or modified.

  > EXAMPLE: In a comparative advertisement, a tractor company modified and animated the John Deere "leaping deer" logo and gradually diminished its proportional size in a comparative advertisement. This was determined to be dilution and was not excused under the comparative advertising defense. (*Deere & Company v. MTD Prods. Inc.*, 34 U.S.P.Q.2d 1706 (S.D. N.Y., 1995).)

- **Noncommercial use of a mark.** There is no dilution unless the junior use is commercial. Because all uses usually have some commercial aspect, a "commercial use" is considered to be one that is primarily to help sell a product or service.

  > EXAMPLE: A pro-life minister used the Internet domain name plannedparenthood.com and included a misleading opening screen entitled "Welcome to the Planned Parenthood Home Page." The site provided antiabortion information and services. A court determined that the use was commercial because it was primarily being used to identify the source of a product or service, not simply to criticize Planned Parenthood. (*Planned Parenthood v. Bucci*, 42 U.S.P.Q.2d 1430 (S.D. N.Y., 1997) affirmed 152 F.3d 920 (2d Cir. 1998).)

- **News reporting.** Using a trademark in journalism or news commentary is exempt from dilution claims.
- **Federal registration.** There can be no dilution under state or common law if the junior user has a federally registered mark, which provides even more incentive to federally register a mark.

Relief for Dilution

Prior to passage of the 2006 Trademark Dilution Revision Act, the main relief the courts were authorized to provide was injunctive relief—that is, a court would order a company to stop further dilution of the famous mark. Now, a successful trademark owner in a dilution case can collect monetary damages (and attorneys' fees) in cases of willful dilution. This provides the antidilution law with considerable punch, because dilution cases are often willful—deliberately intended to trade off of and blur or tarnish a famous mark—for example, McClaim and McSleep in the case of McDonald's. In summary, do not get caught trying to ride on the coattails of a famous mark belonging to someone else. It might end up costing you a bundle.

State Trademark Dilution Laws

Since 1996, dilution lawsuits have relied primarily on the federal dilution statute (rather than state laws). The Trademark Dilution Revision Act of 2006 further enhanced the power of federal registration by barring any state dilution claims against the owner of a federally registered mark. In other words, after 2006, the owner of a federally registered mark cannot be sued for state dilution claims. The states that have dilution statutes are: Alabama, Arizona, Arkansas, California, Connecticut, Delaware, Florida, Georgia, Hawaii, Idaho, Illinois, Indiana, Iowa, Kansas, Louisiana, Maine, Massachusetts, Minnesota, Missouri, Montana, Nebraska, New Hampshire, New Mexico, New York, Oregon, Pennsylvania, Puerto Rico, Rhode Island, Tennessee, Texas, and Washington. An additional five states recognize the dilution doctrine under cases decided by their courts: Kentucky, Maryland, Michigan, New Jersey, and Ohio.

You can find the dilution statutes of most states by visiting the All About Trademarks website (www.ggmark.com) and clicking on "State Trademark Laws."

Cybersquatting

A cybersquatter is a person who registers a well-known trademark as a domain name hoping to later profit by selling the domain name to the trademark owner. The practice of cybersquatting began when most businesses were not savvy about the commercial opportunities on the Internet. Some entrepreneurial souls registered the names of well-known companies as domain names—the now familiar www.companyname.com—with the intent of selling the names back to the companies when they finally realized the economic potential of the Internet. Panasonic, Fry's Electronics, Hertz, and Avon were among the "victims" of cybersquatters. Opportunities for cybersquatters are rapidly diminishing, because most businesses now know that registering and protecting their domain names is essential.

Keep in mind that, in some instances, a conflict over the use of a domain name is due to an honest mistake and might not involve the degree of bad faith required to prove cybersquatting. When we talk about cybersquatters, we are referring to those who deliberately stake out domain names with the intent of profiting from the use of someone else's trademark. (For more on domain names, see Chapter 2.)

Federal Anticybersquatting Consumer Protection Act

The new federal anticybersquatting law authorizes a trademark owner to sue an alleged cybersquatter in federal court and obtain a court order transferring the domain name back to the mark's owner. In some cases, the cybersquatter must pay money damages. To stop a cybersquatter, the mark's true owner must prove all of the following:

- The domain name registrant had a bad-faith intent to profit from the mark.
- The mark was distinctive at the time the domain name was first registered.
- The domain name is identical to or confusingly similar to the mark.
- The mark qualifies for protection under federal trademark laws— that is, the mark is distinctive and its owner was the first to use the mark in commerce.

If the person or company that registered the domain name had reasonable grounds to believe that the use of the domain name was fair and lawful, it has not acted in bad faith. In other words, if the accused cybersquatter can show a judge that it had reason to register the domain name other than to sell it back to the trademark owner for a profit, then a court will probably allow the person or company to keep the domain name.

The Long Reach of the ACPA

One nice feature of the federal Anticybersquatting Consumer Protection Act (ACPA) is that a trademark owner does not need to obtain personal jurisdiction over the cybersquatter. Personal jurisdiction refers to the court's right to bind the defendant (in this case, the cybersquatter). In order to establish personal jurisdiction, courts normally need to find that the defendant lives or works within the court's geographic reach, or took some action (such as signing a contract) within that area.

Because cybersquatters can operate from any place in the world, let alone any state, it could be difficult to obtain personal jurisdiction over most of them. No problem: Courtesy of the ACPA, the trademark owner can proceed under a legal principle known as "in rem," in which the court focuses on the "thing" (the domain name) and not its owner. The court can then declare that it has control over the property—the domain name—and the court can award the domain name to the winning party. In a 2002 case involving Harrods and 60 domain names registered by an Argentinean company, this approach was expanded when a federal court ruled that courts could use the in rem provisions when considering claims of infringement and dilution against cybersquatters. (*Harrods Ltd. v. Sixty Internet Domain Names*, 302 F.3d 214 (4th Cir. 2002).)

Congress has developed some guidelines for the courts to use in looking for bad faith. They include:

- Is the registrant using the domain name to divert users from the mark owner's site to another site, where customer confusion is likely to result or the mark's reputation for quality is harmed? In other words, is the domain name being used in a way that negatively affects the mark owner's website or the value of its trademark?
- Has the registrant offered to sell the domain name to the mark owner without ever legitimately using the domain name on a commercial website?

- Has the registrant provided false or misleading contact information to the domain name registrar or failed to keep this information up to date?
- Has the registrant registered multiple names that are the same as or confusingly similar to distinctive marks? In other words, is there an apparent pattern of cybersquatting?
- Is the mark in question famous or highly distinctive? The more distinctive or famous the mark, the more the court is likely to conclude that the registrant acted in bad faith.

The Uniform Domain Name Dispute Resolution Policy

All domain name registrars require their registrants to agree that any dispute between a trademark owner and a domain name registrant over the right to use the domain name will be submitted to arbitration. The arbitration system was created and is run by the Internet Corporation for Assigned Names and Numbers (ICANN), the same international organization that is now in charge of domain name registrations in general. The arbitration system is referred to as the Uniform Domain Name Dispute Resolution Policy, or UDRP.

Under the UDRP, the arbitrator can order the domain name transferred to the trademark owner if the owner proves all of the following elements:

- The domain name at issue is identical or confusingly similar to the trademark in question.
- The registrant has no rights or legitimate interests in the domain name.
- The domain name was registered and/or is being used in bad faith.

Similar proof is required to prevail in a lawsuit based on the federal Anticybersquatting Consumer Protection Act. The ICANN procedure can be used against domain name registrants inside and outside the United States.

Here's a look at each of the three elements that must be established by trademark owners in order to prevail under the UDRP:

- **The domain name is confusingly similar to the trademark.** The trademark owner must prove ownership (the exclusive right to use the mark) and must also establish that the domain name is confusingly similar to the mark. The "identical or confusingly similar" test will probably be satisfied if the domain name at issue is preventing the trademark owner from using its mark as its own domain name.

- **The domain name registrant has no rights or legitimate interests in the domain name.** To prove this element, the trademark owner must show three things:

  - The registrant has never tried to use the domain name (or a similar one) in connection with legitimate commerce, on or off the Internet.

  - The registrant was never generally known by the domain name, even if the name wasn't used in commerce as a trademark.

  - The registrant isn't using the domain name in any legitimate way. A legitimate use would, for example, consist of use on a non-commercial website that engages in satire or criticism. But the use would not be legitimate if the registrant's actual intent is to divert consumers from the mark owner's website or business location, or to tarnish the mark by lessening its reputation for quality.

- **The domain name registrant acted in bad faith when registering or using the domain name.** This one is really the flip side of the second item. The registrant has acted in bad faith if any of the following is shown:

  - The registrant acquired the domain name with the intent to sell it back to the mark's owner—or to a competitor of the mark's owner—for profit. This wouldn't apply to those who acquire domain names with the intent to auction them off to the highest bidder later, because such a plan is not directed specifically at a mark's owner.

- The registrant has a pattern of acquiring domain names with the intent to block their use by legitimate trademark owners. That is, the registrant is a true cybersquatter.
- The registrant is a competitor who acquired the domain name primarily to disrupt the mark owner's business.
- The registrant is using the domain name to attract users to the registrant's website by creating customer confusion. (See Chapter 6 for more on the likelihood of confusion.)

For example, bad faith was demonstrated where a cybersquatter purchased domain names in anticipation of a major bank merger. The defendant in that case registered domain names that combined elements of Bank of America and Merrill Lynch—for example, bofaml.com. In its defense, the defendant argued that it had never profited from the sale of any of the domain names. The court rejected that argument, finding that the defendant earned considerable sums by "parking" the domains—that is, by generating pay-per-click revenue. (*Webadviso v. Bank of America Corp.,* S.D. N.Y., No. 09-cv-05769-DC, 2/16/09.)

Using the UDRP

To initiate and prosecute a complaint under the UDRP, a trademark owner chooses a dispute resolution "provider," which is an organization approved by ICANN. So far, ICANN has approved four providers. Each provider has its own supplemental rules for dispute resolution, which you must follow in addition to ICANN's procedural rules (available on the ICANN website at www.icann.com). You can check them out at each provider's website, which can be located through the ICANN website (select "Domain Name Resolution" at the bottom of the page). These sites offer detailed discussions about how to navigate the UDRP.

To begin a case, the mark owner sends a complaint to the provider, setting out specific facts that prove the three elements discussed above. As a general rule, the mark owner (the initiator of the process) will be responsible for paying the provider's fees, although the fees will be shared if the domain name registrant asks for three arbitrators instead of allowing the case to be presented to a single arbitrator.

After reviewing the complaint for completeness, the provider will send the registrant a copy of the complaint, along with directions on how the registrant can respond and by what deadline. The domain name registrant can continue to use the name until the dispute is resolved.

The provider will usually issue a decision based solely on the complaint and the response. If unhappy with the decision, either party may go to court. However, if the decision is in the trademark owner's favor, the domain name will be transferred to the owner unless the registrant promptly files a lawsuit to prevent it.

When It's Cheaper Not to Fight

The fees for the UDRP procedure are typically in the $1,000 to $1,500 range for one arbitrator adjudicating one domain name. For that reason, many cybersquatters offer domain names at a price in the $1,500 range. It's a tough call, especially when a trademark owner prefers not to pay off a speculator. But there's an appealing aspect to buying off the cybersquatter—you get the domain name immediately and without any guesswork as to the final decision. If you do pay off a cybersquatter, make sure you use an online escrow service to avoid any funny business.

 FREQUENTLY ASKED QUESTION
Infringing Domain Name?

"My wife recently started selling her handmade jewelry in a local shop and asked me to help her get an email address. Knowing a thing or two about the Internet, I decided the best way to do this was to register a domain name and then set up a Google account to host the mail. Everything was fine and then last week, I received an email from a law firm saying that the domain I had registered was an 'infringing domain' because it incorporates their client's trademark. Now they say that I have seven days to respond, transfer the domain name to them, and provide a sworn affidavit attesting that I ceased selling any goods that infringe on their trademark. If my wife's little side business is not related to anything that the other company sells, do they have any right to order me to turn over my domain name? I didn't think that anyone could come after you for just requesting a domain name."

The short answer to your question is "More information is needed." You're correct about the basic trademark principles—if you're not likely to confuse consumers, then there's no trademark infringement. That's why, for example, different companies can use Arrow as a trademark for shirts and staplers and electronics (although only one company can have the domain name, www.arrow.com). Under another theory (dilution), a company with a famous trademark can stop you from using a similar trademark even if the goods or services are not related—for example, Microsoft could stop a company from selling Microsoft Vista dog food.

If you acquired the domain name in bad faith—for example, you intended to hold the domain hostage in the hopes of selling it back to the trademark owner—then the trademark owner can pursue you in federal court under anti-cybersquatting laws (or can force you to arbitrate under international domain name rules). We're not saying you're doing any of these things (and it appears from your letter that you're not). But if the big company is hassling you, we're not sure where that will lead. Keep in mind that there's a financial benefit for the law firm if you fight. (Law firms love people who drive up their billable hours.) We don't want you to cave to a bullying law firm, but we're not sure of all the facts in your case and we're not sure that a $10 domain name is worth the hassle. (Unfortunately, it would cost you at least ten times that amount for a half-hour consultation with a trademark attorney.)

The Odds of Success Under ICANN

In a review of over 14,000 proceedings involving domain names brought under the ICANN UDRP system, more than 85% of cases were decided in favor of the petitioner (which is almost always the trademark owner). (Many of these cases were defaults—the other side failed to respond.) The ICANN website offers a searchable database of all decisions rendered under the UDRP as well as a statistical summary. You can access this information at www.icann.org/udrp/udrp.htm.

When Someone Infringes Your Mark

S uppose that you encounter another business that is using a name for its product or service that is identical or very similar to yours, and you feel you are losing customers and profits as a result. How can you stop them?

Before you go on the Internet to find an attorney, take a minute to look at how and whether a lawsuit is likely to solve your problems.

If, at the end of this chapter, you still feel you want to litigate, then grab that phone—after reading Chapter 14 for suggestions on finding a lawyer—and good luck!

What Litigation Costs

Start by reminding yourself that lawsuits usually cost a bundle—a big bundle. Typically, lawyers who handle trademark cases charge $250 per hour and up. It doesn't take a genius to understand that if you hire a lawyer for a month's worth of work (surely a low estimate for a full-blown trademark fight) it will cost you close to $40,000. From start to finish, a trademark infringement lawsuit costs between $120,000 and $750,00 for each party.

Perhaps these figures will help you understand why we have great respect for the ancient curse that says, "May you be involved in a lawsuit in which you know you are right."

How Much Is Your Mark Really Worth to You?

Given the horrendous costs, it pays to carefully consider whether a particular dispute over a mark is worth litigating. Let's look at this issue a little closer.

Can You Recover Attorneys' Fees in State Court?

If your mark is being used in one state only, your infringement suit will most likely be brought in state court, and the laws of your state will determine how attorneys' fees will be paid. In most states, the courts will not require the loser of a lawsuit to pay the winner's attorneys' fees. Or stated bluntly, even if you win, you'll have to pay your own lawyer and risk ending up in the poorhouse. However, in a few jurisdictions, such as Colorado, North Carolina, Wisconsin, and Puerto Rico, the prevailing party is awarded attorneys' fees as a matter of course, and in a few others (Alaska, Iowa, Maine, Minnesota, Missouri, Oklahoma, Texas, and Washington), the court has discretion to award attorneys' fees, usually in exceptional cases only.

Can You Recover Attorneys' Fees in Federal Court?

If you use your mark across state, territorial, or international boundaries, you will probably end up in federal court. Federal law permits an award of attorneys' fees to a victorious plaintiff, but only in exceptional trademark infringement lawsuits. To qualify as such a case, the defendant must have acted willfully, intentionally, or maliciously. In 2014, the Supreme Court ruled on a similar attorney fee provision in patent law and redefined "exceptional" as "simply [a dispute] that stands out from others with regards to the strength of a company's case or the 'unreasonable manner' in which they made it." This ruling gave judges more leeway to decide when a litigant is entitled to attorneys' fees. (*Octane Fitness v. Icon Health and Fitness and Highmark v. Allcare Health*, 134 S.Ct. 1749 (2014).) It was unclear whether the Supreme Court's holding also applied to trademark law, especially in light of a Ninth Circuit ruling that held otherwise. However, in an *en banc* (11-judge court) ruling, the Ninth Circuit held that it agreed with "the majority of our sister circuits" that *Octane* had "altered the analysis of fee applications under the Lanham Act." (*SunEarth Inc. v. Sun Earth Solar Power Co.*, F.3d (9th Cir. 2016).) The bottom line is this: Unless you are dealing with a clear case of bad intentions, don't count on attorneys' fees in federal trademark litigation.

How Treble Damages Can Help Pay Attorneys' Fees

Although courts have discretion to award attorneys' fees in unusual cases, they are required to award treble damages (triple your actual damages)—and order the defendant to disgorge any profits caused by the infringement—in cases where willful infringement is proven. Willful infringement cases therefore have the potential to generate a considerable sum of money above and beyond what the true trademark owner actually suffered from the infringement. Because the goal in most cases is to stop the infringing use—which will happen if the court finds that infringement occurred—the trademark owner can use the damages to pay its legal fees. Trademark lawyers understand this and might therefore be willing to represent plaintiffs in willful infringement cases and defer payment of their fees until the case settles or they get a judgment. This arrangement is not a contingency fee, because the fee isn't based on the outcome of the case. It's merely a method of deferring fees until the plaintiff is in a better position to pay them.

Litigation Short of Trial

A common strategy is to file an infringement lawsuit and ask the court to grant emergency relief until the case can be fully litigated and decided in a trial. This type of relief—termed a preliminary or temporary injunction—typically orders the alleged infringer to stop using the mark in question pending the outcome of the lawsuit. Because, as a practical matter, getting slapped with an order of this type puts the alleged infringer in an untenable position from the outset, the party bringing the suit can usually secure a settlement on very favorable terms.

To obtain a preliminary injunction, you must convince the court of two basic facts:

- Your business will suffer irreparable injury if the emergency relief isn't granted.
- Your case is strong enough on the face of things to make it probable that you'll win if and when a trial eventually takes place.

The first fact is very easy to show. The mere existence and daily use of an infringing mark robs the owner of its customer base and the goodwill that the mark represents. Because there is no real way to measure the loss of goodwill in monetary terms, judges usually consider this type of injury to be irreparable as a matter of course.

The second fact—probable success—is another matter. Here the judge has to be convinced that the plaintiff's infringement claim is strong enough to warrant depriving the infringer of the right to use its mark without first holding a trial. Some judges are more willing to do this than others, and it is impossible to predict whether an attempt to get a preliminary injunction will be successful.

Once the court rules on a request for a preliminary injunction, the losing party has a powerful incentive to settle. When the judge has prohibited the defendant from using the disputed mark pending trial, it means that the judge has found it probable that infringement has occurred. That's a pretty good clue as to what the eventual judgment will be. Furthermore, the injunction leaves the defendant little choice but to adopt a new mark to use during the pendency of the case. These facts usually drive the defendant to cave in, unless the plaintiff is seeking treble damages and refuses to settle the case (which is unusual).

Conversely, if the plaintiff loses in its attempt to get an injunction, it means that the defendant will be able to continue using the disputed mark during the pendency of the trial, and that the judge has concluded that infringement probably hasn't occurred. Many plaintiffs are willing to settle because the bottom line analysis—the cost of a full trial versus the potential of losing in trial—favors the predictability of a settlement. Such settlements can "legitimize" the defendant's use of the mark through licensing agreements.

Because the outcome of the preliminary injunction request usually results in an early termination of the case, the legal fees associated with the normal trademark case often are much less than if the case were fully litigated. But they can still be high—routinely between $10,000 and $25,000—because it takes a lot of preparation to successfully handle the preliminary injunction proceeding.

The Mental State of the Infringer Matters in Trademark Litigation

When an infringer knew about the first user's mark at the time the infringement began, he or she will be considered a willful infringer. This knowledge is either something that is proven in a trial (such as continued use by the infringer after having been notified of the infringement), or is presumed to have existed if the mark was on the federal Principal Register when the infringement began and the owner of the infringed mark properly used the registration notice with the mark (an ® or a statement to the effect of "This is a registered trademark belonging to Rackafrax Company"). Once the willful label attaches to an infringer, the infringer can be forced to pay treble damages and surrender its profits made from the goods or services carrying the infringing mark.

On the other hand, if the infringer is considered innocent—the business had no knowledge of the infringed mark—the plaintiff-owner usually cannot collect treble damages or the defendant's profits, and in some cases cannot even prevent the infringer from continuing to use the mark, at least in a limited geographical area.

Beware of Being Right

Whether a preliminary injunction and settlement are obtained or the case goes to trial (tack on at least another $50,000), using the courts to resolve an infringement claim is usually very costly. But many otherwise reasonable people insist on it. Why? Probably for the same reason many otherwise reasonable people behave like pit bulls in divorce proceedings—emotional attachment to being right. And remember the old curse we discussed earlier—many lawyers get rich because of clients trying to vindicate their positions.

Sadly, the question of who has the right to use a mark often affects people in an emotional way that doesn't always serve their long-term economic interests. They get addicted to their mark, and as with any addiction, they may be willing to spend way beyond what common sense would dictate to keep it. In fairness, it can be hard to know if your urge toward litigation is motivated by ego, principle, or a sense of outrage when the name of your business (which might even get confused with the existence of the business itself) is threatened. If you're unsure of your attorney's motivation, get a second opinion, if possible.

Negotiate—Don't Litigate

Negotiation offers you lots of options that litigation doesn't. For one, it's cheaper; for two, it's quicker; and for three, you help fashion the outcome. It gives you a chance to devise a solution both parties can live with rather than wasting time and money trying to allocate fault.

How do you get a purported infringer to the negotiating table? As mentioned, some would advocate a lawsuit to seek a preliminary injunction for that purpose. But that is obviously an expensive method of getting the defendant's attention. And, of course, whenever litigation is started, there is a risk that it will gain too much of its own momentum and escalate.

A better way to start is to send the infringing business a letter, stating the problem and proposing that you negotiate. The fact that both parties must bear the high cost of a lawsuit might even become part of the common ground on which you build a solution, instead of a threatening weapon. But you need not give up all your weapons at once. Even if you don't plan to litigate (or would only do so reluctantly), your opponent doesn't need to know that at the start.

On the other hand, negotiation necessarily implies give and take. You have to decide what you are willing to give up and what you need in exchange. For example, must the infringer change the mark completely, or can you live with it if the infringer makes modifications? Do you need the matter resolved right now, or are you able to provide the infringer with some time to make necessary changes? What's the maximum you're willing to spend on this dispute? How much would you pay to buy the right to use the name, even if you think you already own it?

Insurance for Trademark Litigation

If you are reading this chapter prospectively and have not yet suffered any harm by another's infringement, check into the option of trademark litigation insurance. This is a rider that can be purchased to augment the coverage of a comprehensive general liability policy, which all businesses have. The rider offers "advertising injury coverage," which is the coverage that courts have interpreted to extend to trademark and unfair competition claims. Coverage like this is not yet available in all states, but California, Illinois, and Minnesota permit it, among others. Even if you don't have such a rider, there's no harm in asking your agent whether the risk is covered by your regular policy.

You might even consider this: How many dollars would it take for you to change your mark?

Let us add our personal perspective: Changing your mark need not be a disaster. In fact, depending on who you are and how you do it, it might hardly cause a ripple.

For example, a very popular Berkeley restaurant had to change from Fat Albert's to Fat Apple's as a result of an ownership dispute. It never lost a beat in the local restaurant scene and still has 45-minute waits out the door for weekend breakfasts.

Even Nolo, the publisher of this book, has had to change its marks from time to time. Its computerized will-writing program, now called *WillMaker*, was originally called *WillWriter*. After Nolo had launched the product and established it in the market, it received a series of threatening letters from a New York law firm stating that Will Writer was a federally registered trademark belonging to a company in New York City that registered wills and printed will forms.

Admittedly, Nolo should have done a more thorough check of the mark before using it, but even if it had, it might have gone ahead and used the mark, because the other company's use was different. It did not make wills or sell computer programs. In addition, the other company's trademark was weak, because it described what the product did— provide a form on which to write a will.

Nolo's first response was to write back to each of these letters, which arrived about six months apart, to say basically, "Don't bother us; you don't have a case." However, the letters kept coming, and the idea of having to defend a suit on the other coast—even one that it might win—loomed as a waste of time and money. So against the almost universal advice of friends and business associates ("You'll lose thousands of sales, confuse your customers, and make yourself a commercial laughingstock"), Nolo cast about for a new name, and came up with *WillMaker*, a mark that was similar to the old one but with a crisper edge to it.

The company notified everyone they could of the change and placed ads that prominently featured their company's trademark (Nolo) to provide continuity. A few trade journals noted the change, but the upshot was that nobody cared one way or the other.

WillMaker flourished, despite the change, perhaps because of Nolo's reputation, perhaps because it was a distinctive product in a narrow field, and perhaps because Nolo's main competitors didn't yet have a comparable product on the market. Still another possibility is that there was nothing all that distinctive about the name WillWriter in the first place.

Whether a name change would be similarly trouble free for another company depends on the business, the product or service, and the nature of competition in that field. It might be harder for a fledgling business than for an established one to weather a change in a trademark. A main concern would be how expensive and feasible it would be to notify all the customers, distributors, or suppliers who would need to know about the change. And for manufacturers of products, the expense of restamping the products or obtaining new containers could be prohibitive.

Certainly, the Internet complicates this issue. If you are using the mark in dispute as your Internet domain name, the cost and hassle associated with changing a domain name (such as getting other websites and search engines to change their links to your site) could be so great that changing it might not be a viable option for you.

If you are a small business in a specific market, you can probably contact your client list either through mailings, in-store flyers, or targeted advertising. You will be surprised how much conversation the name change will generate.

If you are a larger business, perhaps you can make the name change into a news story that industry magazines or newsletters would mention, either as a story or in a column. You might make the name change the basis of a new and different ad campaign. While it does appear a little careless to have adopted someone else's mark, most customers can relate to the misfortune of inadvertently stepping on the toes of some unknown business in a distant city. So it need not ruin your reputation at all. In fact, it may be a shot in the arm. In the metaphor of the self-help therapy industry, you got lemons, so get busy selling lemonade.

How to Handle an Infringer

Regardless of how your dispute is finally resolved, you will want to take some or all of the following steps when dealing with infringement of your mark. Obviously, because no two infringement situations are exactly the same, you'll need to adopt and change these steps to fit your needs.

Step 1: Discover the Registration and Use Status of Your Opponent's Mark

Your first order of business is to discover:
- whether the mark is federally registered and/or registered in your state
- when the other mark was first used anywhere, and
- when the mark was first used in a manner that came into conflict with your mark.

You can get the registration information by doing a trademark search in the manner described in Chapter 5. If the mark is federally registered, your trademark search can also tell you the date the owner claimed it was first used anywhere. To find out when the mark was first used anywhere and in a manner that conflicts with your mark, you will need to do a little investigation.

Step 2: Read Chapter 10, "Sorting Out Trademark Disputes," to Discover Who Is the Infringer

That chapter explains who has priority when two marks conflict in the marketplace. It will teach you which mark owner—you or your opponent—has the stronger legal case. This information is vital in the negotiation process, because your negotiating position is likely to be far different if you are clearly the top dog from a legal point of view than if you are just as clearly the infringer.

Step 3: Research as Much as You Can About the Business With Which You Will Be Negotiating

You need to know its size, financial health, ownership, market share, products or services, and, most importantly, its litigation history. Obviously, this information will help greatly when you have to decide on a negotiating strategy. For example, if the company is on shaky financial ground, you can play harder ball than if they have a robust balance sheet. And if the other business has gone to court before on this or another mark, you should be very cautious in your dealings with it, unless you too are willing to invest a great deal in your favorite law firm. Also, you need to know what kind of product the company makes and how and where they market it to properly evaluate its use of the mark in question. If its use is an obvious case of infringement (identical mark, closely related markets) and you have legal priority, you have a much stronger negotiation position than if it is a borderline case.

These pieces of information are not as hard to find as you might think. The computer databases that are available for your use (see Chapters 4 and 5) contain a great deal of information on businesses, in the form of business descriptions and revenue.

For either large or small businesses, litigation history is available in state or federal court files, which are public records and increasingly available on the Internet. (See Chapter 14 for more on Internet resources.) They are usually indexed by the names of the parties. In this way, you can discover most cases that the business has initiated (assuming it filed in the county in which it operates), but not necessarily those in which it has been sued (which is also relevant to its financial health) because that could have happened anywhere.

You can do all this yourself or hire a lawyer, business investigator, or information broker to do it for you. Of course, you may not need all the pieces of information we've discussed, so just obtain the facts you think are relevant or you can afford.

Public Access to the Federal Court Database

Public Access to Court Electronic Records (PACER) is an electronic public access service that allows users to obtain case and docket information online from federal appellate, district, and bankruptcy courts. Access to case information costs $0.10 per page. The cost to access a single document is capped at $3.00, the equivalent of 30 pages. The cap does not apply to name searches, reports that are not case specific, and transcripts of federal court proceedings. If your usage does not exceed $15 in a quarter, fees are waived. For more information go to: www.pacer.gov.

Step 4: Write a Letter

The next step is to write a letter to the infringer (sometimes called a "cease and desist" letter). This is what attorneys do; if you are more comfortable having an attorney write the letter, find one to do it. (See Chapter 14, "Help Beyond This Book.") Write to the owner or president or whatever person is the highest level of management for which you can obtain a name, address, and phone number.

The letter should be businesslike and firm but not accusatory, and it should state the key facts in a clear and concise way. "It has come to our attention that your business is using [_____] trademark or trade name in [_____] manner" is an acceptable way to start. State your claim that your mark has legal priority—including the nature of your business, how you use the mark, when and where you began using it, when you registered it (if you registered it), and whatever else you think is relevant. Then state that you believe the use of the mark by the other business infringes on your rights, and firmly ask the business to stop its use of the mark.

> **CAUTION**
> **Let sleeping dogs lie.** If the material in Chapter 10, "Sorting Out Trademark Disputes," indicates that you are clearly in the wrong, the worst thing you can do is bring the conflict to the opponent's attention. Here, the old adage of "Let sleeping dogs lie" is very appropriate.

Make sure you provide the other business with enough information, including, for example, a copy of your registration certificate, so it can independently verify the basic facts that you allege and respond appropriately. But you need not exhaustively recount your business history or give extraneous information. Whatever you put in this letter must be accurate, because it can be used against you later in court if you subsequently offer evidence or make claims that are inconsistent with the letter's contents.

> **CAUTION**
> **Don't set deadlines or make threats.** Refrain from setting deadlines or making threats of litigation in this first letter. If you do, you will feel compelled to take some action if the business doesn't comply with your demand, in order to show that you are serious. And it is likely that your action will be premature. Better to give yourself room and expect to write a second or even a third letter before giving your opponent an ultimatum.

Another potential downside to threatening litigation might surprise you. The infringing party could interpret your threat as a statement that litigation is inevitable. Hoping to get the jump on you, it might file an action for declaratory judgment in its local federal court. If that court is in a different part of the country than you are, you will be at a significant disadvantage and will no longer have a choice about whether to litigate or use some other, less costly method of resolving the dispute.

Sample Letter

[Date] _____

[Infringer's Name] _____
[Infringer's Address] _____

_____

Dear [Infringer's Name],

It has recently come to our attention that your business is using [describe the infringer's trademark] trademark or trade name on [service or product]. We believe that this use infringes on our ownership rights in [describe your trademark] trademark. We first became aware of your mark [state the circumstances—e.g., at the 2009 Weaving Trade Show in Albuquerque].

We have the exclusive right to use this trademark based on the following facts: [Now list the bases of your rights—federal or state registration numbers, date of first use, date of registration, federal or state registration numbers, on what products or services you use it, and in what geographical areas. Attach copies of your registration papers and samples of how you use the mark.]

We believe that your use of this mark is likely to confuse our customers [and suppliers] and will damage the good reputation that our [goods, services] have enjoyed until now. Therefore, we request that you cease any further use of this mark.

Please reply with an acknowledgment of the ownership right that we claim in this mark and a proposed timetable for halting its continued use.

Sincerely,

[Your name] _____
[Your title] _____
[Your address] _____

_____

When There Is No Actual Conflict—Yet

Sometimes the use of a mark that—on its face—overlaps with another mark does not result in a conflict in the marketplace. For instance, if you own the national right to a mark but are using it only in the Southwest, an infringing use in the Northeast won't affect you. However, if you later decide to move into that region, the dual use of the marks would be very confusing. Also, as we indicated in Chapter 8, it is important for you to police the use of your mark so it won't be weakened by overuse or considered abandoned.

If you discover an infringer whose use of the mark isn't in conflict with yours right now, consider writing a letter pointing out that you own the exclusive national right to the mark and intend to enforce your right when you start using your mark in that part of the country. You need not demand that their use cease immediately. If you never expand in that direction, no harm is done. But if you do want to start using your mark in that part of the country, you've at least preserved your right to force the other user to adopt a different mark at that time. The Internet makes these kinds of situations less likely because use on the Internet often immediately creates a national or international market.

Step 5: Negotiate

This process can be as flexible as you wish it to be. The outcome is limited only by the creativity of the negotiators. But once you reach an agreement, it makes sense to be aware of all its ramifications. For instance, if you agree to let the defendant continue using the mark in exchange for a license fee, your pocketbook might be in better shape, but you might lose control of the mark (it will be considered abandoned) if it no longer serves its function of uniquely identifying the source of goods or products in the marketplace. On the other hand, if the mark is being used on entirely different goods and services and no customer confusion is likely, it might not hurt to assign the defendant all rights to the mark for that other purpose in exchange for cash. The bottom line is, have a trademark attorney read over the agreement before you commit to it.

Here are five possible negotiation strategies:

1. **Bluff your opponent into thinking you are about to file a lawsuit.** This strategy works best when your mark is federally registered and the other mark is not, and it appears that your opponent began to use its mark after your mark's registration date. The reason for this is that under these facts, your opponent is legally liable to you for treble (triple) damages, the profits they realized from the sale of the goods or services carrying the mark, and possibly your attorneys' fees. You might scare your opponent into stopping use of the mark entirely. Or you might just get your opponent to agree to modify its mark. Of course, you must be prepared to spend a fair amount of energy (and attorneys' fees if you use an attorney as part of your bluff) to convince the other side that you're not bluffing. And you ought to be prepared to go to court if the bluff fails.

> ⊘ CAUTION
> **Don't put your bluff in writing.** If you send a written letter threatening litigation, you run the risk of finding that letter as an exhibit on a complaint for declaratory judgment filed by the other party in a federal court far from your place of business. If you decide to threaten litigation as part of your bluff, make sure you do it orally unless the infringing party is located in the same part of the country as you are and, as mentioned, you are prepared to litigate if the other party calls your bluff.

2. **Compromise on use.** A good fallback position is to suggest an agreement on territory or manner of usage—such as, "You can have the name in Nebraska and Kansas, and I'll use it in Oklahoma and Texas," or "You use it only as a trade name for your crockery-manufacturing business, and I'll use it only as a mark on my line of stuffed animals."

3. **Modify the marks.** Perhaps you and the other party can make a few modifications to the way your marks appear to distinguish each more clearly from the other. For instance, you change your mark from the Homemade Cafe to Homemade Diner, and the other party changes from HomeMade Cafe to the Home Cooking Cafe.

4. **Offer a buy-out.** You could offer to buy your opponent's rights in the trademark. It might seem unfair to have to pay the other party to change its name, but that might solve your problem in an economical way, considering that you are saving everyone the cost of litigating over the trademark.

5. **Offer to sell your mark.** Conversely, you might even sell your rights to the mark to the other party for a handsome sum in exchange for adopting a new mark. The money could serve as a much-needed capital infusion, as well as the means to afford an advertising campaign around your new name.

Step 6: Consider Other Dispute Resolution Options

Traditionally, trademark-related disputes have been settled by negotiation or ended up in court before a judge or jury. However, in recent years several alternative, informal, and private ways to handle these and other types of disputes have become popular. They are faster and cheaper than traditional court processes; they often produce superior solutions; and, because of their informality, they don't necessarily require representation by an attorney.

Unless a written contract provides that a particular approach to dispute resolution must be followed, these alternative approaches are usually voluntary, which means all parties have to agree to use them. However, some courts are beginning to require litigants to first attempt one of these alternative approaches before the judges allow the cases to proceed to a trial.

The two common ways to resolve disputes are arbitration and mediation. Although arbitration and mediation are often mentioned in the same breath and are frequently confused with each other, they are actually quite distinct in the way they approach disputes. The most striking difference between them is that in arbitration you still present your case to a third party (called an arbitrator) for a decision, while in mediation you enlist the aid of a third party (called a mediator) to help you and the other party reach a voluntary solution, without any particular resolution being imposed on you. Think of mediation as structured negotiation. Let's take a closer look at how each approach works.

Arbitration

In arbitration, the parties agree to select and pay one arbitrator—or a panel of three arbitrators—to hear the dispute. If the parties want three arbitrators, the usual selection method is for each party to select its own arbitrator and then leave it to these arbitrators to pick the third.

As a general rule, arbitrators come from panels put together by large national organizations like the American Arbitration Association (www.adr.org) and JAMS (Judicial Arbitration and Mediation Services; www.jamsadr.com). However, smaller, more specialized groups of arbitrators might also be available in your locality (check the Internet).

Although many of the arbitrators offered by the larger organizations are attorneys or retired judges, many are not. It is up to the parties to decide whether their particular dispute should be decided by someone with a legal background or someone who perhaps has a more appropriate expertise—such as a contractor in a construction dispute, or an insurance broker if the dispute involves the interpretation of an insurance contract. In the case of a trademark dispute, it is likely that you will, in fact, want at least one experienced trademark lawyer to arbitrate the dispute.

The rules used to choose the arbitrator(s) and conduct the arbitration are usually provided by the organization you have selected to arbitrate the dispute. For instance, it is common to agree to have the arbitration conducted under the "rules of the American Arbitration Association."

Unlike court, arbitration can proceed very rapidly and conclude in a matter of weeks, although several months is more common. Obviously, the length of time a particular arbitration will take depends on the complexity of the dispute and the eagerness of the parties to push the matter forward. Even if one party to an arbitration is in a hurry, it is usually possible for the other party to slow things down.

As a general rule, the arbitrator's fees are paid equally by the parties, by agreement. These fees can be considerable. If the arbitration takes only an hour or two of the arbitrator's time, the fees might be reasonable. However, if the arbitration takes days, then the expense will mount accordingly. The arbitrator's fees are in addition to what each side is paying its attorney, if it decides to use one.

Probably the biggest issue in any arbitration is whether the decision of the arbitrator(s) will be final or if the loser will be permitted to go to court for a regular trial.

This issue is typically decided by the parties when they agree to arbitrate, unless the matter has already been addressed in a contract. Because a decision to arbitrate usually is based on a wish to resolve the dispute quickly and cheaply, most parties opt to make the arbitrator's decision final, meaning that it can be entered in a court with competent jurisdiction as a final, unappealable judgment, which makes it enforceable.

> **CAUTION**
>
> **Beware of binding arbitration.** The finality of an arbitration can be troublesome if the arbitrator strays far from established legal principles in arriving at the decision. Under most court rules dealing with binding arbitration, an arbitrator's departure from the law cannot be challenged in an appeal. For that reason, businesses that believe they are legally in the right are often reluctant to turn their fate over to a decision maker who is, in essence, unconstrained by the law. Better to pay costs of litigation, these businesses believe, than create the risk of a runaway and crippling arbitration result.

If you are asserting your trademark rights against the owner of a domain name, you may invoke nonbinding arbitration under rules established by an international body known as ICANN. See Chapter 10 for more on how this procedure works.

Mediation

The central idea underlying mediation is simple. Most disputes can be settled in a manner that is at least minimally satisfactory to each of the disputing parties—the colloquial win-win scenario. Mediators use a number of techniques to identify potential points of agreement and help the parties move toward these points on a voluntary basis.

If the mediation does not produce a settlement, the parties are free to pursue other avenues, including litigation.

The same organizations that provide arbitrators usually also furnish mediators. Also, a number of individual business attorneys and law firms are beginning to offer mediation services to people engaged in business disputes—including disputes over trademarks. The best way to locate these services is to use the Internet and look for announcements that emphasize business mediation.

Another good way to find potential mediators is to visit the websites maintained by the Association of Intellectual Property Law Attorneys (AIPLA; www.aipla.org) and the International Trademark Association (INTA; www.inta.org). A list of business mediators in your area can also be obtained from the Mediation Information and Resource Center (www.mediate.com).

Because mediation is about reaching an agreement rather than trying to convince a decision maker, it is not necessary to involve an attorney. However, attorneys often can help you find an appropriate mediator. They can also be helpful as advisers during the course of the mediation, and, assuming an agreement is reached, can create a detailed binding written agreement that both you and the other party will feel comfortable signing.

Step 7: Consult an Attorney

If none of the above gets you anywhere, by all means call a trademark lawyer. The lawyer might have a better letter-writing technique, or might tell you to forget about the conflict. The lawyer probably will be able to help you find a mediator or arbitrator, if you want to pursue one of these options, or the lawyer might advise that your best shot is to go to court. If you've tried everything else first, the lawyer might be right. (See Chapter 14, "Help Beyond This Book.")

When Someone Claims That You Infringed a Trademark

Here's a scenario that you wouldn't relish: You receive an irate letter from Ms. Blowhard in North Noluk demanding not only that you immediately cease using your new mark for clothing designs, Nines, but also that you account for all your profits derived from the use of that name. She also demands that you pay her treble (triple) damages for the insult, or she will see you in court. What to do? Stay calm.

First, be assured that no matter how threatening the letter, the world won't fall on your head today, tomorrow, or even next week. However, legal entanglements might eventually follow. So, first, we'll tell you what those are. Next, we will explain your options and help you decide which ones make sense for you. But, before you actually adopt a strategy, you'll need to think about the big picture—how valuable is the trademark you've been using and, given the legal realities, how much energy and money are you willing to spend to protect it?

Much of this discussion is very similar to the information in Chapter 11, "When Someone Infringes Your Mark." It's a good idea to read that whole chapter (it's short) to get an idea of the other party's point of view.

Start by understanding that trademark lawsuits are extremely expensive. From the point of view of either the infringer or the infringee, negotiation is a more pragmatic, cost-effective, and often more fruitful way to resolve a trademark dispute. With that guiding principle, let us help you respond to someone's claim that you infringed on his or her mark.

What the Complaining Party Can Do to You

Right away, you should know that your opponent can stop your use of your mark only with a court order (known as a temporary injunction). To get this, your opponent must clear two legal hurdles:

1. Your opponent must convince a judge that he or she has suffered, or will suffer, irreparable damage unless the judge issues an immediate court order barring your continued use of the mark.

2. Your opponent must convince a judge that he or she is likely to eventually win in court (that is, by proving that he or she has superior rights to the mark and that you infringed on those rights).

In cases where the two names compete in the marketplace, a judge will often assume that the first hurdle has been cleared, because trademark infringements siphon off goodwill in a way that cannot easily be measured and repaired in a later action for damages (which is why the injury is called irreparable).

The second hurdle is much more difficult to overcome, because the judge, without the benefit of a full trial, is being asked to make an important finding about the primary issue in the case: Has infringement really occurred? To develop and prove the facts that the judge will need to arrive at this conclusion normally involves quite a bit of (always expensive) legal time. So unless your opponents are both solvent and determined, they will not likely leap into court without first: (1) finding out as much about you and your use of the mark as possible, and (2) testing your reaction to their infringement claims. The upshot is, you probably have a little time to figure out what to do.

Steps You Should Take

We don't mean to imply that you should ignore the letter. On the contrary, you should get busy with the following steps, lest you end up with a process server at your door, serving you with a lawsuit.

Step 1: Find Out What You Can About the Complaining Business and Its Use and Registration of the Mark at Issue

Here we echo the discussion in Chapter 11 on the same issue from the opposite perspective. Please read that material. In essence, the more you know about the other party, the better you can evaluate how to respond to his or her allegations. In addition, it's essential to the development of your case that you know exactly how your opponent uses its mark, and where and how long the party has used it.

Once you get all that information, you should reread Chapter 10 to help you decide if your opponent has a case against you.

Step 2: Get Advice

After you have gathered as much information as possible, consult a trademark attorney to confirm or correct your understanding of the situation, as well as to get the point of view of a disinterested experienced party. Although you might understandably want to avoid attorneys and their attendant costs, paying several hundred dollars for a reasoned legal opinion about your situation is cost-effective, given the probable cost of ending up on the losing side of a lawsuit or even retooling your stationery and marketing materials if you decide to switch rather than fight. You might also want to get the advice of friends or business associates whom you trust. They may have had comparable experiences, or they might simply have reliable common sense and good tactical suggestions.

Once you fully inform yourself of the legal and practical implications of the trademark dispute, listen to your gut. It's almost always a mistake to follow a course of action you don't feel comfortable about. Fortunately, because the complaining business is likely to write you several letters before taking legal action, you probably have enough time to consider your next step carefully.

Step 3: Choose Your Tactical Responses

Here are some common responses, and at least some of the possible consequences of each:

- **The ostrich technique.** You can bury your head in the sand and ignore the infringement claim. In fact, if you are convinced that the other business doesn't have a case and knows it, this might work. Otherwise, it's probably a mistake, as it risks your being sued just to get your attention.

- **The German Shepherd response.** You can send back a letter full of sound and fury, informing the complainer that under no circumstances will you ever stop using your mark, and the mere suggestion that you are infringing is an insult. Remember, however, that this is a typical lawyerly tactic, which some lawyers adopt with the hopes of fanning the flames of a small dispute, turning it into a true conflagration with the promise of lots of billable hours.

- **The elephantine response.** You reply in a calm and polite letter, stating the facts as you see them and explaining why you disagree with the infringement claim. Your tone makes it clear that you are reasonable and flexible and perfectly willing to engage in further discussion and to hear more information on the subject. This sort of letter does not predispose you to any particular strategy, because you can always dig in your heels later, but in our view, it's most likely to put you farther along the road to fruitful discussion than does either of the other two responses.

Step 4: Plan Your Negotiation Strategy

Now let's assume that negotiation by letter, fax, or phone has begun. What sort of strategies should you consider? These are identical to the ones discussed in Chapter 11, which we suggest you read (or reread). Also, once again let us make the point that changing your name need not be a disaster and might even be a marketing opportunity.

Step 5: Seek Mediation or Arbitration

One approach that may help you reach an agreement without being dragged into court is to seek arbitration or mediation. These alternative approaches to dispute resolution are described in more detail in Chapter 11.

FREQUENTLY ASKED QUESTION
Overzealous Zazzler zeeks TM advice.

"I'm a Zazzle (www.zazzle.com) entrepreneur. From my understanding, a registered trademark is a pretty specific thing (I could be wrong). So, for example, if you get a trademark for the words 'First Kiss,' the trademark would specify the font in which the words would be written, the colors if any other than black, as well as whatever else you specify to make your trademark original and how it will be used. 'First Kiss' is now your registered trademark! Now for the questions: (1) You come across someone who uses the words 'First Kiss' in a graffiti styled design with all sort of frills and embellishments and plasters it on a T-shirt, mug, etc. Now, although the words used are the same, they are written in completely different style (font), it looks nothing like the trademarked words, and would never be confused as having anything to do with the company/individual that registered the trademark …. is that a trademark violation? (2) 'First' and 'Kiss' are pretty common words and are used frequently. You come across someone who has used those words in a sentence and plastered it on a T-shirt, mug, etc. 'Remembering our very first kiss'"… is that a trademark violation?"

You're starting with some incorrect information; we need to back up a few steps.

Square One Dept. A trademark registration for a name or text is usually not limited to a specific font; if that were the case, Nike, Gucci, and Coca-Cola would have problems stopping ripoffs. Even if someone registers the word mark in connection with a design, courts won't limit protection to the design. They will apply common sense to determine whether someone is trading off the mark unfairly and consumers are likely to be confused. So changing colors and fonts doesn't get you off the hook for infringement.

As for your questions … Someone who registered First Kiss for T-shirts and cups would have priority over subsequent users on similar merchandise and could stop them regardless of the font. You claim that customers "would never be confused." If you can prove that in court, you might be able to get off the hook for infringement, but we believe that the chances of proving an identical word mark on identical goods does not infringe are slim to none.

Trademark fair use. Your second question is a little more complex and relies on interpreting the rules for trademark fair use. As a general rule, descriptive use of terms is permissible. Again, common sense prevails here, as a competitor's repetitive use of a descriptive term might be an illegal attempt to siphon customers.

International Trademark Protection

Your mark could become so well-known that you'll want to protect it in another country. If so, you should take some steps now to do that, or at least look into the process.

Trademark laws are different abroad. Many countries follow the U.S. principle and require actual use in commerce before registration. These "use" countries include the United Kingdom, Canada, Australia, New Zealand, and other current and former British Commonwealth members.

But in the majority of nations, registration alone forms a basis for ownership rights. In these countries, anyone can get a registration on your mark without having used it there first. This presents a serious problem for marks that appear to be headed for international use after becoming well known in this country. Some businesses have made money by spotting these types of marks, preemptively registering them in key countries, and then demanding large fees to transfer (assign) the names back to their original U.S. owners. Also, in some countries you might not be able to import your goods without first registering your mark there.

In this chapter, we discuss the two basic issues to resolve if you're considering seeking foreign trademark rights: (1) Where will you seek protection, and (2) what method will you use to register your trademark abroad?

> **CAUTION**
>
> **Our basic advice about international trademarks is that when in doubt about how to proceed, get an experienced trademark attorney who has done international registrations to help.** It is possible, as explained below, for a layperson to accomplish international registrations under the Madrid Protocol, but you could have difficulty assessing your likelihood of success unless you consult with a trademark expert.

Where Will You Seek Protection?

Where you seek protection depends, obviously, on where you plan to market your services or products. All countries require that you use the mark within a period of time after registration or it will lapse, so register only in those countries where you can reasonably foresee sales in the next several years.

Unfortunately, you might not yet know into which countries you will be expanding. If so, consider registering your trademark in Canada and Mexico, which are natural choices. Mexico, like most of the international community belongs to the Madrid Protocol, a group of nations that uses a simplified system for international registrations, described below. Canada will join on June 17, 2019.

The nature of your product and how it might fit into the international market will inform your choice of additional countries for international registration. Because you can't foresee all contingencies, your basic business philosophy will dictate this decision: Either cover as many possibilities as you can by registering in several countries (the expensive choice), or restrict your international registrations to your one or two best choices and hope your decision pays off.

Once you're certain about foreign registration, you must arrange for or conduct an international trademark search. In those countries in which registration alone forms a basis for ownership rights, such searches are much simpler to do than in "use" countries, because all potential conflicts will be found on the national register of trademarks, without the need to search for unregistered trademarks.

Free and Fee-Based Resources for International Trademark Searching

You may search the trademark registries of many foreign countries for free. Visit WIPO (World Intellectual Property Organization) at its database of international trademark registries (www.wipo.int/madrid/en/members/ipoffices_info.html). You may also use the fee-based services identified in Chapter 4 and have a search company perform these national searches.

What Does It Mean in Italian?

Check to see if your mark has an unintended meaning in the country in which you plan to register. For example, Pschitt was a French mark that could not be marketed as a soft drink in the United States. This suggestion also applies to English-speaking countries—in Australia, a "Whopper" (a U.S. trademark for a hamburger) is slang for male genitalia and, so, not advisable as a trademark there. To get an opinion on your mark, consult a native speaker of the country you are considering.

Making Money (But Losing Your Name)

In 1971, a young, recently divorced mother and her friend started a unique low-profile company in the U.S. that:
- sold pure and simple cosmetics, lotions, and perfumes
- offered its products in small-size, recyclable bottles with no extraneous ingredients, and
- didn't test its products on animals.

The business was named The Body Shop (because its first place of business was in a former auto repair shop). The owners had the foresight to register the name with the USPTO not long after business started to blossom. It was a timely enterprise and a great success, eventually opening several outlets within its region. It was the kind of business that made people who moved

Making Money (But Losing Your Name) (continued)

out of the area beg friends traveling back there to bring them some Body Shop products. Soon, it also had a booming catalog business.

Years passed. Meanwhile, in London, another entrepreneur (who reportedly had visited the Bay Area store) created similar products and chose the same name. The second Body Shop also took off, even faster and on a wider basis than the original had in the United States. Eventually, the Body Shop (U.K.) had over 500 flourishing franchises throughout Europe. It was confusing to travelers, but because the U.S. company had obtained only the exclusive rights to the name in the United States, they could not stop the British Body Shop's use.

Then came the day when the British store owners sought to enter the U.S. market. The U.S. corporation had the legal right to the name and therefore potent weapons at its disposal. But the British firm had many times the capital of its U.S. counterpart and threatened an expensive lawsuit that the U.S. company could not afford. Like reasonable businesspeople, the U.S.-based Body Shop heeded the bottom line, settling the dispute. It sold the U.S. rights to its name to the British company, agreeing to change its name within 18 months, in exchange for an undisclosed (but sizable) sum of money.

The point of this story depends on your perspective. Some might say: Trademark your name everywhere you can at once! Others could reflect that the protagonists in our story, by federally registering their trademark, showed foresight that was unusual at the time for a small "New Age" concern. That act gave them the leverage they needed to extract a price from the English company for use of the trademark in the United States.

In the end, the U.S. company suffered the inconvenience of changing its name, but that's something that many companies do willingly when their circumstances change. Although bitter over the misappropriation, they weren't, as a practical matter, deprived of expansion opportunities. They hadn't expanded much before the conflict arose, and existed as a relatively small—but profitable—concern with a few regional outlets and a catalog. The owners bargained for enough time to reach all their regular customers and notify them of the new name Body Time, and they received a handy infusion of capital from the sale of their trademark. In 2018, after 48 years in business, the original Body Shop (aka Body Time) closed.

How Do You Register Abroad?

The owner of a U.S. trademark registration can use one of three ways to secure a foreign registration: under the Madrid Protocol (among 120 member nations), as a Community Trademark (among 28 European nations), or via separately filed registrations in each nation.

The Madrid Protocol

The Madrid Protocol is a system that allows an applicant to file simultaneous registration applications in any of the 120 nations that belong to the Madrid Protocol treaty. You can find a list of all member nations at the World Intellectual Property Organization (WIPO) website (www.wipo.int/madrid/en/members).

The Madrid Protocol, adopted in the United States in November 2003, is administered by the WIPO. When compared to filing separate registrations in several foreign countries, the Madrid Protocol is considered a more efficient and less expensive route.

For U.S. applicants, the first step under the Madrid Protocol is to federally register your mark with the USPTO. (We explain this procedure in Chapter 7.) The administrators of the Madrid Protocol refer to this application/registration as either the basic application or basic registration, and they refer to the nations in which you choose to register after the United States to as nations for which "extension of protection" is sought.

Each of these nations will decide, using its national criteria, whether to register the mark. If one of these countries refuses registration, that refusal will not affect the main Madrid Protocol application. For example, if you apply to register in Denmark and Estonia but are rejected in Estonia, the rejection will not affect the status of your application in Denmark. Only if the basic registration (the U.S. registration) is abandoned or declared invalid within the first five years of the international registration will the other registrations be terminated.

To file, go to the USPTO home page (www.uspto.gov) and click "Trademarks." On the upper right side of the page, click "Madrid Protocol."

The Community Trademark

The Community Trademark is a method of registering for a trademark that is good in the 28 European countries that belong to the European Union. To qualify for Community Trademark status, the proposed mark must be acceptable in all countries. If your application is rejected by even one country, you must file separate national applications for trademark registration in each country.

Unlike a trademark issued under the Madrid Protocol, the CTM is good throughout the European Union nations and can be enforced throughout the EU. So, instead of having to file separate lawsuits in each member nation, you can file one lawsuit for infringement in many nations.

Generally, trademark lawyers advise that a CTM is worthwhile if you would want registration in more than three of the EU nations. You can apply for an application for a Community Trademark at the Office for Harmonization of the Internal Market, in Alicante, Spain. For more information about how the community mark works and how to apply for one, visit http://oami.europa.eu.

Brexit, Britain, and Trade Marks

Although Britain has voted to leave the European Union, the country has not—at the time this book went to press—formally entered into an agreement for departure from the EU. Anticipating concerns, the British government has issued a statement regarding trade mark status ("trademark" is two words in the UK). The following is an excerpt from the statement:

"The existing UK system for protecting trade mark rights will remain largely unaffected by the UK's decision to leave the EU. While the UK remains a full member of the EU then EU Trade Marks (EUTM) continue to be valid in the UK. When the UK leaves the EU, in any scenario, an EUTM will continue to be valid in the remaining EU Member States and UK businesses will still be able to register an EU trade mark, which will cover all remaining EU Member States."

For more information, check the UK's website (www.gov.uk).

Registering on a Country-by-Country Basis

If you are filing separate trademark applications in foreign countries, the good news is that most nations where you will file belong to the International Convention for the Protection of Industrial Property (known as the Paris Convention).

This law has standardized a few things. One of the most important is that trademark owners from one Paris Convention country who register their trademarks in another Paris Convention country are entitled to the same rights as are native trademark owners of that country. Although each country's laws are different, the convention at least puts all trademark owners in any one Paris Convention country on the same legal footing.

Another important benefit is that once a U.S. citizen applies to register a federal trademark in the United States, the date of that application serves as the effective date of application in all other Paris Convention countries in which that citizen applies, if done so within six months of the U.S. application. This is important because in most of those countries rights are based on registration, and the effective date of application (or priority date) is an important method of determining rights. Thus, it is imperative to file an international registration soon after filing one in the United States, if you plan to do so at all.

If you plan on handling the filing in a foreign country, you'll need to research the trademark laws of that nation. You can do this online— start at either the WIPO website (www.wipo.org) or the All About Trademarks site (www.ggmark.com). These foreign laws are usually summarized at each nation's trademark office website and will inform you how soon you must begin to use your mark after registration, and whether special licensing and tax rules might apply to your service or product and its mark. Again, this is why you should consult an experienced international trademark attorney—to make sure you find out about and comply with all applicable laws.

Help Beyond This Book

W‌e hope that this book provides all the information you will need to choose and protect your trademark, service mark, or trade name. But you might need additional help, either in the form of more advanced legal resources or a trademark attorney's assistance.

Don't Be Afraid of Legal Research

Looking up the law for yourself needn't be scary. By reading this book you will have already learned the basic trademark vocabulary necessary to understand the more technical legal materials we discuss. In addition, Nolo publishes a basic legal research guide, *Legal Research: How to Find & Understand the Law,* by the Editors at Nolo (Nolo), which teaches you how to efficiently do basic legal research. You will also find most law librarians to be of great help.

Nolo: Your One-Stop Trademark Resource

Nolo, the publisher of this book, offers the following trademark resources:

- **Legal information.** Nolo's website (www.nolo.com) provides detailed legal information about acquiring and protecting trademarks. Nolo also provides helpful information on conducting legal research, with links to sites where you can locate case law and statutes.
- **Trademark attorneys.** Nolo operates a national lawyer directory that provides in-depth profiles of attorneys, as well as verification that each lawyer is in good standing with the state licensing agency. The directory includes many trademark attorneys (go to www.nolo.com/lawyers and select "Intellectual Property"). Note: It might not be necessary that the trademark attorney you choose be in your local area, because many trademark actions—for example, appealing from a trademark objection—can be done from anywhere in the United States.

Finding Trademark Laws and Information on the Internet

The Internet offers convenient access to an enormous amount of trademark materials, including:

- the federal trademark database
- the federal trademark statutes and regulations
- informative articles by trademark experts
- the USPTO's *Trademark Manual of Examining Procedure*
- the *Design Search Code Manual*
- the *Acceptable Identification of Goods and Services Manual*
- guides to various aspects of trademark practice
- recent changes in USPTO rules and procedures, and
- much, much more.

Here is a brief list of sites that will either have the information you are looking for or will provide you with links to other sites that do.

www.uspto.gov. The U.S. Patent and Trademark Office is the place to go for recent policy and statutory changes and transcripts of hearings on various trademark law issues. This site also lets you do your own trademark search for free, search the *Trademark Manual of Examining Procedure* (the guide the USPTO examiners use when processing trademark applications and handling other proceedings), complete your trademark registration application online, and check the status of any trademark. This site also links to other useful trademark-related sites.

www.ggmark.com. This site, maintained by a trademark lawyer, provides basic national and international trademark information and a fine collection of links to other trademark resources.

www.schwimmer.legal.com. The Trademark blog, written by Martin Schwimmer, has become the leading site on the Web for current news about trademark law.

www.thettablog.blogspot.com. The TTAB blog by John Welch is the most comprehensive source on the activities of the Trademark Trial and Appeals Board.

Doing Your Own Research in a Law Library

When seeking answers in a law library, you will find useful the three-step approach that we describe below:

1. Read one or more discussions by experts in the field to get a background and overview of the topic being researched. In this case, you will already have a basic background from this book and will be looking for additional details on a particular topic.
2. Read the law itself (cases and statutes) upon which the experts base their opinions. (Reading primary materials such as these can be confusing without first digesting an expert's analysis.)
3. Make sure the law you read is completely up to date.

Read One or More Discussions by Experts

The following are some recommended publications written by trademark law experts.

The most authoritative book on trademark law is the multivolume set entitled *McCarthy on Trademarks and Unfair Competition*, by J. Thomas McCarthy, published by Thomson Reuters. You can find this treatise in many law libraries.

Trademark Associations and Legal Publishers

Two associations of trademark lawyers offer other materials that you might find helpful. You can get a list of their publications by writing or calling them:

International Trademark
  Association (INTA)
655 Third Avenue, 10th Floor
New York, NY 10017
212-642-1700
www.inta.org

American Intellectual Property
  Law Association (AIPLA)
241 18th Street South, Suite 700
Arlington, VA 22202
703-415-0780
www.aipla.org

Read the Law Itself

The main law governing trademarks in the United States is the Lanham Act, also known as the Federal Trademark Act of 1946 (as amended in 1988). It is located at Title 15, Chapters 1051 through 1127, of the *United States Code*. You can find it in either of two series of books, *United States Code Annotated* (U.S.C.A.) or *United States Code Service*, Lawyers Edition (U.S.C.S.). All law libraries carry at least one of these series. To find a specific section of the Lanham Act, consult either the index at the end of Title 15, or the index at the end of the entire code.

Finding a Lawyer

If you become involved in a trademark dispute, are having trouble getting your mark registered, or simply want some advice from a professional about a trademark issue, you will want to consult a trademark lawyer. You want a trademark lawyer who:

- knows the trademark field well
- is willing to acknowledge your competence gained from using this book, and
- is honest and conscientious.

Fortunately, by arming yourself with the information in this book, you have a good shot at finding a lawyer with all of these characteristics.

Find a Lawyer Who Knows the Trademark Field Well

Trademark lawyers usually advertise online as intellectual property specialists able to handle patent, trademark, copyright, and trade secret cases. Because each of these fields is increasingly becoming a complicated legal world all to itself, most intellectual property law specialists tend to be very knowledgeable in one or two of these areas and only passingly familiar with the others.

For instance, it is common for patent lawyers to be far more knowledgeable in that area than in trademark law, even though both patents and trademarks involve practice before the USPTO. Similarly, some lawyers specialize in trademarks and do little or no patent work.

The point of knowing this, of course, is that you want a trademark lawyer who really knows trademarks, not someone willing to brush up on trademarks at your expense.

When you call on the intellectual property specialist, ask these questions:

- What percentage of your practice involves trademark work?
- Are you a member of the International Trademark Association or the American Intellectual Property Law Association?

The first inquiry will help you find a true specialist in this area, while the second will help you find a lawyer who is curious enough about the subject of trademarks to join these associations of trademark specialists.

Find a Lawyer Who Is Willing to Acknowledge Your Competence

In addition to satisfying yourself that a lawyer is competent, you want to find someone who is reasonably congenial to work with. You don't need us to tell you that lawyers tend to look down on laypersons when it comes to the lawyer's area of expertise. This means that many of the lawyers you initially encounter are likely to be turned off by your understanding of trademark law. Fortunately, however, some lawyers are willing to respect their clients' knowledge and know-how to work with them rather than against them. This is the type of lawyer you should be looking for.

You can find a lawyer who isn't intimidated by a competent client if you:

- explain over the phone that you have been using this book
- articulate exactly what you want the lawyer to do, and
- carefully monitor the lawyer's reaction.

If the lawyer scoffs at the idea of a self-help law book or you get a whiff of, "Don't tell me what you need, I'm the lawyer," go on to the next name on the list. If the response appears to respect your self-help efforts and admits the possibility that you are a competent human being, make an appointment.

Find a Lawyer Who Is Honest and Conscientious

If you are just seeking advice, then you needn't worry much about the lawyer's character. But if you are looking for someone to represent you in a dispute, the human being you are dealing with becomes paramount. The best analytical trademark lawyers in the world can bring you to financial and emotional ruin if they lack the ability to understand your needs and to represent you with your best interests in mind.

Honesty

While some would argue that there's no such thing as an honest lawyer, we maintain that it is possible to have honest dealings with your lawyer. Start by clearly understanding that the lawyer's financial interest is to run up lots of billable hours over a period of time. This interest is the opposite of yours, which is to arrive at a fast, cost-efficient, and reasonably livable resolution of the problem.

Once you understand this tension, you'll also understand that it is essential that you and your lawyer agree up front about what the lawyer will do and the amount of control you will have over the lawyer's activities. Rule Number One is that the lawyer is working for you, not vice versa; and Rule Number Two is that you have a right to understand the reason for every minute of the lawyer's time that will be billed to you.

Conscientiousness

Your lawyer must be willing to agree to consult you on all phases of the case and to promptly return your phone calls. Although nothing leads to a ruinous relationship faster than bad communication, too few lawyers keep their clients well posted. Lawyers faced with complaints about their lousy client contact habits often reply that many clients call or expect too much. But because the client is paying for the lawyer's time, this seems like a pretty weak excuse. Our experience tells us that the usual reason lawyers don't return phone calls is that they have neglected some facet of the case and simply don't want to face the client.

Your lawyer must also be willing to follow through on your case to its completion. This one is tricky to monitor, because it involves predicting the future. However, as long as good communication is established at the outset, there's an improved chance that your lawyer will give you good service.

Find a Lawyer Who Is Open to Dispute Resolution Alternatives

In recent years, many lawyers have discovered that there often are better ways to resolve disputes than the old "haul 'em into court" technique. The two most common of these alternative approaches are arbitration and mediation. When you search for an attorney, make sure that the attorney is fully up to speed on these private, fast, inexpensive, and often successful techniques and is willing to help you explore them as a potential way to solve your problem. Arbitration and mediation are discussed in Chapter 11, "When Someone Infringes Your Mark."

Internet Resources

A number of websites offer listings for domestic and international trademark lawyers, including:
- the International Trademark Association (www.inta.org)
- the American Intellectual Property Law Association (www.aipla.org), and
- Nolo's lawyer directory (www.nolo.com).

International Classifications
of Goods and Services

A

The following classifications are from the *International Classification of Goods and Services under the Nice Agreement*. A more detailed version of the *Classification* can be found at the WIPO website at www.wipo.int/classifications/nice/en.

GOODS

CLASS 1 (Chemicals)

Chemicals used in industry, science, and photography, as well as in agriculture, horticulture, and forestry; unprocessed artificial resins, unprocessed plastics; manures; fire extinguishing compositions; tempering and soldering preparations; chemical substances for preserving foodstuffs; tanning substances; adhesives used in industry.

Explanatory Note: This class includes mainly chemical products used in industry, science, and agriculture, including those which go to the making of products belonging to other classes.

Includes, in particular:
- compost;
- salt for preserving other than for foodstuffs; certain additives for the food industry.

Does not include, in particular:
- raw natural resins (CL 02);
- chemical products for use in medical science (CL 05);
- fungicides, herbicides, and preparations for destroying vermin (CL 05);
- adhesives for stationery or household purposes (CL 16);
- salt for preserving foodstuffs (CL 30);
- straw mulch (CL 31).

CLASS 2 (Paints)

Paints, varnishes, lacquers; preservatives against rust and against deterioration of wood; colorants; mordants; raw natural resins; metals in foil and powder form for painters, decorators, printers, and artists.

Explanatory Note: This class includes mainly paints, colorants, and preparations used for the protection against corrosion.

Includes, in particular:
- paints, varnishes, and lacquers for industry, handicrafts, and arts;
- dyestuffs for clothing;
- colorants for foodstuffs and beverages.

Does not include, in particular:
- unprocessed artificial resins (CL 01);
- laundry bluing (CL 03);
- cosmetic dyes (CL 03);
- paint boxes (articles for use in school) (CL 16);
- insulating paints and varnishes (CL 17).

CLASS 3 (Cosmetics and cleaning preparations)

Bleaching preparations and other substances for laundry use; cleaning, polishing, scouring, and abrasive preparations; soaps; perfumery, essential oils, cosmetics, hair lotions; dentifrices.

Explanatory Note: This class includes mainly cleaning preparations and toilet preparations.

Includes, in particular:
- deodorants for human or animal use;
- room fragrancing preparations;
- sanitary preparations being toiletries.

Does not include, in particular:
- chemical chimney cleaners (CL 01);
- degreasing preparations for use in manufacturing processes (CL 01);
- deodorants other than for human or animal use (CL 05);
- sharpening stones and grindstones (hand tools) (CL 08).

CLASS 4 (Lubricants and fuels)

Industrial oils and greases; lubricants; dust absorbing, wetting, and binding compositions; fuels (including motor spirit) and illuminants; candles, wicks.

Explanatory Note: This class includes mainly industrial oils and greases, fuels, and illuminants.

Does not include, in particular:

- certain special industrial oils and greases (consult the Alphabetical List of Goods).

CLASS 5 (Pharmaceuticals)

Pharmaceutical, veterinary, and sanitary preparations; dietetic substances adapted for medical use, food for babies; plasters, materials for dressings; material for stopping teeth, dental wax; disinfectants; preparations for destroying vermin; fungicides, herbicides.

Explanatory Note: This class includes mainly pharmaceuticals and other preparations for medical purposes.

Includes, in particular:

- sanitary preparations for medical purposes and for personal hygiene;
- deodorants other than for personal use;
- cigarettes without tobacco, for medical purposes.

Does not include, in particular:

- sanitary preparations being toiletries (CL 03);
- deodorants for human or animal use (CL 03);
- supportive bandages (CL 10).

CLASS 6 (Metal goods)

Common metals and their alloys; metal building materials; transportable buildings of metal; materials of metal for railway tracks; nonelectric cables and wires of common metal; iron mongery, small items of metal hardware; pipes and tubes of metal; safes; goods of common metal not included in other classes; ores.

Explanatory Note: This class includes mainly unwrought and partly wrought common metals as well as simple products made of them.

Does not include, in particular:
- bauxite (CL 01);
- mercury, antimony, alkaline and alkaline-earth metals (CL 01);
- metals in foil and powder form for painters, decorators, printers, and artists (CL 02).

CLASS 7 (Machinery)

Machines and machine tools; motors and engines (except for land vehicles); machine coupling and transmission components (except for land vehicles); agricultural implements other than hand-operated; incubators for eggs; automatic vending machines.

Explanatory Note: This class includes mainly machines, machine tools, motors, and engines.

Includes, in particular:
- parts of motors and engines (of all kinds);
- electric cleaning machines and apparatus.

Does not include, in particular:
- certain special machines and machine tools (consult the Alphabetical List of Goods);
- hand tools and implements, hand operated (CL 08);
- motors and engines for land vehicles (CL 12).

CLASS 8 (Hand tools)

Hand tools and implements (hand operated); cutlery; side arms; razors.

Explanatory Note: This class includes mainly hand-operated implements used as tools in the respective professions.

Includes, in particular:
- cutlery of precious metals;
- electric razors and clippers (hand instruments).

Does not include, in particular:
- certain special instruments (consult the Alphabetical List of Goods);

- machine tools and implements driven by a motor (CL 07);
- surgical cutlery (CL 10);
- paper knives (CL 16);
- fencing weapons (CL 28).

CLASS 9 (Electrical and scientific apparatus)

Scientific, nautical, surveying, electric, photographic, cinematographic, optical, weighing, measuring, signaling, checking (supervision), life-saving, and teaching apparatus and instruments; apparatus for recording, transmission, or reproduction of sound or images; magnetic data carriers, recording discs; automatic vending machines and mechanisms for coin-operated apparatus; cash registers, calculating machines, data processing equipment and computers; fire-extinguishing apparatus.

Explanatory Note

Includes, in particular:

- apparatus and instruments for scientific research in laboratories;
- apparatus and instruments for controlling ships, such as apparatus and instruments, for measuring, and for transmitting orders;
- the following electrical apparatus and instruments:
  - certain electrothermic tools and apparatus, such as electric soldering irons, electric flatirons which, if they were not electric, would belong to Class 8;
  - apparatus and devices which, if not electrical, would be listed in various classes, i.e., electrically heated clothing, cigar-lighters for automobiles;
- protractors; punched card office machines; amusement apparatus adapted for use with television receivers only.

Does not include, in particular:

- the following electrical apparatus and instruments:
  - electromechanical apparatus for the kitchen (grinders and mixers for foodstuffs, fruit-presses, electrical coffee mills, etc.), and certain other apparatus and instruments driven by an electrical motor, all coming under Class 7;

- electric razors and clippers (hand instruments) (CL 08); electric toothbrushes and combs (CL 21);
- electrical apparatus for space heating or for the heating of liquids, for cooking, ventilating, etc. (CL 11);
- clocks and watches and other chronometric instruments (CL 14);
- control clocks (CL 14).

CLASS 10 (Medical apparatus)

Surgical, medical, dental, and veterinary apparatus and instruments, artificial limbs, eyes, and teeth; orthopedic articles; suture materials.

Explanatory Note: This class includes mainly medical apparatus, instruments and articles.

Includes, in particular:
- special furniture for medical use;
- hygienic rubber articles (consult the Alphabetical List of Goods);
- supportive bandages.

CLASS 11 (Environmental control apparatus)

Apparatus for lighting, heating, steam generating, cooking, refrigerating, drying, ventilating, water supply, and sanitary purposes.

Explanatory Note

Includes, in particular:
- air conditioning apparatus;
- bedwarmers, hot water bottles, warming pans, electric or non-electric;
- electrically heated cushions (pads) and blankets, not for medical purposes;
- electric kettles;
- electric cooking utensils.

Does not include, in particular:
- steam producing apparatus (parts of machines) (CL 07);
- electrically heated clothing (CL 09).

CLASS 12 (Vehicles)

Vehicles; apparatus for locomotion by land, air, or water.

Explanatory Note

Includes, in particular:

- motors and engines for land vehicles;
- couplings and transmission components for land vehicles;
- air cushion vehicles.

Does not include, in particular:

- certain parts of vehicles (consult the Alphabetical List of Goods);
- railway material of metal (CL 06);
- motors, engines, couplings, and transmission components other than for land vehicles (CL 07);
- parts of motors and engines (of all kinds) (CL 07).

CLASS 13 (Firearms)

Firearms; ammunition and projectiles; explosives; fireworks.

Explanatory Note: This class includes mainly firearms and pyrotechnical products.

Does not include, in particular:

- matches (CL 34).

CLASS 14 (Jewelry)

Precious metals and their alloys and goods in precious metals or coated therewith, not included in other classes; jewelry, precious stones; horological and chronometric instruments.

Explanatory Note: This class includes mainly precious metals, goods in precious metals, and, in general, jewelry, clocks, and watches.

Includes, in particular:

- jewelry (i.e. imitation jewelry and jewelry of precious metal and stones);
- cuff links, tie pins.

Does not include, in particular:
- certain goods in precious metals (classified according to their function or purpose), for example:
- metals in foil and powder form for painters, decorators, printers, and artists (CL 02);
- amalgam of gold for dentists (CL 05);
- cutlery (CL 08);
- electric contacts (CL 09);
- pen nibs of gold (CL 16);
- objects of art not in precious metals (classified according to the material of which they consist).

CLASS 15 (Musical instruments)

Musical instruments.

Explanatory Note

Includes, in particular:
- mechanical pianos and their accessories;
- musical boxes;
- electrical and electronic musical instruments.

Does not include, in particular:
- apparatus for the recording, transmission, amplification, and reproduction of sound (CL 09).

CLASS 16 (Paper goods and printed matter)

Paper, cardboard, and goods made from these materials, not included in other classes; printed matter; bookbinding material; photographs; stationery; adhesives for stationery or household purposes; artists' materials; paintbrushes; typewriters and office requisites (except furniture); instructional and teaching material (except apparatus); plastic materials for packaging (not included in other classes); playing cards; printers' type; printing blocks.

Explanatory Note: This class includes mainly paper, goods made from that material, and office requisites.

Includes, in particular:
- paper knives;
- duplicators;
- plastic sheets, sacks and bags for wrapping and packaging.

Does not include, in particular:
- certain goods made of paper and cardboard
  (consult the Alphabetical List of Goods);
- colors (CL 02);
- hand tools for artists (for example: spatulas, sculptors' chisels)
  (CL 08).

CLASS 17 (Rubber goods)

Rubber, gutta-percha, gum, asbestos, mica, and goods made from these materials and not included in other classes; plastics in extruded form for use in manufacture; packing, stopping, and insulating materials; flexible pipes, not of metal.

Explanatory Note: This class includes mainly electrical, thermal, and acoustic insulating materials and plastics, being for use in manufacture in the form of sheets, blocks, and rods.

Includes, in particular:
- rubber material for recapping tires;
- padding and stuffing materials of rubber or plastics;
- floating antipollution barriers.

CLASS 18 (Leather goods)

Leather and imitations of leather, and goods made of these materials and not included in other classes; animal skins, hides; trunks and traveling bags; umbrellas, parasols, and walking sticks; whips, harness, and saddlery.

Explanatory Note: This class includes mainly leather, leather imitations, travel goods not included in other classes, and saddlery.

Does not include, in particular:
- clothing, footwear, headgear (consult the Alphabetical List
  of Goods).

CLASS 19 (Nonmetallic building materials)

Building materials (nonmetallic); nonmetallic rigid pipes for building; asphalt, pitch, and bitumen; nonmetallic transportable buildings; monuments, not of metal.

Explanatory Note: This class includes mainly nonmetallic building materials.

Includes, in particular:

- semiworked woods (for example: beams, planks, panels);
- veneers;
- building glass (for example: floor slabs, glass tiles);
- glass granules for marking out roads;
- letter boxes of masonry.

Does not include, in particular:

- cement preservatives and cement-waterproofing preparations (CL 01);
- fireproofing preparations (CL 01).

CLASS 20 (Furniture and articles not otherwise classified)

Furniture, mirrors, picture frames; goods (not included in other classes) of wood, cork, reed, cane, wicker, horn, bone, ivory, whalebone, shell, amber, mother-of-pearl, meerschaum, and substitutes for all these materials, or of plastics.

Explanatory Note: This class includes mainly furniture and its parts and plastic goods, not included in other classes.

Includes, in particular:

- metal furniture and furniture for camping;
- bedding (for example: mattresses, spring mattresses, pillows);
- looking glasses and furnishing or toilet mirrors;
- registration number plates not of metal;
- letter boxes not of metal or masonry.

Does not include, in particular:

- certain special types of mirrors, classified according to their function or purpose (consult the Alphabetical List of Goods);
- special furniture for laboratories (CL 09);

- special furniture for medical use (CL 10);
- bedding linen (CL 24);
- eiderdowns (CL 24).

CLASS 21 (Housewares and glass)

Household or kitchen utensils and containers (not of precious metal or coated therewith); combs and sponges; brushes (except paintbrushes); brush-making materials; articles for cleaning purposes; steel wool; un-worked or semiworked glass (except glass used in building); glassware, porcelain, and earthenware not included in other classes.

Explanatory Note: This class includes mainly small, hand-operated utensils and apparatus for household and kitchen use as well as toilet utensils, glassware, and articles in porcelain.

Includes, in particular:

- utensils and containers for household and kitchen use, for example: kitchen utensils, pails, and pans of iron, aluminum, plastics, and other materials, small hand-operated apparatus for mincing, grinding, pressing, etc.;
- candle extinguishers, not of precious metal;
- electric combs;
- electric toothbrushes;
- dish stands and decanter stands.

Does not include, in particular:

- certain goods made of glass, porcelain, and earthenware (consult the Alphabetical List of Goods);
- cleaning preparations, soaps, etc. (CL 03);
- small apparatus for mincing, grinding, pressing, etc., driven by electricity (CL 07);
- razors and shaving apparatus, clippers (hand instruments);
- metal implements and utensils for manicure and pedicure (CL 08);
- cooking utensils, electric (CL 11);
- toilet mirrors (CL 20).

CLASS 22 (Cordage and fibers)

Ropes, string, nets, tents, awnings, tarpaulins, sails, sacks, and bags (not included in other classes); padding and stuffing materials (except of rubber or plastics); raw fibrous textile materials.

Explanatory Note: This class includes mainly rope and sail manufacture products, padding and stuffing materials, and raw fibrous textile materials.

Includes, in particular:

- cords and twines in natural or artificial textile fibres, paper, or plastics.

Does not include, in particular:

- certain nets, sacks, and bags (consult the Alphabetical List of Goods);
- strings for musical instruments (CL 15).

CLASS 23 (Yarns and threads)

Yarns and threads, for textile use.

CLASS 24 (Fabrics)

Textiles and textile goods, not included in other classes; bed and table covers.

Explanatory Note: This class includes mainly textiles (piece goods) and textile covers for household use.

Includes, in particular:

- bedding linen of paper.

Does not include, in particular:

- certain special textiles (consult the Alphabetical List of Goods);
- electrically heated blankets (CL 10);
- table linen of paper (CL 16);
- horse blankets (CL 18).

CLASS 25 (Clothing)

Clothing, footwear, headgear.

Explanatory Note
   Does not include, in particular:
   • certain clothing and footwear for special use
     (consult the Alphabetical List of Goods).

CLASS 26 (Fancy goods)

Lace and embroidery, ribbons and braid; buttons, hooks, and eyes, pins and needles; artificial flowers.

Explanatory Note: This class includes mainly dressmakers' articles.
   Includes, in particular:
   • slide fasteners.
   Does not include, in particular:
   • certain special types of hooks (consult the Alphabetical List of Goods);
   • certain special types of needles (consult the Alphabetical List of Goods);
   • yarns and threads for textile use (CL 23).

CLASS 27 (Floor coverings)

Carpets, rugs, mats and matting, linoleum, and other materials for covering existing floors; wall hangings (nontextile).

Explanatory Note: This class includes mainly products intended to be added as furnishings to previously constructed floors and walls. Does not include wooden flooring (CL 19).

CLASS 28 (Toys and sporting goods)

Games and playthings; gymnastic and sporting articles not included in other classes; decorations for Christmas trees.

Explanatory Note
   Includes, in particular:
   • amusement and game apparatus adapted for use with an external display screen or monitor;
   • fishing tackle;
   • equipment for various sports and games.

Does not include, in particular:
- Christmas tree candles (CL 04);
- diving equipment (CL 09);
- amusement apparatus adapted for use with television receivers only (CL 09);
- electrical lamps (garlands) for Christmas trees (CL 11);
- playing cards (CL 16);
- fishing nets (CL 22);
- clothing for gymnastics and sports (CL 25);
- confectionery and chocolate decorations for Christmas trees (CL 30).

CLASS 29 (Meats and processed foods)

Meat, fish, poultry, and game; meat extracts; preserved, dried, and cooked fruits and vegetables; jellies, jams, fruit sauces; eggs, milk, and milk products; edible oils and fats.

Explanatory Note: This class includes mainly foodstuffs of animal origin as well as vegetables and other horticultural comestible products which are prepared for consumption or conservation.

Includes, in particular:
- milk beverages (milk predominating).

Does not include, in particular:
- certain foodstuffs of plant origin (consult the Alphabetical List of Goods);
- baby food (CL 05);
- dietetic substances adapted for medical use (CL 05);
- salad dressings (CL 30);
- fertilized eggs for hatching (CL 31);
- foodstuffs for animals (CL 31);
- living animals (CL 31).

CLASS 30 (Staple foods)

Coffee, tea, cocoa, sugar, rice, tapioca, sago, artificial coffee; flour and preparations made from cereals, bread, pastry, and confectionery, ices;

honey, treacle; yeast, baking-powder; salt, mustard; vinegar, sauces (condiments); spices; ice.

Explanatory Note: This class includes mainly foodstuffs of plant origin prepared for consumption or conservation as well as auxiliaries intended for the improvement of the flavor of food.

Includes, in particular:

- beverages with coffee, cocoa, or chocolate base;
- cereals prepared for human consumption (for example: oat flakes and those made of other cereals).

Does not include, in particular:

- certain foodstuffs of plant origin (consult the Alphabetical List of Goods);
- salt for preserving other than for foodstuffs (CL 01);
- medicinal teas and dietetic substances adapted for medical use (CL 05);
- baby food (CL 05);
- raw cereals (CL 31);
- foodstuffs for animals (CL 31).

CLASS 31 (Natural agricultural products)

Agricultural, horticultural, and forestry products and grains not included in other classes; living animals; fresh fruits and vegetables; seeds, natural plants, and flowers; foodstuffs for animals, malt.

Explanatory Note: This class includes mainly land products not having been subjected to any form of preparation for consumption, living animals and plants, as well as foodstuffs for animals.

Includes, in particular:

- raw woods;
- raw cereals;
- fertilized eggs for hatching;
- mollusca and crustacea (live).

Does not include, in particular:

- cultures of microorganisms and leeches for medical purposes (CL 05);

- dietary supplements for animals (CL 05);
- semiworked woods (CL 19);
- artificial fishing bait (CL 28);
- rice (CL 30);
- tobacco (CL 34).

CLASS 32 (Light beverages)

Beers; mineral and aerated waters and other nonalcoholic drinks; fruit drinks and fruit juices; syrups and other preparations for making beverages.

Explanatory Note: This class includes mainly nonalcoholic beverages, as well as beer.

Includes, in particular:
- dealcoholized drinks.

Does not include, in particular:
- beverages for medical purposes (CL 05);
- milk beverages (milk predominating) (CL 29);
- beverages with coffee, cocoa, or chocolate base (CL 30).

CLASS 33 (Wine and spirits)

Alcoholic beverages (except beers).

Explanatory Note:

Does not include, in particular:
- medicinal drinks (CL 05);
- dealcoholized drinks (CL 32).

CLASS 34 (Smokers' articles)

Tobacco; smokers' articles; matches.

Explanatory Note:

Includes, in particular:
- tobacco substitutes (not for medical purposes).

Does not include, in particular:
* cigarettes without tobacco, for medical purposes (CL 05);
* certain smokers' articles in precious metal (CL 14) (consult the Alphabetical List of Goods).

SERVICES

CLASS 35 (Advertising and business)

Advertising; business management; business administration; office functions.

Explanatory Note: This class includes mainly services rendered by persons or organizations principally with the object of:
* help in the working or management of a commercial undertaking, or
* help in the management of the business affairs or commercial functions of an industrial or commercial enterprise, as well as services rendered by advertising establishments primarily undertaking communications to the public, declarations or announcements by all means of diffusion and concerning all kinds of goods or services.

Includes, in particular:
* services consisting of the registration, transcription, composition, compilation, or systematization of written communications and registrations, and also the exploitation or compilation of mathematical or statistical data;
* services of advertising agencies and services such as the distribution of prospectuses, directly or through the post, or the distribution of samples. This class may refer to advertising in connection with other services, such as those concerning bank loans or advertising by radio; the bringing together, for the benefit of others, of a variety of goods (excluding the transport thereof), enabling customers to conveniently view and purchase those goods.

Does not include, in particular:

- activity of an enterprise the primary function of which is the sale of goods, i.e., of a so-called commercial enterprise;
- services such as evaluations and reports of engineers which do not directly refer to the working or management of affairs in a commercial or industrial enterprise (consult the Alphabetical List of Services);
- professional consultations and the drawing up of plans not connected with the conduct of business (CL 42).

CLASS 36 (Insurance and financial)

Insurance; financial affairs; monetary affairs; real estate affairs.

Explanatory Note: This class includes mainly services rendered in financial and monetary affairs and services rendered in relation to insurance contracts of all kinds.

Includes, in particular:

- services relating to financial or monetary affairs that comprise the following:
  - services of all the banking establishments, or institutions connected with them such as exchange brokers or clearing services;
  - services of credit institutions other than banks such as cooperative credit associations, individual financial companies, lenders, etc.;
  - services of "investment trusts," of holding companies;
  - services of brokers dealing in shares and property;
  - services connected with monetary affairs vouched for by trustees;
  - services rendered in connection with the issue of travelers' checks and letters of credit;
- services of realty administrators of buildings, i.e., services of letting or valuation, or financing;
- services dealing with insurance such as services rendered by agents or brokers engaged in insurance, services rendered to the insured, and insurance underwriting services.

CLASS 37 (Building construction and repair)

Building construction; repair; installation services.

Explanatory Note: This class includes mainly services rendered by contractors or subcontractors in the construction or making of permanent buildings, as well as services rendered by persons or organizations engaged in the restoration of objects to their original condition or in their preservation without altering their physical or chemical properties.

Includes, in particular:
- services relating to the construction of buildings, roads, bridges, dams, or transmission lines, and services of undertakings specializing in the field of construction such as those of painters, plumbers, heating installers, or roofers;
- services auxiliary to construction services like inspections of construction plans;
- services of shipbuilding;
- services consisting of hiring of tools or building materials;
- repair services, i.e., services which undertake to put any object into good condition after wear, damage, deterioration, or partial destruction (restoration of an existing building or another object that has become imperfect and is to be restored to its original condition);
- various repair services such as those in the fields of electricity, furniture, instruments, tools, etc.;
- services of maintenance for preserving an object in its original condition without changing any of its properties (for the difference between this class and Class 40 see the Explanatory Note of Class 40).

Does not include, in particular:
- services consisting of storage of goods such as clothes or vehicles (CL 39);
- services connected with dyeing of cloth or clothes (CL 40).

CLASS 38 (Telecommunications)

Explanatory Note: This class includes mainly services allowing at least one person to communicate with another by a sensory means. Such services include those which:
- allow a person to talk to another,
- transmit messages from one person to another, and
- place a person in oral or visual communication with another (radio and television).

Includes, in particular:
- services which consist essentially of the diffusion of radio or television programs.

Does not include, in particular:
- radio advertising services (CL 35);
- telemarketing services (CL 35).

CLASS 39 (Transportation and storage)

Transport; packaging and storage of goods; travel arrangement.

Explanatory Note: This class includes mainly services rendered in transporting people or goods from one place to another (by rail, road, water, air, or pipeline) and services necessarily connected with such transport, as well as services relating to the storing of goods in a warehouse or other building for their preservation or guarding.

Includes, in particular:
- services rendered by companies exploiting stations, bridges, railroad ferries, etc., used by the transporter;
- services connected with the hiring of transport vehicles;
- services connected with maritime tugs, unloading, the functioning of ports and docks, and the salvaging of wrecked ships and their cargoes;
- services connected with the functioning of airports;
- services connected with the packaging and parceling of goods before dispatch;

- services consisting of information about journeys or the transport of goods by brokers and tourist agencies, information relating to tariffs, timetables, and methods of transport;
- services relating to the inspection of vehicles or goods before transport.

Does not include, in particular:

- services relating to advertising transport undertakings such as the distribution of prospectuses or advertising on the radio (CL 35);
- services relating to the issuing of travelers' checks or letters of credit by brokers or travel agents (CL 36);
- services relating to insurance (commercial, fire, or life) during the transport of persons or goods (CL 36);
- services rendered by the maintenance and repair of vehicles, nor the maintenance or repair of objects connected with the transport of persons or goods (CL 37);
- services relating to reservation of rooms in a hotel by travel agents or brokers (CL 42).

CLASS 40 (Treatment of materials)

Treatment of materials.

Explanatory Note: This class includes mainly services not included in other classes, rendered by the mechanical or chemical processing or transformation of objects or inorganic or organic substances.

For the purposes of classification, the mark is considered a service mark only in cases where processing or transformation is effected for the account of another person. A mark is considered a trademark in all cases where the substance or object is marketed by the person who processed or transformed it.

Includes, in particular:

- services relating to transformation of an object or substance and any process involving a change in its essential properties (for example, dyeing a garment); consequently, a maintenance service, although usually in Class 37, is included in Class 40 if it entails such a change (for example, the chroming of motor vehicle bumpers);

- services of material treatment which may be present during the production of any substance or object other than a building; for example, services which involve cutting, shaping, polishing by abrasion, or metal coating.

Does not include, in particular:

- repair services (CL 37).

CLASS 41 (Education and entertainment)

Education; providing of training; entertainment; sporting and cultural activities.

Explanatory Note: This class contains mainly services rendered by persons or institutions in the development of the mental faculties of persons or animals, as well as services intended to entertain or to engage the attention.

Includes, in particular:

- services consisting of all forms of education of persons or training of animals;
- services having the basic aim of the entertainment, amusement, or recreation of people.

CLASS 42 (Science and technology)

Scientific and technological services and research and design relating thereto: industrial analysis and research services; design and development of computer hardware and software.

Explanatory Note: Class 42 includes mainly services provided by persons, individually or collectively, in relation to the theoretical and practical aspects of complex fields of activities; such services are provided by members of professions such as chemists, physicists, engineers, computer programmers, etc.

Includes, in particular:

- the services of engineers and scientists who undertake evaluations, estimates, research, and reports in the scientific and technological fields;
- scientific research services for medical purposes.

Does not include, in particular:
- business research and evaluations (CL 35);
- word processing and computer file management services (CL 35);
- financial and fiscal evaluations (CL 36);
- mining and oil extraction (CL 37);
- computer (hardware) installation and repair services (CL 37);
- services provided by the members of professions such as medical doctors, veterinary surgeons, psychoanalysts (CL 44);
- medical treatment services (CL 44);
- garden design (CL 44);
- legal services (CL 45).

CLASS 43 (Hotels and restaurants)

Services for providing food and drink; temporary accommodations.

Explanatory Note: Class 43 includes mainly services provided by persons or establishments whose aim is to prepare food and drink for consumption and services provided to obtain bed and board in hotels, boarding houses, or other establishments providing temporary accommodations.

Includes, in particular:
- reservation services for travelers' accommodations, particularly through travel agencies or brokers;
- boarding for animals.

Does not include, in particular:
- rental services for real estate such as houses, flats, etc., for permanent use (CL 36);
- arranging travel by tourist agencies (CL 39);
- preservation services for food and drink (CL 40);
- discotheque services (CL 41);
- boarding schools (CL 41);
- rest and convalescent homes (CL 44).

CLASS 44 (Medical, beauty, and agricultural)

Medical services; veterinary services; hygienic and beauty care for human beings or animals; agriculture, horticulture, and forestry services.

Explanatory Note: Class 44 includes mainly medical care, hygienic and beauty care given by persons or establishments to human beings, and animals; it also includes services relating to the fields of agriculture, horticulture, and forestry.

Includes, in particular:

- medical analysis services relating to the treatment of persons (such as X-ray examinations and taking of blood samples);
- artificial insemination services;
- pharmacy advice;
- animal breeding;
- services relating to the growing of plants such as gardening;
- services relating to floral art such as floral compositions as well as garden design.

Does not include, in particular:

- vermin extermination (other than for agriculture, horticulture, and forestry) (CL 37);
- installation and repair services for irrigation systems (CL 37);
- ambulance transport (CL 39);
- animal slaughtering services and taxidermy (CL 40);
- timber felling and processing (CL 40);
- animal training services (CL 41);
- health clubs for physical exercise (CL 41);
- scientific research services for medical purposes (CL 42);
- boarding for animals (CL 43);
- retirement homes (CL 43).

CLASS 45 (Legal and personal services)

Legal services; personal and social services rendered by others to meet the needs of individuals; security services for the protection of property and individuals.

Explanatory Note

Includes, in particular:
- services rendered by lawyers, legal assistants, and personal advocates, to individuals, groups of individuals, organizations, and enterprises;
- investigation and surveillance services relating to the safety of persons and entities;
- services provided to individuals in relation with social events, such as social escort services, matrimonial agencies, funeral services.

Does not include, in particular:
- professional services giving direct aid in the operations or functions of a commercial undertaking (CL 35);
- services relating to financial or monetary affairs and services dealing with insurance (CL 36);
- escorting of travelers (CL 39);
- security transport (CL 39);
- services consisting of all forms of education of persons (CL 41);
- performances of singers and dancers (CL 41);
- computer services for the protection of software (CL 42);
- services provided by others to give medical, hygienic, or beauty care for human beings or animals (CL 44);
- certain rental services (consult the Alphabetical List of Services and relating to the classification of services).

Glossary of Terms

Abandonment. Loss of trademark rights resulting from nonuse of a mark and demonstrated by sufficient evidence that the owner intends to discontinue use of the mark; may also occur when mark has lost its distinctiveness through owner's misuse of trademark rights or as a result of naked license.

Allegation of Use. A USPTO form that combines the Statement of Use and Amendment to Allege Use.

Amendment to Allege Use. An amendment to an intent-to-use application indicating use of a mark in commerce; it can only be filed before the USPTO approves the mark for publication (or if there is a rejection, within six months of the response period). An applicant would complete the Allegation of Use form when filing an Amendment to Allege Use.

Answer. A written response to a court complaint in which the defendant admits or denies the allegations and provides a list of defenses.

Arbitrary mark. A word or group of words that has a dictionary meaning that does not pertain to the goods or services with which it is associated.

Assignment. A permanent transfer of trademark rights and goodwill.

Blurring. A form of dilution in which a famous mark loses some of its distinctiveness due to the use of a similar mark.

Cancellation proceeding. An action brought before the Trademark Trial and Appeal Board to cancel a federal registration of a mark; must be based upon one of the statutory grounds provided in the Lanham Act, and the party bringing the action must prove that it would be damaged.

Certification mark. A mark that indicates that third-party goods and services meet certain standards such as regional origin, material, mode of manufacture, quality, accuracy, or that the work or labor was performed by a member of a certain organization.

Civil cover sheet. A form required at the time of filing of the complaint for use by the court in maintaining certain statistical records.

Collateral estoppel. A defense to infringement; a senior user is required to abide by factual or legal determinations made in a previous lawsuit.

Collective mark. Used by members of a cooperative, an association, or other collective group or organization to indicate membership or to indicate the source of the organization's products or services.

Commerce. For purposes of protection of U.S. trademarks, any trade or business lawfully regulated by the United States.

Common law. A system of legal rules derived from the precedents and principles established by court decisions.

Concurrent use. A legal determination that more than one person is entitled to use a similar mark.

Confidentiality agreement (also known as nondisclosure agreement or disclosure agreement). A contract that restricts or prohibits the disclosure of confidential information.

Counterfeiting. The act of making or selling look-alike goods or services bearing fake trademarks

Cybersquatter. A person who registers a well-known trademark as a domain name hoping to later profit by selling the domain name to the trademark owner.

Declaratory relief. Request that the court sort out the rights and legal obligations of the parties in the midst of an actual controversy.

Defamation of business. False statements that injure a business's reputation. Defamation affects the manner in which the public perceives the company's trademarked products.

Descriptive mark. A name or term that merely describes a product or service (or its nature, quality, characteristics, ingredients, or origin) and is considered "weak."

Design patent. Legal protection granted for a new, original, and ornamental design for an article of manufacture; it protects only the aesthetic appearance of an article, not its structure or utilitarian features.

Dilution. A form of trademark injury that occurs when a famous mark's reputation is blurred or tarnished by the commercial use of a similar mark. Unlike traditional trademark infringement, there is no requirement of consumer confusion, and the parties do not have to be competitors selling similar goods or services.

Disclaimer. A statement that a trademark owner asserts no exclusive right in a specific portion of a mark, apart from its use within the mark.

Disparagement. False statements that interfere with a company's business relations and negatively affect a company's ability to do business.

Distinctive mark. A mark that is either immediately distinguishable, such as an arbitrary, fanciful, or suggestive mark or a descriptive mark that has acquired secondary meaning.

Diversity. The right to file a lawsuit based upon nonfederal claims in federal court; parties must be from different states and the matter in controversy over $50,000.

Domain name. An identifier of a website location consisting of two parts: a generic top-level domain (such as .com or .org) and a second level that is the name of the business or organization (such as amazon or eBay).

Drawing. A substantially exact representation of the mark as used or (in the case of intent-to-use applications) as intended to be used. A drawing is required for all federal trademark applications and for many state trademark applications.

Estoppel. A defense to infringement in which the junior user prevents the senior user from contradicting behavior upon which the junior user has justifiably relied. To assert an estoppel defense successfully, the senior user must know the facts of the junior user's conduct, and the junior user must have a justifiable belief that the infringing conduct is permitted.

Fair use. A company may defend its use of a trademarked term (owned by someone else) when the term is used to describe products or services. For example, an ad for a dishwashing machine may refer to the "joy of dishwashing" without infringing the trademark "Joy" as used for dishwashing soap. In 2005, the U.S. Supreme Court ruled that the fair-use defense can be made even when the use results in consumer confusion.

Famous mark. A mark that is widely recognized by the general consuming public as a designation of the source of the goods or services. Factors that determine whether a mark is famous include: (1) the duration, extent, and geographic reach of advertising and publicity of the mark; (2) the amount, volume, and geographic extent of sales of goods or services offered under the mark; (3) the extent of actual customer recognition of the mark; and (4) whether the mark was registered on the Principal Register.

Fanciful marks. An invented word that is created solely to be used as a trademark or service mark, for example, Exxon or Kodak. These fanciful coined marks are immediately distinctive and are considered to be the strongest of all marks.

Franchise agreement. A contract in which a trademark owner (the "franchiser") permits another business (the "franchisee") to operate under the trademark and offer trademarked (or "branded") products and services, for example a Ford dealership, a Baskin & Robbins ice cream store, or an H&R Block tax preparation business.

Functionality. The usability of a product feature or design; functional features or design will not be protected under trademark law.

Generic term. A term that describes an entire group or class of goods.

Genericide. The process by which trademark rights are abandoned because consumers have begun to think of the trademark as the descriptive name for the goods; results from a judicial determination or inter partes proceeding at the Patent and Trademark Office.

Geographically descriptive (weak). A geographic term describes the origin, location, or source of the product or service, for example, First National Bank of Bloomington for a bank located in Bloomington, Indiana.

Geographically misdescriptive (unprotectable). A geographic term that misleads consumers into believing that the product originates from a region when it does not. For example, Danish Maid Cultured Products is geographically misdescriptive of products that are not from Denmark.

Goodwill. The tendency or likelihood of a consumer to repurchase goods or services based upon the name or source of the goods or services.

Gray-market goods. When goods are manufactured abroad with the authorization of the trademark owner but are imported into the United States without authorization of the trademark owner.

House mark. A word or group of words that functions as the source for various products or services from one company; it is often used in conjunction with other trademarks.

Incontestable. A trademark that is immune from challenge except for certain grounds specified in Section 33(b) of the Lanham Act; conclusive evidence of the registrant's exclusive right to use the registered mark in commerce in connection with the specified goods or services.

Infringement. Occurs when the junior user's goods or services create a likelihood of confusion with the senior user's goods or services.

Inherently distinctive. A mark that is immediately distinguishable, such as an arbitrary, fanciful, or suggestive mark. Marks that are not immediately distinguishable but describe some quality or aspect of the goods or services may acquire distinctiveness through sales and advertising (see *secondary meaning*).

Injunction. A court order directing the defendant to stop certain activities.

Intellectual property. Any product of the human mind that is protectable under law.

Intent to use. An application for federal trademark registration based upon the trademark owner's bona fide intention to use the mark in commerce.

Inter partes. A formal administrative hearing governed by federal rules of civil procedure and evidence.

Interference proceeding. A minitrial before the Trademark Trial and Appeal Board brought when two pending trademark applications conflict or when a pending application conflicts with a registered mark that is not incontestable; only permitted under extraordinary circumstances.

Interference with business relations. A defendant intentionally interferes with the plaintiff's business relationship with a third party.

Interference with prospective economic advantage. A defendant intentionally interferes with a probable business relationship between the plaintiff and a third party.

International schedule of classes of goods and services. A system for classification of goods and services applicable to federal trademark applications filed on or after September 1, 1973.

Junior user. A party who adopts and uses a trademark similar to a mark previously adopted and used by a senior user.

Jurisdiction. The right of a court to hear a type of case or to bind the participants.

Laches. A defense to infringement in which the junior user argues that the senior user's delay in bringing the lawsuit is so unreasonable that the senior user should be barred from proceeding.

Likelihood of confusion. The probability of whether consumers will be confused as to the sponsorship, affiliation, or connection between the products or services of companies with similar marks; a standard for infringement, registration, and inter partes proceedings.

Merchandise license. A contract between the trademark owner and licensee permitting the licensee to apply the trademark to certain consumer goods, for example, coffee mugs featuring images of Bugs Bunny or the logo of a university.

Merely descriptive. See *descriptive mark.*

Motion for preliminary injunction. A request that the court order the defendant to halt the infringing activity until the outcome of the trial.

Motion for summary judgment. A request that the court grant a judgment without having a trial because there is no dispute as to the facts.

Naked license. A trademark license in which a trademark owner fails to supervise the nature and quality of the goods or services being produced under the license. A naked license can result in loss of all trademark rights.

Opposition proceeding. An action brought before the Trademark Trial and Appeal Board to prevent the federal registration of a mark; must be based upon one of the statutory grounds provided in the Lanham Act, and the party bringing the action must prove that it would be damaged.

Parody. A defense used by a junior user who seeks to justify its imitation on the premise of humor or satirical social commentary. As a general rule, the same likelihood of confusion standards are applied in a case involving parody as in any other type of infringement. The difference is that the junior user attempts to argue that consumers could not be confused because the use is obviously a joke.

Permanent injunction. A court order issued after a final judgment on the merits of the case; it permanently restrains the defendant from engaging in the infringing activity.

Preliminary injunction. A court order granted after a noticed hearing when the parties have an opportunity to present evidence as to the likelihood of plaintiff's success on the merits and irreparability of the harm to be suffered if the injunction is not granted; it lasts until a final judgment has been rendered.

Priority. A senior user's right to prevent a junior user from using a mark.

Related goods or services. Goods or services that the consuming public is likely to believe come from a certain company.

Remedies. Forms of judicial relief available in a lawsuit, for example, damages, injunctions, or attorneys' fees.

Request to divide out. A statement included in an Allegation of Use asking to separate from the application certain goods for which the trademark has not been used.

Reverse confusion. When a junior user, usually a larger, more powerful company, attempts to usurp the power of the senior user's mark and create the impression that the senior user is the infringer.

Right of publicity. The legal right to control the commercial exploitation of a person's name, image, or persona.

Secondary meaning. Demonstration that the consuming public associates a mark with a single source; it's usually proved by advertising, promotion, and sales. A weak (descriptive) mark is said to acquire distinctiveness when it takes on a secondary meaning.

Section 8 declaration (also known as a Declaration of Continued Use). A declaration by a trademark owner that the mark is still in use. Filed between the fifth and sixth year following registration and at the time of each trademark renewal. Failure to file in this time period or within the six-month grace period may result in loss of trademark rights.

Section 9 application for renewal. An application seeking renewal of a federal trademark registration; it must be filed within six months of the expiration of the initial term of trademark registration.

Section 15 declaration (also known as a Declaration of Incontestability). A declaration that a trademark has been in continuous use for five years since registration. Filed between the fifth and sixth year following registration. If filed and accepted by the Patent and Trademark Office the mark becomes incontestable.

Section 44 application. An application for federal trademark registration by the owner of a mark registered in a foreign country, provided that country is a party to an international convention or treaty of which the United States is a member.

Senior user. The first party to adopt and use a particular mark in connection with its goods or services.

Service mark. A mark used in the sale or advertising of services to identify and distinguish services.

Statement of Use. A declaration indicating use of a mark in commerce; it can only be filed after a Notice of Allowance has been issued. An applicant would complete the Allegation of Use form when filing a Statement of Use.

Strong mark. Achieved by an inherently distinctive mark or by a nondistinctive mark that has achieved secondary meaning.

Suggestive mark. A mark that alludes to or hints at (without describing) the nature or quality of the goods.

Summons. A document served with the complaint that explains that the defendant has been sued and has a certain time limit in which to respond.

Sweetheart sales. Shipments or transactions within a company and performed solely to qualify for registration or for a claim of priority.

Tarnishment. A form of dilution that occurs when a famous mark is damaged by an unpleasant or unwholesome use of a similar mark.

TEAS (Trademark Electronic Application System). A USPTO database available to the public (at www.uspto.gov) that allows the user to apply for a trademark, a collective mark, or certification mark or file a Statement of Use/Amendment to Allege Use or another application and postregistration forms.

Temporary restraining order (TRO). An injunction, often granted *ex parte*, that is short in duration and only remains in effect until the court has an opportunity to schedule a hearing for the preliminary injunction.

TESS (Trademark Electronic Search System). A USPTO database available to the public (at www.uspto.gov) that allows the user to search through federal trademark registrations and prior-filed applications.

Trade dress. A distinctive combination of elements, many of which may not be protectable by themselves under trademark law.

Trade secret. Any business information that is kept in confidence and that gives the business an advantage over competitors who do not know it.

Trademark. Any word, symbol, design, device, logo, or slogan that identifies and distinguishes one product or service from another.

Trademark license. An agreement granting limited trademark rights.

TSDR (Trademark Status and Document Retrieval). A USPTO database that enables a user to retrieve information about the status of applications or federally registered marks, as well as to view and download hundreds of thousands of trademark documents.

Unclean hands. A defense asserted when the senior user has committed a serious act of wrongdoing in regard to the lawsuit or the activity precipitating the lawsuit.

Unfair competition. A collection of common law principles and precedents, many of which are adopted as state laws, that protect against unethical business practices.

URL (Uniform Resource Locator). A system for locating a website; it generally begins with http://www. followed by a domain name.

Use in commerce. Actual use of a mark in the ordinary course of trade (or, if otherwise impracticable, on documents associated with the goods). For federal registration, commerce is any commerce lawfully regulated by the federal government. For state registration, it is generally any commerce occurring within the state of registration. A service mark is deemed to be in use in commerce when it is used or displayed in the sale or advertising of services and the services are rendered in commerce.

Weak. Nondistinctive name or term that cannot be registered or protected as a trademark unless the owner proves a consumer awareness or "secondary meaning."

Selected Pages From Thomson CompuMark Trademark Research Report

Search: Incorporator Pro

Reprinted with permission of Thomson CompuMark

Thomson CompuMark

Trademark Research Report

Mark Searched: INCORPORATOR PRO

Client Name:	THOMSON COMPUMARK
Type Of Search:	FULL SEARCH
Formatted:	By Source

Attention: **SCOTT RUTHERFORD**

Our File:	136177611 -78
Date Completed:	February 26, 2007
Date Received:	February 22, 2007
Received by:	Telephone

Goods/Services:

SOFTWARE PRODUCT

Table of Contents

Mark Searched: INCORPORATOR PRO

INCORPORATOR PRO

Group One Summary

Citation	Status	Class(es)	Owner	Source	Page	Record of Interest
			GROUP ONE			
1. INCORPORATOR PRO	Abandoned	9	NOLO	USPTO	18	☐
2. INCORPORATOR PRO	N/A	9	NOLO PRESS	Common Law Database	165	☐
3. INCORPORATORPRO.COM	N/A	N/A	N/A	Domain Name	202	☐

Search: 136177611   Analyst: ANDREA SLATER   Report Summary Page: 6

INCORPORATOR PRO

USPTO Summary Page

Citation	Status	Class(es)	Owner	Reg/Serial Number	Page	Record of Interest

GROUP ONE

1. INCORPORATOR PRO

	Abandoned	9	NOLO	SN-76-463,346	18	☐

GROUP TWO

No Group Two Matches

GROUP THREE

2. NATIONWIDE INCORPORATORS THE INCORPORATION PROFESSIONALS

	Registered	42	CALIFORNIA INCORPORATORS	RN-2,801,326 SN-78-090,464	19	☐

3. MARIPRO INCORPORATED

	Registered	9, 40, 42	MARIPRO INCORPORATED	RN-2,706,549 SN-76-363,473	20	☐

4. CAPRO INCORPORATED

	Cancelled	9, 16	CAPRO INCORPORATED	RN-1,268,994 SN-73-407,856	22	☐

5. PROSYNAPTIC TECHNOLOGIES, INCORPORATED

	Pending	9, 42	PROSYNAPTIC TECHNOLOGIES, INCORPORATED	SN-77-067,918	24	☐

6. PROMED SYSTEMS INCORPORATED

	Abandoned	42	PROMED SYSTEMS, INC.	SN-73-493,128	26	☐

7. COMPUTER SERVICE PROFESSIONALS INCORPORATED

	Abandoned	42	COMPUTER SERVICE PROFESSIONALS INCORPORA ...	SN-74-346,720	28	☐

8. SHOWPRO INCORPORATED

	Abandoned	35	SHOWPRO, INC.	SN-73-553,149	30	☐

9. PROFESSIONAL TECHNOLOGIES, INCORPORATED

	Misassigned	35	PROFESSIONAL TECHNOLOGIES, INCORPORATED	SN-74-043,051	31	☐

10. COMMUNICATIONS PROFESSIONALS OF SOUTH CAROLINA INCORPORATED

	Abandoned	37	COMMUNICATIONS PROFESSIONALS OF SOUTH CA ...	SN-75-052,275	32	☐

Search: 136177611   **Analyst: ANDREA SLATER**   USPTO Summary Page: 7

INCORPORATOR PRO

Citation	Status	Class(es)	Owner	Reg/Serial Number	Page	Record of Interest
			GROUP FOUR			
11. PROSOFT LEARNING CORPORATION						
	Pending	9	PROSOFT LEARNING CORPORATION	SN-78-822,486	33	☐
12. PRL PROSOFT LEARNING CORPORATION						
	Pending	9	PROSOFT LEARNING CORPORATION	SN-78-822,479	35	☐
13. VIPRO CORPORATION THE INTERNET SURETY COMPANY						
	Abandoned	35	VIPRO CORPORATION	SN-75-899,602	37	☐
14. PROSOFT LEARNING CORPORATION						
	Pending	16	PROSOFT LEARNING CORPORATION	SN-78-822,484	38	☐
15. PLC PROSOFT LEARNING CORPORATION						
	Pending	16	PROSOFT LEARNING CORPORATION	SN-78-822,476	40	☐
16. HIRSCHLER FLEISCHER A PROFESSIONAL CORPORATION						
	Registered	16	HIRSCHLER FLEISCHER	RN-2,708,709 SN-76-340,064	42	☐
17. PTC PROFESSIONAL TESTING CORPORATION						
	Registered	16, 42	PROFESSIONAL TESTING CORPORATION	RN-2,133,782 SN-75-100,729	43	☐
18. CORPORATE PRO BONO						
	Pending	35	PRO BONO INSTITUTE	SN-78-762,830	45	☐
19. SOLUTIONS BUTZEL LONG A PROFESSIONAL CORPORATION						
	Registered	42	BUTZEL LONG	RN-2,570,908 SN-76-088,200	46	☐
20. PROSOFT LEARNING CORPORATION						
	Pending	41	PROSOFT LEARNING CORPORATION	SN-78-822,482	47	☐
21. PLC PROSOFT LEARNING CORPORATION						
	Pending	41	PROSOFT LEARNING CORPORATION	SN-78-822,473	49	☐
22. PROACTIVE INFORMATION CORPORATION						
	Abandoned	41	PROACTIVE INFORMATION CORPORATION	SN-75-614,879	51	☐

Search: 136177611   Analyst: ANDREA SLATER   USPTO Summary Page: 8

INCORPORATOR PRO

Citation	Status	Class(es)	Owner	Reg/Serial Number	Page	Record of Interest
23. MYCORPORATION.COM PROFESSIONALS NETWORK						
	Registered	35, 42	MY CORPORATION BUSINESS SERVICES, INC.	RN-2,897,331 SN-78-293,665	52	☐
24. PGC ISO9001 PROGATE GROUP U.S.A. CORPORATION						
	Registered	42	PROGATE GROUP U.S.A. CORPORATION	RN-2,674,346 SN-76-316,857	53	☐
25. PROVIS CORPORATION						
	Abandoned	9	PROVIS CORPORATION	SN-75-174,338	55	☐
26. DIGITAL PRO CORPORATION						
	Abandoned	9	DIGITAL-PRO, CORP.	SN-73-492,585	56	☐
27. SMART FORMS CORPORATION PERMITPRO FOR WINDOWS CORPORATION, NEW YORK, NY.						
	Misassigned	9	SMART FORMS CORPORATION	SN-75-760,799	57	☐
28. PSC PROFESSIONAL SOUND CORPORATION						
	Cancelled	9	PROFESSIONAL SOUND CORPORATION	RN-2,092,736 SN-75-080,421	58	☐
29. MORETIME THE CORPORATE TIME MANAGEMENT SYSTEM DESIGNED FOR MANAGERS AND PROFESSIONALS A PRODUCT OF LYNN-ARTHUR ASSOCIATES						
	Abandoned	42	LYNN-ARTHUR ASSOCIATES	SN-73-404,692	59	☐
30. INTERNET INCORPORATORS						
	Registered	42	WICKFORD EQUITIES, LLC.	RN-2,458,702 SN-75-404,152	60	☐
31. INTERNET INCORPORATORS						
	Registered	42	WICKFORD EQUITIES, LLC.	RN-2,679,110 SN-75-124,945	62	☐
32. WORLDWIDE INCORPORATORS LTD.						
	Registered	35	WORLDWIDE INCORPORATORS LTD.	RN-2,299,102 SN-75-570,111	65	☐
33. INCORPORATORS USA, LLC						
	Pending	35	REGISTERED AGENTS, LTD.	SN-78-808,595	66	☐
34. AMERICAN INCORPORATORS						
	Registered	35	AMERICAN INCORPORATORS LTD.	RN-2,536,840 SN-78-068,934	67	☐
35. FASTINCORPORATORS						
	Abandoned	35	FAST INCORPORATORS INC.	SN-76-519,811	68	☐

Search: 136177611   Analyst: ANDREA SLATER   USPTO Summary Page: 9

INCORPORATOR PRO

Citation	Status	Class(es)	Owner	Reg/Serial Number	Page	Record of Interest
36. GEEKS INCORPORATED						
	Registered	42	GEEKS ONSITE LTD.	RN-2,783,731 SN-76-391,514	69	☐
37. PCO INCORPORATED						
	Published	9	PC OPEN INC.	SN-78-704,318	71	☐
38. GVP INCORPORATED NETWORK & SYSTEMS CONSULTING						
	Registered	42	PC MALL, INC.	RN-2,361,713 SN-75-628,860	73	☐
39. INCORPORATETIME						
	Registered	42	WALSH, KERRY	RN-3,004,229 SN-78-464,888	75	☐
40. INCORPORATE						
	Cancelled	9	UNABRIDGED SOFTWARE, INC.	RN-2,085,108 SN-75-128,694	76	☐
41. MICROPRO INTERNATIONAL CORPORATION						
	Cancelled	9, 16	MICRON PC, LLC	RN-1,233,332 SN-73-267,413	77	☐
42. CORPRO						
	Registered	9	CORSTAR BUSINESS COMPUTING CO., INC.	RN-1,450,424 SN-73-588,242	82	☐
43. MEMBERPRO						
	Registered	9	REDESIGN TECHNOLOGIES INC.	RN-3,008,149 SN-76-417,408	83	☐
44. INSTALLPRO						
	Registered	9	RELEASE ENGINEERING INC.	RN-2,800,234 SN-78-115,518	85	☐
45. INTRUPRO						
	Registered	9	INTOTO, INC.	RN-3,040,878 SN-78-503,676	86	☐
46. INTERACTIVEPRO						
	Registered	9	SIGMATECH, INC.	RN-2,798,237 SN-76-103,632	87	☐
47. PARTNER PRO						
	Registered	42	VMG TECHNOLOGIES, INC.	RN-2,706,944 SN-76-426,736	88	☐
48. PRESENTERPRO						
TTAB	Registered	9	SIGMATECH, INC.	RN-2,854,043 SN-75-728,431	89	☐

Search: 136177611   Analyst: ANDREA SLATER   USPTO Summary Page: 10

INCORPORATOR PRO

Citation	Status	Class(es)	Owner	Reg/Serial Number	Page	Record of Interest
49. INFO-PRO						
	Registered	9	INFORMATION PROFESSION ALS COMPANY	RN-3,019,036 SN-76-546,245	91	☐
50. INDUSTRYPRO						
	Registered	35, 42	ZIRKLE & CO.	RN-2,406,037 SN-75-840,779	92	☐
51. INSTALLATIONPRO						
	Registered	37	METRON NORTH AMERICA, LTD.	RN-2,869,799 SN-78-298,485	93	☐
52. PROFILERPRO						
	Published	9	CALIPER LIFE SCIENCES, INC.	SN-77-000,497	95	☐
53. ALLOCATOR PRO						
	Registered	9	FMR CORP.	RN-2,269,948 SN-75-311,768	96	☐
54. LAWYER PRO						
	Renewed	9	HARLAND FINANCIAL SOLUTI ONS, INC.	RN-1,874,579 SN-74-399,446	98	☐
55. SMALL BIZ PRO						
	Pending	35	BESACK & ASSOCIATES	SN-78-886,070	102	☐
56. EBUSINESS PRO						
	Abandoned	9, 16, 42	ZD INC.	SN-75-514,100	103	☐
57. COMPANYDATA PRO						
	Abandoned	9, 16, 35, 36, 38, 42	DEUTSCHE TELEKOM AG	SN-78-166,920	106	☐
58. BIZPRO						
	Pending	16	APEX BUSINESS SOLUTION S, LLC	SN-76-665,761	108	☐
59. PRO BUSINESS TOOLS						
	Registered	42	PROSITE BUSINESS SOLUTI ONS, LLC	RN-3,131,366 SN-78-467,030	109	☐
60. BIZPRO						
	Cancelled	35	APTAN, INC.	RN-2,136,707 SN-75-138,818	110	☐
61. BUSINESS PLAN PRO						
	Registered	9	PALO ALTO SOFTWARE, INC.	RN-2,165,157 SN-75-167,857	111	☐

INCORPORATOR PRO

Citation	Status	Class(es)	Owner	Reg/Serial Number	Page	Record of Interest
			GROUP FIVE			
62. THE INCORPORATOR WWW.INCBYPRO.COM						
	Registered	42	THE INCORPORATOR INCORPORATED	RN-3,201,257 SN-78-795,446	112	☐
63. PROS INCORPORATED						
	Abandoned	35	PROS INCORPORATED	SN-75-288,910	113	☐

INCORPORATOR PRO

US-1
Group: One

INCORPORATOR PRO

INCORPORATOR PRO

Status: ABANDONED
INTENT TO USE

USPTO Status: ABANDONED-FAILURE TO RESPOND
USPTO Status Date: MAY 27, 2004

Goods/Services:
International Class 9: COMPUTER SOFTWARE FOR USE IN
CREATING STATE CORPORATION DOCUMENTS

Last Reported Owner:
NOLO
CALIFORNIA CORPORATION
950 PARKER STREET
BERKELEY, CALIFORNIA 94710

Chronology:
Filed: OCT 31, 2002   **Serial Number:** 76-463,346
Abandoned: MAY 27, 2004

Ownership Details:
Applicant:
NOLO
CALIFORNIA CORPORATION
950 PARKER STREET
BERKELEY, CALIFORNIA 94710
Filing Correspondent:
NOLO
950 PARKER STREET
BERKELEY CA 94710

In-Use Information
Citation Link: None Found
Owner Link: None Found
In-Use Link: None Found

INCORPORATOR PRO

US-2
Group: Three

NATIONWIDE INCORPORATORS THE INCORPORATION PROFESSIONALS

Status: REGISTERED

USPTO Status: REGISTERED
USPTO Status Date: DEC 30, 2003

Goods/Services:

International Class 42: PREPARATION AND FILINGS TO STATE AGENCIES ON BEHALF OF BUSINESS OWNERS TO FORM CORPORATIONS AND LIMITED LIABILITY COMPANIES
First Used: DEC 15, 2001 (INTL. CL. 42)
In Commerce: DEC 15, 2001

Disclaimers:

"NATIONWIDE INCORPORATORS" AND "THE INCORPORATION PROFESSIONALS"

Last Reported Owner:

CALIFORNIA INCORPORATORS
CALIFORNIA CORPORATION
15928 VENTURA BLVD., SUITE 224
ENCINO, CALIFORNIA 91436

We Have Located Other Marks With This Owner

CALIFORNIA INCORPORATORS THE   State   Page 123
PROFESSIONAL SOLUTION

Chronology:

Filed: OCT 26, 2001   **Serial Number:** 78-090,464
Published For Opposition: NOV 05, 2002
Registered: DEC 30, 2003   **Registration Number:** 2,801,326

Ownership Details:

Registrant:

CALIFORNIA INCORPORATORS
CALIFORNIA CORPORATION
15928 VENTURA BLVD., SUITE 224
ENCINO, CALIFORNIA 91436

Filing Correspondent:

CALIFORNIA INCORPORATORS
15928 VENTURA BLVD STE 224
ENCINO CA 91436-4413

INCORPORATOR PRO

US-4
Group: Three

CAPRO
INCORPORATED

CAPRO INCORPORATED

Status: CANCELLED   **Cancellation Section:** 8

USPTO Status: CANCELLED - SECTION 8
USPTO Status Date: JUL 12, 1990

Goods/Services:

International Class 9: COMPUTERS AND PERIPHERAL EQUIPMENT
FOR COMPUTERS-NAMELY, PRINTERS AND VIDEO DISPLAY
TERMINALS
International Class 16: INSTRUCTION MANUALS FOR COMPUTER
HARDWARE AND SOFTWARE
First Used: JUN 01, 1982 (INTL. CL. 9)
In Commerce: JUL 30, 1982
First Used: JUN 01, 1982 (INTL. CL. 16)
In Commerce: JUL 30, 1982

Disclaimers:

NO CLAIM IS MADE TO THE EXCLUSIVE RIGHT TO USE "INCORPO
RATED", APART FROM THE MARK AS SHOWN.

Last Reported Owner:

CAPRO INCORPORATED
CALIFORNIA CORPORATION
12781 PALA DR.
GARDEN GROVE, CALIFORNIA 92641

We Have Located Other Marks With This Owner

CAPRO INCORPORATED	State	Page 133
CAPRO INCORPORATED	State	Page 134

Chronology:

Filed: JAN 03, 1983   **Serial Number:** 73-407,856
Published For Opposition: DEC 13, 1983
Registered: MAR 06, 1984   **Registration Number:** 1,268,994
Cancelled: AUG 21, 1990

Ownership Details:
Registrant:

CAPRO INCORPORATED
CALIFORNIA CORPORATION
12781 PALA DR.
GARDEN GROVE, CALIFORNIA 92641

Filing Correspondent:

HOWARD J. KLEIN
KLEIN & SZEKERES

INCORPORATOR PRO

US-30
Group: Four

INTERNET INCORPORATORS

Status: REGISTERED
SUPPLEMENTAL REGISTER

USPTO Status: SECTION 8 - ACCEPTED
USPTO Status Date: NOV 18, 2006

Goods/Services:

International Class 42: LEGAL SERVICES, NAMELY, FORMATION
OF CORPORATIONS, RESIDENT AGENT SERVICES AND OFFICE
HEADQUARTERS SERVICES FOR OTHERS
First Used: APR 11, 1998 (INTL. CL. 42)
In Commerce: APR 11, 1998

Disclaimers:

"INTERNET INCORPORATORS"

Last Reported Owner:

WICKFORD EQUITIES, LLC.
NEVADA LIMITED LIABILITY COMPANY
1151 AIRPORT RD., STE. 02
MINDEN, NEW YORK 89423

We Have Located Other Marks With This Owner

INTERNET INCORPORATORS   USPTO   Page 62

Chronology:

Filed: DEC 11, 1997   **Serial Number:** 75-404,152
Application Amended: SEP 13, 1999
Registered: JUN 05, 2001   **Registration Number:** 2,458,702
Affidavit Section: REGISTERED - SEC. 8 (6-YR) ACCEPTED NOV
18, 2006

Ownership Details:
Registrant:

SIERRA HOLDINGS LIMITED
NEVADA CORPORATION
PO BOX 1490
VERDI, NEVADA 89438

INCORPORATOR PRO

US-31
Group: Four

INTERNET
INCORPORATORS

INTERNET INCORPORATORS

Status: REGISTERED
SUPPLEMENTAL REGISTER

USPTO Status: REGISTERED
USPTO Status Date: JAN 21, 2003

Goods/Services:

International Class 42: LEGAL SERVICES, NAMELY, FORMATION
OF CORPORATION, ESTABLISHMENT OF RESIDENT AGENTS AND
OFFICE AND HEADQUARTERS FOR CORPORATIONS
First Used: APR 11, 1998 (INTL. CL. 42)
In Commerce: APR 11, 1998

Disclaimers:
"INCORPORATORS"

Last Reported Owner:

WICKFORD EQUITIES, LLC.
NEVADA LIMITED LIABILITY COMPANY
1151 AIRPORT RD., STE. 02
MINDEN, NEW YORK 89423

We Have Located Other Marks With This Owner

INTERNET INCORPORATORS   USPTO   Page 60

Chronology:

Filed: JUN 25, 1996   **Serial Number:** 75-124,945
Application Amended: OCT 26, 1998
Registered: JAN 21, 2003   **Registration Number:** 2,679,110
Date Revived/Reinstated: AUG 14, 2001

Ownership Details:

Registrant:

SIERRA HOLDINGS LIMITED
ANGUILLA CORPORATION
P.O. BOX 801
THE VALLEY, ANGUILLA

INCORPORATOR PRO

US-40
Group: Four

INCORPORATE

INCORPORATE

Status: CANCELLED   **Cancellation Section:** 8
SUPPLEMENTAL REGISTER

USPTO Status: CANCELLED - SECTION 8
USPTO Status Date: MAY 01, 2004

Goods/Services:

International Class 9: SOFTWARE FOR CREATING THE LEGAL DOCUMENTS TO FORM A CORPORATION AND INSTALLATION AND INSTRUCTION MANUALS SOLD AS A UNIT THEREWITH
First Used: MAR 23, 1995 (INTL. CL. 9)
In Commerce: APR 13, 1995

Last Reported Owner:

UNABRIDGED SOFTWARE, INC.
TEXAS CORPORATION
5959 WEST LOOP SOUTH, SUITE 300
BELLAIRE, TEXAS 77401

Chronology:

Filed: JUN 10, 1996   **Serial Number:** 75-128,694
Application Amended: FEB 17, 1997
Registered: JUL 29, 1997   **Registration Number:** 2,085,108
Cancelled: JUN 15, 2004

Ownership Details:

Registrant:

UNABRIDGED SOFTWARE, INC.
TEXAS CORPORATION
5959 WEST LOOP SOUTH, SUITE 300
BELLAIRE, TEXAS 77401

Filing Correspondent:

RITA M. IRANI
PRAVEL, HEWITT, KIMBALL & KRIEGER
1177 WEST LOOP SOUTH, TENTH FLOOR
HOUSTON, TX 77027-9095

INCORPORATOR PRO

US-42
Group: Four

CORPRO

CORPRO

Status: REGISTERED

   USPTO Status: SECTION 8 & 15 - ACCEPTED AND
   ACKNOWLEDGED
   USPTO Status Date: DEC 11, 1992

Goods/Services:
   International Class 9: COMPUTER PROGRAMS RECORDED ON
   MAGNETIC MEDIA
   First Used: OCT 09, 1985 (INTL. CL. 9)
   In Commerce: OCT 09, 1985

Last Reported Owner:
   CORSTAR BUSINESS COMPUTING CO., INC.
   NEW YORK CORPORATION
   1 AQUEDUCT ROAD
   WHITE PLAINS, NEW YORK 10606

Chronology:
   Filed: MAR 17, 1986   **Serial Number:** 73-588,242
   Published For Opposition: JUL 01, 1986
   Registered: AUG 04, 1987   **Registration Number:** 1,450,424
   Affidavit Section: REGISTERED - SEC. 8 (6-YR) ACCEPTED &
                SEC. 15 ACK. DEC 11, 1992

Ownership Details:
Registrant:
   CORSTAR BUSINESS COMPUTING CO., INC.
   NEW YORK CORPORATION
   1 AQUEDUCT ROAD
   WHITE PLAINS, NEW YORK 10606

Filing Correspondent:
   MARILYN MATTHES BROGAN
   CURTIS, MORRIS & SAFFORD
   530 FIFTH AVENUE
   NEW YORK, NY 10036

INCORPORATOR PRO

US-63
Group: Five

PROS
INCORPORATED

PROS INCORPORATED

Status: ABANDONED
                SUPPLEMENTAL REGISTER
                AMENDED TO USE APPLICATION

USPTO Status: ABANDONED-FAILURE TO RESPOND
USPTO Status Date: MAR 28, 2000
Goods/Services:
    International Class 35: PROVIDING BUSINESS AGENT SERVICES
    FOR PROFESSIONAL ATHLETES AND OTHER CELEBRITIES
    First Used: MAR 02, 1973 (INTL. CL. 35)
    In Commerce: APR 01, 1973
Last Reported Owner:
    PROS INCORPORATED
    VIRGINIA CORPORATION
    9 SOUTH 12TH STREET
    P.O. BOX 673
    RICHMOND, VIRGINIA 23218

Chronology:
    Filed: MAY 08, 1997   **Serial Number:** 75-288,910
    Abandoned: MAR 28, 2000

Ownership Details:
Applicant:
    PROS INCORPORATED
    VIRGINIA CORPORATION
    9 SOUTH 12TH STREET
    P.O. BOX 673
    RICHMOND, VIRGINIA 23218
Filing Correspondent:
    ALLEN S MELSER
    REID & PRIEST LLP
    701 PENNSYLVANIA AVE NW
    WASHINGTON DC 20004

INCORPORATOR PRO

State Summary Page

Citation	Status	Class(es) Owner		Registration Number	State	Page	Record of Interest
			GROUP ONE				
			No Group One Matches				
			GROUP TWO				
			No Group Two Matches				
			GROUP THREE				
1. CALIFORNIA INCORPORATORS THE PROFESSIONAL SOLUTION							
	Registered	42	CALIFORNIA INCORPOR ATORS	47569	CA	123	☐
2. PROMED SYSTEMS INCORPORATED							
	Not renewed	9, 16	PROMED SYSTEMS, IN C.	5946	CT	124	☐
3. PROMEDSYSTEMS INCORPORATED							
	Expired	35, 36, 41, 42	PROMED SYSTEMS, IN C.	5947	CT	125	☐
4. PROWEST INCORPORATED							
	Not renewed	35, 42	PROWEST INCORPORAT ED ALBUQUERQUE	40407	NM	126	☐
5. CSPI COMPUTER SERVICE PROFESSIONALS INCORPORATED							
	Not renewed	35	COMPUTER SERVICE PROFESSIONALS INC.	S12095	MO	127	☐
6. MPPA MINNESOTA PROFESSIONAL PHOTOGRAPHERS' ASSOCIATION, INCORPORATED							
	Not renewed	9, 40, 42	MINNESOTA PROFESSIO NAL PHOTOGRAPHERS ASS ...	13818	MN	128	☐
7. THE POWERPRO'S, INCORPORATED							
	Registered	37	THE POWERPRO'S INCO RPORATED	20020719	RI	129	☐
8. PRO PRINT INCORPORATED							
	Renewed	35	PRO-PRINT, INCORPOR ATED	N/A	KS	130	☐
9. NATIONAL PROMOTIONS INCORPORATED "PROFESSIONALS IN CREATIVE PRODUCTIONS"							
	Registered	35	NATIONAL PROMOTIO NS INCORPORATED	N/A	WI	131	☐

INCORPORATOR PRO

Citation	Status	Class(es)	Owner	Registration Number	State	Page	Record of Interest
10. PROFESSIONAL DATA RESOURCES INCORPORATED PDR							
	Registered	42	PROFESSIONAL DATA ETC CINCINNATI	63157	OH	132	☐
11. CAPRO INCORPORATED							
	Expired	9	CAPRO INCORPORATED	68265	CA	133	☐
12. CAPRO INCORPORATED							
	Expired	9, 16	CAPRO INCORPORATED	68269	CA	134	☐
13. INCORPORATOR							
	Registered	7, 8, 9	DYNAMICS CORP OF AMERICA GREENWICH	9457	OH	135	☐

GROUP FOUR

Citation	Status	Class(es)	Owner	Registration Number	State	Page	Record of Interest
14. FLORIDA BUSINESS "INCORPORATORS"							
	Registered	35	FLORIDA BUSINESS INCORPORATORS LLC	T20061110	FL	136	☐
15. PROVISTA CORPORATION							
	Not renewed	35	PROVISTA CORPORATION	50101689	IN	137	☐
16. PROFESSIONAL CADD CONCEPTS CORPORATION-PLANT THE SEED OF EXCELLENCE PCC							
	Not renewed	42	PROFESSIONAL CADD CONCEPTS CORPORATION	1993S3126	MD	138	☐
17. THE INCORPORATOR							
	Not renewed	16	KITCO, INC.	11385	SC	139	☐
18. THE INCORPORATOR							
	Not renewed	42	THE INCORPORATOR, INC.	N/A	WI	140	☐
19. DELAWARE BUSINESS INCORPORATORS, INC.							
	Expired	35	DELAWARE BUSINESS INCORPORATORS, INC.	1708	DE	141	☐
20. JOHNSON, MILLER & CO. CERTIFIED PUBLIC ACCOUNTANTS A PROFESSIONAL CORPORATION							
	Registered	35, 36	MOHNSON, MILLER & CO. CERTIFIED PUBLIC A ...	TK97032802	NM	142	☐
21. PSC PROFESSIONAL SOUND CORPORATION							
	Expired	9	PROFESSIONAL SOUND CORPORATION	101033	CA	143	☐

INCORPORATOR PRO

Citation	Status	Class(es) Owner	Registration Number	State	Page	Record of Interest
22. IMPORTPRO						
	Registered	9, 42 TRANS MOUNTAIN CONSULTING CO.	19971132681	CO	144	☐
23. BUSINESSPRO						
	Registered	35 RECOMPUTE! CORPORATION	56075	TX	145	☐

GROUP FIVE

Citation	Status	Class(es) Owner	Registration Number	State	Page	Record of Interest
24. PRO INCORPORATED						
	Not renewed	20 PROFESSIONAL REPRESENTATION ORGANIZATION ...	19891021749	CO	146	☐

INCORPORATOR PRO

ST-1
Group: Three

CALIFORNIA INCORPORATORS™
"The Professional Solution"

CALIFORNIA INCORPORATORS THE PROFESSIONAL SOLUTION

State: CALIFORNIA

Status: REGISTERED
Date Registered: MAR 20, 1997
Registration No.: 47569

Goods/Services: **International Class: 42**
NEW BUSINESS IN CALIFORNIA
State Class: 42

First Use In State:	**First Use Anywhere:**
FEB, 1996	FEB, 1996

Design Phrase: THE WORDS "CALIFORNIA INCORPORATORS" WITH THE
FIRST LETTERS OF EACH NAME IN A DROP CAP STYLE,
THE NAME IS ACCOMPANIED WITH A LOGO IN THE STYLE
OF TWO CRESCENTS FACING EACH OTHER (LOCATED
ABOVE THE NAME) AND THE WORDS "THE
PROFESSIONAL SOLUTION" (LOCATED B ELOW THE
NAME)

Registrant:

CALIFORNIA INCORPORATORS
CALIFORNIA CORPORATION
15928 VENTURA BOULEVARD, SUITE 108
ENCINO, CALIFORNIA 91436

We Have Located Other Marks With This Owner

NATIONWIDE INCORPO RATORS THE INCORPO RATION PROFESSIONALS	USPTO	Page 19

Manner Of Display:

USED ON ADVERTISING BROCHURES, ON ADVERTISING
LEAFLETS, ON BUSINESS CARDS, ON LETTERHEADS.

Index